Secondary School Teaching:

Modes for Reflective Thinking

HERBERT F. A. SMITH

Professor of Education
Southern Illinois University

WM. C. BROWN COMPANY PUBLISHERS
135 SOUTH LOCUST STREET • DUBUQUE, IOWA 52003

Manufactured by WM. C. BROWN CO. INC., Dubuque, Iowa
Printed in U. S. A.

Preface

Practically all of those who are concerned with secondary education feel that the purpose of the school is to produce graduates who can think independently. This book is an effort to bring to teachers in high schools, and to those who hope to be secondary school teachers, concepts that will help them make such an outcome a reality rather than an ideal. Current theory and practice of methodology are examined to determine the most valuable techniques available and more advanced concepts from which success can be expected are presented.

The school, as an agent of a society, must adapt itself to the changes brought about by time. The presently evolving social order will demand increased flexibility of its members in their vocational pursuits while it grants them much more leisure time than their ancestors enjoyed. In both these aspects of their lives, the ability to think independently is a key to success. As the agent of society responsible for the preparation of its youth, the high school, to fulfill its purpose, must accept the responsibility of fostering independent thinking on the part of its students.

Because the term "independent thinking" sometimes connotes rebellious thinking, the term "reflective thinking" is used in this work. One can think reflectively only to the extent that he can utilize the skills of thinking. Such skills depend for their development on instruction and practice. If they can be taught, it is an important part of the function of the secondary school to teach them. There has been a good deal of research done which indicates the feasibility of teaching specific skills of thinking and the schools of the country, here and there, have made some progress in this direction. The secondary school, as opposed to the elementary, has been somewhat hampered in this respect both through its organization of staff and its curriculum. Narrowness of preparation on the part of the teachers and restrictions on the use of time and space in school are the factors involved.

The fragmentation of the curriculum brought about by the restrictions mentioned—in this case methodology has clearly dictated to curriculum—has produced a confusion which is marked by an absence of clearly cut aims acceptable to both teachers and the general public. It is in this culture that the many adverse criticisms of the high schools have flourished. The call for a return to scholarship, demands for "tougher" courses, and more homework are expressions of concern for an essential recognized by both professsional and lay people. A unified approach to secondary school teaching will not only clarify the task of the faculty but will also answer many criticisms.

The unified approach, by the thesis of this book, can best be based on teaching through thought processes to generalizations that are functional in light of the demands of the day.

Table of Contents

CHAPTER 1

Foundations of
Secondary School Teaching Method

OVERVIEW

Throughout the ages man has struggled ceaselessly to teach his children the essentials of his culture. As he has progressed he has felt the essentials go beyond the satisfying of the basic needs of food and shelter. He has learned the use of language containing words such as "love," "happiness," "freedom," "atom," and "space." He has grasped, to some degree, the great ideas expressed by these words. As these ideas develop, the teaching of the young becomes more difficult.

If past efforts to teach are studied, if man's attempts to understand how he learns are considered, will guidelines for the instruction of our boys and girls be found? Can we use these guidelines, if we can find them, in our schools?

A thorough study of the history of education, psychology, and philosophy would doubtlessly lead to many answers for some of these questions. Of necessity, however, the treatment of these fields for the immediate purpose is of a fragmented nature—only the barest minimum has been chosen for the paramount purpose of showing some of the roots of the various high school methods found in our American schools.

LEARNING AND TEACHING

Learning and teaching are interacting activities. Although learning occurs to a degree without teaching, most learning is a result of teaching. It goes without saying that there is no teaching without learning. The aim of both learning and teaching, the desired outcome of the interaction, is scholarship. Scholarship can be defined as the attainment of knowledge and the development of wisdom in its use.

The Beginning: The Seventh Grader Is Friendly, Curious, and Eager

The Greek Period

Long ago Chaucer wrote the simple and often quoted definition of a scholar—a man who would gladly learn and gladly teach. Yet that definition was written at a time when scholarship was far from its best. The scholars of his time were prone to learn from the ancients without a great deal of application to the needs of the times and without inquiring into the world about them. This period was 1500 years after the third century before Christ which witnessed a great flow of thought in the little city of Athens. Socrates, Aristotle, Plato, and others searched their literature and that of other societies, questioned all comers, and collected and studied specimens and occurrences of vast numbers of natural phenomena. They delved into every brand of learning and questioned their findings, and their conclusions, at every turn. The students who listened to them were expected to follow this rigorous pattern. Few were able to do so. In the first place, most of the people of the time were bound by necessity to daily toil that left little time for following a man like Socrates around the city. In the second place, of the few who could afford the luxury of scholarship only some were fitted by nature to be able to utilize it. In the third place, it was not fashionable to be seen with men who had no respectable means of support and who went out into the streets and markets to engage in conversation with the populace. The love of learning, like all other loves, has its price and its price is high. It is characteristic of the scholar that he writes. These leaders of Greek thought wrote an amazing number of books. One of the greatest of the Athenian scholars was Aristotle who wrote in many fields and formulated knowledge that was to be revered for many ages. As a matter of fact, he studied so thoroughly and wrote so convincingly that he became an authority who, for centuries, could not be doubted.

The Roman Period

Although the Romans were near the Greeks geographically and in time, they were, in general, law makers and organizers. Their philosophers have not reached the place in history accorded to those of Greece. During the Roman domination of the western world, however, there occurred the birth of Christ. Centuries before Abraham had spoken to the children of Israel of one God who reigned supreme. Other groups had worshipped gods, and the concept of beings beyond the physical perception of man was not new. The idea of one God, however, the creator of all things and the beginning of all wisdom, was new and was the contribution of the Hebrews to the world. With the great teaching of Jesus, the concept of one God was greatly strengthened and spread in spite of adversity and persecution. The essential teachings of Jesus, however, were intellectualized in the several centuries after His birth and the teachings of the Church became a great body of authoritative dogma. In the violently disordered period of history which followed the decline of the Roman Empire, the power of the Church was upheld and the knowledge protected by it survived. Much of the secular knowledge not protected by it, and this included a large part of the contributions of the Greeks, was lost to Christendom. Even in the Dark Ages, though, men were thinking and wondering. Away from the disrupted center, men like Augustine and Patrick contributed to the thought of the centuries, and in the Mohammedan culture scholars pursued the study of the Greek writers and kept their works alive.

The Great Reconciliation

By the thirteenth century the Church recognized that there were two sources of thought open to the teachers of the time. On the one hand were the teachings of the Church, and on the other, the secular teachings based largely on the works of Aristotle. St. Thomas Aquinas was able to show that the two channels could run together. In spiritual matters, the Church was supreme, but in secular matters, the knowledge of the Greeks and others could be recognized. This great reconciliation meant that the scholars of the time had authority on which to depend and for several centuries scholars did depend on it almost entirely. This was the time of Chaucer and the very fact that the Canterbury Tales were so called is indicative. The ride to Canterbury was essentially a pilgrimage. As Canterbury was the center to which pilgrims came, so was the Church the center to which all ideas adhered.

The Age of Discovery

It is an axiom that no great power in history goes unchallenged. Even the Church has not been exempt and, as time went on, forces arose to challenge its stand on many things. The Crusades had intermingled the ideas of the East and West and it is apparent that there was some movement of scholars from Greece into the European world. In the three centuries after St. Thomas' reconciliation, upheavals occurred in philosophy, science, and in geographical knowledge—Copernicus shook the world with his concept of the universe, Magellan added new horizons to man's knowledge of his own sphere and, later, Luther established a new concept of religion. All of these men were questioning the teaching of the past. Each was striving toward a new idea in his own field. It must be remembered that there were others who worked equally hard whose work did not receive attention and who have been forgotten. One man was able to see this striving on the part of his fellows and to identify the elements of it. He was Francis Bacon (1561-1626) who lived in England about the time of Shakespeare. Bacon made no great discovery but laid the foundation for much discovery of truth in his description of a method of thought known by the ancients but not to his world. He asserted that learning begins wtih observable facts and proceeds from these facts to a logical conclusion. Actually his method has been refined greatly over the years and his contribution lay in the stimulation he gave to learning rather than in discovery.

The rise of modern science dates from Bacon's time. It is not necessary to list all the discoveries made to convince the reader that great strides have been made in all branches of science by men who painstakingly studied facts which they had observed, who devised experiments to verify or enlarge these facts, and who reached new conclusions and formulated new theories. One hesitates to point to the stage reached by man in his scientific development today because tomorrow is bound to make today's stage obsolete.

Inductive and Deductive Thinking

The method of thinking outlined by Bacon is technically referred to as inductive and its converse is deductive. In the inductive method, the learner is led from the particular to the general. He is presented a question the answer to which he does not know. He then makes observations that lead him to infer an answer. He makes every effort to verify this answer and is willing to have it rejected until it is verified. After verification, an application of the answer, or the principle which it supports, is sought. The successful application of a principle is the ultimate end of the inductive process of thinking. In contrast, in the deductive method of thinking, the learner is led from the general to the particular. He is told the principle and is supplied illustrations as verification of the principle. His thinking then may proceed to other illustrations or may use the principle to account for phenomena he has observed.

It must be understood that deductive thinking is not outmoded or lessened in importance by the use of inductive thinking. Knowledge grows through an interaction of inductive and deductive thought. Separate data or occurrences are studied and from them generalizations are made which are principles in themselves or which lead to principles. The generalizations are in turn used to explain facts otherwise unexplainable or to predict facts if certain procedures are followed. From these facts further generalizations are made and so on. Deductive thought follows inductive thought and inductive follows deductive in man's search for truth. When the search is apparently making little progress, the deductive powers of men's minds are dominant. When both the inductive and the deductive powers are functioning, the search progresses rapidly. The present great wave of scientific invention has grown from the desire of man to find new facts and his successful fulfillment of that desire, the application of old and new principles of science, and deductions made from those principles.

Science Applied to Human Behavior

Because of technological advances which make impressions on us every day, we are inclined to think that scientific work has been directed largely to the development of things. In this work, it must be remembered, that the scientific study of learning and of child development received a great deal of attention in the nineteenth century and the development of these areas continues today. The results of these studies are not as easily delineated nor as easily applied as some of the findings of physical science. Several schools of thought in each area have been developed. Some have been discarded; some have been modified; some continue to be strong and fruitful. All have resulted from the work of sincere men using the best method they know to find knowledge and to apply the results of it. Because there have been many schools of thought in methods of teaching, conflicting methods have been used. The inconsistencies have laid the schools open to criticism.

Conclusion

There have been sincere and effective scholars in almost every period of history. No method of thinking, or teaching, can claim a monopoly on scholarship but some pattern is essential to it. It is the duty of the high school to foster scholarship which means that the school must teach boys and girls to think critically and independently. Some knowledge of how people have been taught and what has been learned from it will aid in understanding how this challenge can be met.

AN HISTORICAL FOUNDATION OF METHOD

"Think! Think for yourself!" How often these words have been spoken to the pupil by his teacher! In various periods of American history they have discouraged, flustered, hindered or helped boys and girls in their pursuit of knowledge.

The Early Colonial Period

"Think! Think for yourself!" roared the master. "If the subjunctive of 'amo' is 'amem,' what is the subjunctive of 'habeo'?" The small figure standing before the crude bench could do anything but remember the subjunctive and certainly could not find it through any path of thought at that time. "Next!" The next boy in line blurted "habem" and consequently was able to move to a position above that of the boy who had missed. The recitation went on.

The year was 1650 and the place was a small settlement not far from Boston. The master was also the preacher of the church across the commons. The eight children lined up before him were the sons of men of local repute and of some wealth. The boys were from twelve to sixteen years of age and would some day, if successful in their studies, go to Harvard College.

The American people very early in their history gave support to the public secondary school. These schools of the early Colonial times generally were taught by men who had been trained for the ministry and who were essentially authoritative in outlook. The philosophy of the time was theocentric, that is, it assumed God to be the center about which the system was built, and left little space for freedom in thought. Psychology, to the extent it was taught, read, and learned, was Aristotelian and, in some cases, Thomistic.

The Aristotelian psychology came from the work of Aristotle (384-322 B.C.) who lived in the Golden Age of Greece and is regarded as one of the greatest of the world's philosophers. He studied and wrote in many fields and, among other matters, was keenly interested in how we learn. His work led him to formulate certain basic theories which are still regarded as sacred by many modern psychologists. He said, essentially, that we remember the relationship of things better when two phenomena occur close together in space or in time rather than when they are more widely separated; we remember things better when there is strong contrast rather than when there is lack of contrast; and we remember recent occasions better than those more remote in time. These teachings had been neglected, or avoided, in Western Europe during the early Christian period and the Middle Ages but were restored with some force during the thirteenth century just prior to the Renaissance. His is considered by some to be the first formal study of the psychology of learning. The Aristotelian philosophy reflected the thought of the Athenians who made such great strides in knowledge centuries before the coming of Christ.

The Thomistic psychology was the work of St. Thomas Aquinas (1225-1274 A.D.), the greatest philosopher of the Middle Ages and the spokesman of the medieval Church. St. Thomas did not repudiate Aristotle's teaching. As a matter of fact, he pointed out that in secular matters it was beneficial to study Aristotelian ideas. To them, however, he said the concept of revelation, a church doctrine, was to be added. By revelation, St. Thomas meant that truths were revealed in the word of God as found in the Old and New Testaments and through the priests of the Church. The "revealed" word of God made possible an understanding of the nature of man which was sought, but not attained, by the early philosophers. This Thomistic psychology was largely the attitude of the Roman Catholic Church as it faced the ferment of thought of the Renaissance.

Great store was placed on the training of the mind and memorization was the cornerstone of method. Not many boys, and fewer girls, attended school in our early history, and the groups were small. In some cases the teachers may have been tyrannical, but here and there were found some true scholars who tried sincerely to instill a love of learning in their pupils and who fostered true scholarship through them.

Scholarship then, as always, meant hour upon hour of consistently hard work. It was considered that the ideas of the culture had been written and the learner was expected to master them. Long selections from the Bible had to be committed to memory; books by the great Greek authors were to be read. Long lists of the subjects that were theoretically available to the pupil can be found[1] but it is probable that the offering of each school was drastically limited by the books available and by the knowledge of the teacher.

Of course, there was no teacher preparation as we know it today. Those teachers who were not preachers were very likely to have been trained to some degree in law or, in some cases, were scholars trying to eke out an existence. It is hardly necessary to say that the pay was low.

Late Colonial Period

"Think! Why were the English able to turn back the Spanish Armada?" The place was Philadelphia in the 1750's. The clean room had white trim and was lighted by large windows with many small panes. The class of boys in the academy was studying English literature. Latin was taught to these boys as to their forefathers, but English and history were also in the curriculum. Benjamin Franklin, a few years before, had urged that the education of our boys and girls be more practical. He pointed out that many children who did not intend to finish high school could go to school beyond the elementary grades. A rich middle class had grown up in the colonies and it was fitting to afford

---

[1]John Franklin Brown, *The American High School* (New York: The MacMillan Company, 1909), p. 27.

their children an education aimed at making them proficient in their own language and cognizant of their own history.

The curriculum had changed somewhat since the time of the first illustration. No longer was the training offered by the early Colonial school sufficient to satisfy the demands of a society grown more sophisticated and more literate. The old school had proved inadequate to meet the needs of the time and was being slowly replaced by a more comprehensive school to be known as the academy.

A Period of Advance in Science

"Think! Why does ice float?" the young science teacher asked the class in a high school in the early 1900's. Thirty-two puzzled young faces looked up to him. The classroom was in a new brick building with round arched windows and hardwood floors. Several pieces of scientific equipment built of varnished hardwood and brass were on a demonstration table in the front of the room. Science had come into the curriculum as the nation became less rural and pioneer and more urban and industralized. Also, following the publication of Darwin's theories and other writings, society became acutely conscious of the world of science and accepted the teaching of it as a proper part of the work of the public high school.

The teacher had recently graduated from a university which had prepared him in science and which had afforded him classes in the methodology of teaching. He was teaching science on the eighth grade level. This was considered a part of the elementary school but some teachers were offering a generalized form of science in this grade. Their efforts were part of the movement that gave rise to the junior high school. The courses in the high school, not only in science but in all fields, were highly specific and the demands on the pupils were vigorous.

Great movements in psychology and philosophy had started by this time and were destined to bring about great things in teaching. William James and Edward Thorndike, among others, were putting forth new and different ideas in the psychology of learning while John Dewey was teaching a new concept of philosophy.[2] The young science teacher was aware of the movements and was anxious to follow their direction.

A Period of Space Technology

"What do you think is the relationship between the cost of electricity produced by an atomic device and the cost of electricity produced by a coal-fired steam generator?" the leader of the high school group asked

---

[2]See Chapter 2.

his fellows. The classroom, in the 1960's, was of concrete block construction and the floor was of tile. The pupils were grouped around tables and many aids to learning were in evidence on the open shelves which lined the room. The teacher was sitting with one of the groups. He was a man well grounded in several academic areas and had done advanced work in a college of education. His pupils came from all levels of society and all had aspirations to achieve much during their lifetimes. Their high school offered them wide opportunities in many fields.

The Common Factor in Teaching

The four illustrations have been chosen to span the history of the country. Of course each is fictional, but each is typical, too, of some of the teaching done during the particular period. In teaching the young, men and women through the ages have tried to inspire their followers to think. Every educational psychologist has tried to describe what thinking is and then has attempted to outline and foster it. The philosophers who have been interested in learning have pondered approaches to it. The aim of all of them is summed up by the teacher who says of his pupils, "I try to teach them to think for themselves." An excellent illustration is provided by Jesus, widely recognized as one of the greatest teachers of all time, when He spoke of things close to those who heard Him. He spoke of a coin being lost, of an ox falling into a pit, of a sower going out to sow. In His wisdom, He guided His people to think toward the great ideas He brought to them.

A Concept of Thinking

Because teachers have not been entirely successful in their efforts to teach what they have struggled to, it is not at all strange that the leading critics of the public schools always cry out that the schools are no longer teaching pupils how to think. They bemoan the empty forms of learning, the useless array of facts, the meaningless repetitions. Of course, to the extent that the critics are perceiving and telling the truth, they are right. The teacher must always watch carefully lest his teaching suffer from these ills. On the other hand, those who support the schools in any era are anxious to point out that the schools are achieving some success in teaching the pupils to think; that the facts taught do lead to sound ideas, and that the many experiences afforded the pupils are meaningful. It is interesting to note that every era has produced both the adverse and the favorable critic and that the criticisms from one era to the next do not change greatly.

Because, then, the guidance of the learner through the thought process is the crux of the task of the teacher, it is necessary that we develop a concept of thinking. The good high school teacher must be able to use the concept in the area of learning which he holds himself fitted to teach, for in this way only can he guide the learner to true scholarship. An attempt will be made to relate this great concept to the teaching of high school curriculum, including the skills and esthetic fields and several fields of study which perhaps should be, but are not generally, found in our high schools.

SUMMARY

Throughout the history of our civilization there have been men devoted to the acquisition and transmission of knowledge. The scholarship attained by them, which has given the world so much in its struggle for civilization, has always been won by hard work. From the effort have come certain skills in thinking which have to be earned all over again by each individual who desires thorough learning and deep wisdom. This indicates a basis for learning and teaching.

In our own history, the teacher has always urged the learner to think. Little help was given in the specific steps involved in our earlier days but in recent times additional knowledge of the learning process has shown that there are very promising ways of helping boys and girls to learn. The psychological aspect and some empirical findings concerning learning and teaching are described in the next chapter.

In subsequent chapters descriptions of methods and their implementation are offered and then particular areas of the curriculum are discussed in terms of particular contributions to the growth of the scholar.

SUGGESTED ACTIVITIES

1. Socrates taught by questioning his listeners and building his precepts on their replies. With one or two other students, prepare and present a dialogue which teaches some simple truth. (Ex. The danger of borrowing from friends.)
2. Select a parable you know and discuss it as a teaching device.
3. Many libraries have copies of old textbooks. If possible, find a text from Colonial days and make a report on it to the class. Emphasize the method probably used in teaching the material found in the book.
4. Discuss the early American schoolteacher as portrayed by Nathaniel Hawthorne in *The Legend of Sleepy Hollow*. If role playing is used, set up a short drama with Ichabod Crane and some of his pupils.
5. From the biography of a well-known American (ex. Lincoln, Edison, Booker T. Washington) determine to what extent persistence in study contributed to his attainment of his goals.

QUESTIONS FOR SELF EVALUATION

1. The "curriculum areas" in the schools of Athens included physical education, drama, and art. Do you see reasons why these subjects, today considered the "frills," should have been important?
2. Before the coming of Jesus, what was the great idea contributed to our civilization by the Hebrews? To what extent had the idea spread over the known world?
3. Compare inductive and deductive thinking, giving examples of each. Indicate their interdependence in the thought process.
4. In our early Colonial times, what strata of society received schooling? Who were the teachers? What qualifications were demanded of them?
5. What was Benjamin Franklin's greatest idea contributed to education? To what extent was his guidance accepted in his time? To what degree has it been used since?

BIBLIOGRAPHY

1. CONANT, JAMES, *The American High School Today*. New York: McGraw-Hill Book Company, 1959.
2. CUBBERLY, ELLWOOD P., *The History of Education*. Boston: Houghton Mifflin Co., 1920.
3. EBY, FREDERICH, *The Development of Modern Education*. New York: Prentice-Hall Inc., 1952.
4. HULLFISCH, H. GORDON, AND SMITH, PHILIP G., *Reflective Thinking: The Method of Education*. New York: Dodd Mead and Company, 1961.
5. PARKER, J. CECIL, EDWARDS, T. BENTLEY, AND STEGEMAN, WILLIAM H., *Curriculum In America*. New York: Thomas Crowell Company, 1962.
6. SAMFORD, CLARENCE ET AL., *Secondary Education*. Dubuque, Iowa: William C. Brown Publishing Company, 1963.
7. WELLINGTON, C. BURLEIGH, AND WELLINGTON, JEAN, *Teaching For Critical Thinking*. New York: McGraw-Hill Book Company, 1960.

CHAPTER 2

Foundations of Secondary
School Teaching Method (Continued)

A PSYCHOLOGICAL FOUNDATION OF METHOD

The pupils stood stiffly in a line stretching from one side of the classroom to the other in front of the teacher's desk. The teacher, seated at the desk, asked the first boy in line to decline the word "mensa." The boy ran through the declension readily. The teacher moved on to the next pupil. "Decline 'bella,'" he said sternly. Not seeing the trap set for him, the boy followed the pattern set by the first student doing "mensa." After the resulting wrong response the teacher asked the third pupil in line if he could decline "bella." This boy, aware of the situation because of the reaction of his fellows, thought for a moment and answered that "bella" was nominative plural and then proceeded to a complete declension. After being notified that he was correct, he stepped around in front of the second boy and thus became the second in line while the formerly second place student was now third. And so the lesson continued with the first pupil struggling to remain first and the others striving to better their positions. After the lesson in Latin others in mathematics, history, and similar subjects followed the same method of teaching. The students who knew their lessons advanced at the expense of those who did not.

Memory Training

This method of teaching was not uncommon half a century ago. An analysis of it reveals a great faith in the training of the memory. Selections from the better-known poets were recited quickly and precisely, if not beautifully; French and Latin verbs were pursued through all their known parts; theories in geometry were presented word perfect with a Q.E.D. flourish at the end. From whence sprang this faith in the memorization of words?

The hearing of lessons has been the cornerstone of method for thousands of years. It is by far the easiest way to teach, or, at least, to take care of children in school. It is characteristic of teaching where only one source is to be considered. In a situation impoverished by a lack of material and a dearth of educated teachers, it is the most logical method imaginable. Because of this, it took a firm hold on schools throughout our Western world, was inherited by us during the Colonial days and has been used extensively ever since.

Faculty Psychology

The psychology of the period before the turn of the century supported this method of teaching in which memorization played such a large part. One of the theories of psychology was Faculty psychology, which dated from the work of Christian Wolff in the first half of the seventeenth century. According to it, the mind is a single thing performing many functions. These functions, including perception, judgment, memory and so on, depend on the different "faculties" of the mind. Because the faculties do perform, it was reasoned, they can be developed. The memorization of a great deal of material develops memory; the study of a subject with rational conclusions develops the ability to arrive at rational conclusions. When one reads of the early schoolmasters of this country, he can readily detect the results of Faculty psychology in the methodology of our professional predecessors.

The organization of the curriculum and the methods of teaching which stemmed from this psychology were termed "formal discipline." The name fits in two meanings of the words. In the first meaning, subjects were supposed to have special powers over the development of the faculties of the mind. As implied in the illustration, Latin was ideally suited to the curriculum because it demanded a great deal of memorization. Mathematics was considered essential in learning accuracy, and the study of geometry in particular developed logical reasoning. The study of literature awakened the esthetic sense. When science was accepted in the curriculum, it was defended on the ground that it was difficult enough to provide a challenge to the students' faculties.

Discipline as control. The methodology was also "formal discipline" in the second meaning of the words. Verbs, theorems, rules of grammar were all memorized. Names of people in history and of battles and dates were all grist for the same mill. Teachers assigned lessons and heard the pupils recite. To "recite" meant to speak back the algebraic solution or the declension of a noun perfectly. The control of the students in such a methodology was "discipline" in the most formal sense of the word.

Fallacies of the method. It is paradoxical that the curriculum, and hence the method, sustained by Faculty psychology was not designed according to it. Everything in the curriculum was first taught to meet a need. Latin was taught because it was essential to the communication system of its time. When the need lessened, Latin was retained as something good for the mind. Parenthetically, one can point out, Latin must yet be retained because it is a window to a great culture and much wisdom that we cannot afford to lose. Other subjects were considered especially good for the mind, too, and were retained until they became dull and lifeless. As has often happened before, and is happening today, culture and snobbery became confused and social status became associated with a certain type of curriculum.

William James was one of the doubters of Faculty psychology and very simply set about to test it. After much effort at training his mind to memorize, he came to the conclusion that it could not be done as the supporters of the theory thought possible. Further experimentation in mathematics and other areas by him and others corroborated his first effort. This attack did not win over all the supporters of the old regime but rather put many of them on a militant defensive. Even today one reads appeals to return to its methods of teaching.

Associationism

With its roots in the laws formulated by Aristotle, a school of psychology known as Associationism had grown up in England. As early as the seventeenth century it had gained strength and a hundred years later was still contributing much to education both in Europe and in this country. According to Associationism, the mind is not a unit but an aggregate of many ideas, feelings, and sensations. All of these are related one to another by association. When one part of the mind is subjected to an impression many other parts are involved because of associations which have been built up by former experience. As one grows older, more and more associations are formed and education has to do with the forming and accumulating of a desirable store of such associations. Hence there are a great number of stories with morals and numerous maxims found in the old readers and copybooks. The more associations formed, the more complete was the education.

Associationism, which still has some support for its later teachings, influenced the psychologists greatly in this country in the last century and sowed seeds which eventually grew into *Connectionism*. Because it has had a very significant influence on our methodology in schools, Connectionism will be discussed later in this chapter.

Herbartianism

The history of education, like that of most areas of learning, contains few examples of spontaneous and rapid growth. Neither Faculty psychology nor any other school of thought held the esteem of all teachers. In the first part of the nineteenth century in Germany, a man named Johann Herbart was attempting to bring about changes in teaching. The mind is a unity, he believed, but its content is determined by many ideas which are elements of the whole. Each idea strives to maintain itself and to grow. The energy maintaining the idea springs from the interest of the learner and hence the essential aspect of learning is the recruiting of interest in the material to be taught when it is presented to the child.

Herbart considered the sources of these ideas to be experience and social intercourse. From the first of these is derived the knowledge of nature, which includes history, science, and mathematics, and from the second are derived our feelings and attitudes toward our fellow men. The ideas, furthermore, are to be thought of as generalizations growing from many small experiences which are essentially sensory. From this basis, teaching must involve an awareness on the part of the learner of the knowledge he possesses; a drive, sustained by interest, to add to that knowledge; the presentation of new material with a recognized relationship to the familiar, and finally an application of new knowledge. One can see in Herbart's work an inductive approach to learning. As a matter of fact, he did suggest a pattern for teaching deductively as well, but it is through his inductive pattern that he is known. His inductive pattern had a wide following in the normal schools of our country in the latter half of the last century and profoundly affected the methods of teaching for many years. It is evident that the promise of Herbart's work was not fulfilled in his time—he died in 1841—and actually much of it was lost in the various interpretations; the term "Herbartian" was applied to many sterile methods stressing the preparation, presenting, and testing of factual materials. Such methods, of course, worked well with Faculty psychology.

Connectionism

In the meantime, Associationism had received a great impetus from the work of Ivan Pavlov who offered the stimulus-response theory of learning. This approach was developed by many psychologists here and in other countries and a great deal of experimental work accrued to the theory that we learn by associating a response to a stimulus. In this country, the work of Edward Thorndike and his students grew out of this idea. Although it is doubtful that Thorndike set out to build a school of psychology, one known as Connectionism did develop from his work. Learning is the result of connections established between receptors of the nervous system and the effectors, it was stated. Much experimentation was done which was used as evidence that we learn through our responses to stimuli. Connectionism and Behaviorism, which was developed a few years later under the leadership of John B. Watson, had a very profound effect on the methodology of schools. Behaviorism held that which was done was learned, that is, the behavior itself was learning. The two theories paved the way to the activity phase of our schools which changed elementary school methods drastically and influenced the secondary schools also, but to a lesser degree.

A belief in Connectionism ruled out credence in Faculty psychology in the individual's mind. Learning is not the development of faculties of the mind which permit it to be directed, with greater power than it had before the learning, toward different fields of knowledge, says the Connectionist. Rather learning is the establishing of satisfying connections between stimuli and responses. The connections are made in the nervous system and once made their recall is far easier than their establishment had been. A mind can be trained in that a system of connections can be built but no subject of the curriculum, or combination of subjects, has any special power in training the mind. Experimentation involving thirteen thousand children provided some of the evidence to substantiate this statement.[1]

The Philosopher and the Psychologist

John Dewey, a philosopher and psychologist of the time, foresaw the acceleration of technical development at the end of the last century and the great social changes that this would bring about. He stated that a sterile curriculum designed for only a part of the population and directed toward the more intelligent would not hold up in a democracy in the twentieth century. A child learns to do what he is doing, he said. If the child receives no satisfaction from learning Latin verbs and is forced to learn them anyway he is learning to dislike Latin. If pressure to get the right answer in arithmetic tests leads to cheating, the school is teaching the child to cheat, not to do arithmetic.

It is more than coincidence that Thorndike and Dewey were members of the same university. They were contributors to a common cause and worked from bases which were mutually acceptable. Thorndike was the psychologist and scientist who declared that we learn from the effects of experience on our nervous systems. His countless experiments moved the study of learning from a speculative to a scientific foundation. He was not the first of the experimental psychologists, but he was one of early ones and certainly one of the most prolific experimenters. Dewey

---

[1]C. R. Broyler, et al. "A Second Study of Mental Discipline in High School Studies," *Journal of Educational Psychology*, 18: 377-404.

was the psychologist and the philosopher who did much to move the philosophic considerations to a pragmatic basis. The work of each man complemented that of the other. Both wrote a great deal and were followed in their thinking by many of the thousands of students who attended Columbia Universtiy, where both taught. It is not strange that their liberal ideas of teaching, with deep philosophical roots and much empirical support, permeated the literature of education in the second and third decades of the century and that they were interpreted to students in colleges of education and teachers' colleges throughout the country. One is more likely to be amazed at the inertia of the schools which resisted the changes the new thinking indicated and the degree to which they remained as they had been rather than rapidly altering. It should be remembered that not all who interpreted, or tried to, were competent and not all of the practitioners of the new methods were aware of the implications of what they were trying to do. Many fools rushed into the fray with resulting disaster; many wiser teachers were too apprehensive to desert their safe methods in favor of the untried.

NEWER PSYCHOLOGIES

When one looks at a checkerboard of white and black squares, he may see it as a black board with white squares on it or as a white board with black squares. While one is gazing at this board, it is likely that the relationship will change from one to the other. Where does the change occur — in the board or in the mind of the perceiver? Obviously it must be in the latter as no change is being made on the board. Max Wertheimer, a psychologist in Germany during the last century, brought attention to this occurrence that is common to most of us and called it the "phi phenomenon." His work was followed by other scholars' efforts and a new concept of the nature of learning started to take form. In a typical experiment a caged chimpanzee had been deprived of food for some time so that his hunger produced a drive. In front of the cage, but out of reach, was a banana. In the cage were two sticks, neither long enough to be used by the chimpanzee to reach the food. These sticks, however, could be put together as are the parts of a fishing rod and the combined length would be enough to reach the banana. Here was a situation far different from that in which a subject is presented with a simple stimulus and his reaction is punished or rewarded or simply recorded. The animal was able, after some time, to put the sticks together and rake in the food. Moreover, when he finally grasped the idea of putting the two sticks together, he seemed to be able to do it quite quickly. In this situation, the animal somehow integrated the factors of the problem and supplied the answer from something other than previous experience. In other words, the learner supplied the integrating factor which related several factors in the situation to each other and led to a solution. The ability to see the various aspects of the problem and then supply an integrating factor has been termed "insight." It is related to the old "aha" theory which was used to explain those flashes of insight many of us have when a problem which has baffled us for some time suddenly seems to solve itself. Many a student has, at one time or another, puzzled over an examination question, answered it knowing the answer was worth little and, when it was far too late to do any good, has become conscious of the correct answer. When the pressure of examination was relieved, he saw the problem in perspective and was able to deal with it. He experienced "insight" but not at the most beneficial time.

Gestaltism

In the foregoing illustration of course, not all the students in any one class would be unable to answer the question during the examination period and have the answer come to them later. Some students would have had the insight previously, probably as the result of conscientious study, and some would never have it. This brings in a very important principle of this newer psychology: each person learns according to his background of experience and associations. All experience is perceived against the background of the learner himself; problems are solved through the interplay of the stimuli presented and the background of the learner. The background is often referred to simply as "ground." When the elements are organized so as to provide a solution through insight, learning takes place. It is easily seen that the newer psychology did not repudiate the findings of Associationism but went a step beyond them. There are several new schools of psychology with the same general approach; the one to which Wolgang Köhler contributed is called the Gestalt school or Gestaltism. The word is the German for pattern or configuration and implies the organization of factors in a problem situation. Whereas Associationism attributed little to insight in the learning process, Gestaltism attributes a great deal to it. This fact in itself has great implications for method and will be brought into discussion many times in this work.

Reward and Punishment

It should be noted that all of the experimenters in the learning process emphasize the drive factor. In Thorndike's animal experiments, as in those of Köhler, the animal was hungry and was offered food as a reward, or some punishment. In experiments with human subjects, some reward or punishment was always one factor of the problem-solving situation. The punishments traditionally associated with the school and the rewards of the reporting system represent the school's attempt to set up a punishment and reward pattern to which the learner responds. The newer psychologies have attempted to replace these with more subtle, and more effective, punishments and rewards based on the principle that motivation is within the learner and cannot be imposed by the teacher.

The Present Situation

Currently we are in a strange position in regard to educational psychology and methodology of teaching in our schools. At least three movements in psychology can be detected as working their influence on methods. The old Faculty psychology proved very tough and never did leave the high school. Through the pressures of progressivism it stood bowed but not defeated through the twenties and thirties. It gained strength in the forties because of the great influx of children and the shortage of teachers. The employment of people with little or no preparation for teaching supported this simplest and most widespread psychology. In the fifties it was reinforced by those critics who would have us put back the clock to the good old times which never, of course, existed. So Faculty psychology is still with us and we still hear that what is unpleasant and hard is good for the learner because it is unpleasant and hard.

Along with this, the Connectionism of Thorndike and the Functionalism of Dewey have left their mark and have dominated much of the elementary school teaching method. In the high school, however, the influence is evidenced by the teaching of some persons who attempt to make learning practical and relative to the individual's need. The field psychologies are beginning to be felt in some geographical areas and in some curriculum areas. To illustrate, the Southern Illinois University School is developing a new program in mathematics in which teaching is based on the learner's comprehension of broad mathematical concepts rather than on the atomistic presentation of algebra, geometry, and trigonometry. In a few years other schools of the area will have participated in the building of a new mathematics course and will use it to some degree. Other schools are experimenting in other subjects and changes will spread out from them. All changes in our high school curriculum, with concomitant changes in method, have followed this pattern to some extent. There will be no deliberate reconciliation of the different schools of psychology in our educational system. Teachers are notoriously poor theorists and will take what seems expedient from each theory and will use it as long as it is usable. Because of this practice, the change from one theory to another will be almost imperceptible. It is logical that the broader approaches of the newer theories, such as those of Köhler and Kurt Lewin, have been the source for the more flexible attitude toward curriculum construction which has been in vogue and the freer methodology stemming from it. Even though criticism from laymen may slow down the trend of broader approaches, both psychological theory and educational practice assure its continuity.

AN EMPIRICAL BASIS OF METHOD

Does it work? When one questions a device or procedure with these words he is putting the evaluation on an empirical basis. It has been said that, according to theory, a bumblebee cannot fly. The theory does not cause the bumblebee to worry, we assume, as he flies from one spot to another. Empirically, we know he flies. In teaching we have to look for evidence of practice to support any method because if it does not work it is of no use. As a matter of fact, the practicing teacher selects and develops most of his methods on empirical rather than theoretical bases.

The Purpose of the High School

The public schools of this country have rather successfully accomplished their aim of teaching every child who has the capacity to read, to write, and to perform the fundamental processes of arithmetic. It is possible to trace the roots of this objective for elementary education back to the Protestant Reformation, from which sprang the ideal that each child has the right and privilege to read the Word of God. The invention of printing made this ideal feasible. It has been in only the last fifty years that the ideal of a secondary education for all youth has been accepted in this country. Although it is not difficult to see the advantage of learning the three R's as the unifying aim of the elementary school in our early history, it has been more difficult to put one's fingers on a like aim for the secondary school. The aims of the secondary school have been expressed in terms of self-realization, economic efficiency, good citizenship, and other such objectives. Basic to all of these is the concept that in high school we should teach boys and girls to think — to think reflectively. In other words, our secondary schools can be expected to produce individuals who are intellectually independent.

Reflective Thinking

Reflective thinking involves seeing the results of one's experiences in relation to one another and drawing conclusions from them. Such conclusions are the generalizations, or concepts, which then function in further thought processes. The essence of teaching, then, is to provide experiences for the learner and develop in him skills by which he can evolve the generalizations which answer his needs.

Various writers have used different names for the process of which we are speaking. Many label it "reflective thinking," some "creative thinking," and a few have used the term "positive thinking." To achieve any proficiency in teaching this, it is first essential to discern the elements which go to make up the thought process and then look for ways in which the teaching can be attacked. Lists of steps of reflective thinking have been compiled by several authors; the classic of these lists is that of John Dewey.[2] For this work, this list is compiled.

1. A difficulty sensed by the thinker.
2. Recognition of the problem involved in the difficulty and the delineation of it.
3. The formation of a hypothesis. This step involves inference and inductive thinking.
4. The gathering of facts to serve as evidence. This step includes a choice of pertinent facts.
5. The use of facts in forming a concept or generalization.
6. The application of the concept or generalization.

These steps were outlined years ago. Since then much research has been done and the implementation of some of the steps has been studied. The results of this research have been garnered and are presented here in a very condensed form.

Some Conclusions Concerning the Elements of Reflective Thinking

Much of the work in the general field of thought pertinent to the high school classroom has been done by science teachers under the heading of scientific thinking. From the psychologies prevalent up to a generation ago, it was thought that the teaching of science itself taught boys and girls to think scientifically. It was surprising to many that research did not bear out this assumption and that scientific thinking was by no means a sure product of the science classes. Tests were devised to measure elements of scientific thinking and, logically enough, it was found that pupils who were taught these elements specifically learned them. Others simply did not. In this work, done in the early thirties, lists of elements of scientific method and of scientific attitude were derived and it was evident from research that each element was separable and could be taught.

---

[2]John Dewey. *How We Think,* Boston: Heath and Company, 1933. p. 12.

Specific Skills. The earliest researchers were soon followed by others who identified skills such as outlining and summarizing. It was reported that good improvement in knowledge was made by pupils receiving specific instruction in these skills. As time went on, skills in making conclusions and evaluating them were identified and declared to be measurable. Several authorities agreed that high levels in these abilities can be reached by boys and girls if they have instruction designed for that purpose. The finding support the generalization that there are no premiums in teaching and in learning—every gain is made at the price of determination and endeavor.

In a technical sense, the skills of which we are speaking are those of inductive thought in which inference plays an important part. Inference can be defined as the perception of the relationship between two or more separate phenomena. To illustrate, if one's car will not start and experimentation shows that the lights will not light and the horn will not sound, one can infer that the battery is either disconnected or dead. Several writers have investigated the possibilities of teaching science by these inductive methods. These men compiled lists of principles in their respective fields and assigned to each several experiments. The experiments lead the learner inductively to a comprehension of the principle involved.

The foregoing paragraphs indicate that those working in the teaching of science have been deeply concerned with the nature of thinking, the elements of it, and the habits and skills involved as well as in the teaching of these things. There is little, if any, significant difference in the teaching of the thought process in one field or another, and the findings of the writers in the science teaching area can be applied with great benefit to the teaching of many subjects in the high school curriculum. The ideas touched upon so far can be expressed in the following conclusions:

The First Conclusion. The ability to do reflective thinking consists of specific skills which can be acquired to varying degrees and, through suitable instruction, by high school pupils of all ability levels.

The Second Conclusion. The abilities which go to make up reflective thinking are separable and measurable.

The Third Conclusion. The ability to do reflective thinking on the part of a high school pupil depends to a large extent on the experience he has had in the elements of the process.

The Fourth Conclusion. The teacher does little to help the learner think reflectively by pointing out generalizations to him.

Reflective Thinking and Measures of Intelligence. Since the turn of the century a great deal of work has been done in the field of tests and measurements, and foremost among the products is the concept of a measurable intelligence and the intelligence quotient. It has been assumed that the ability to perform well on an intelligence test and the ability to think are synonymous. This assumption has to be questioned. An intelligence test is to some extent a memory test based on a background of experience that is common to all those who are given the test. Of course no such common background exists because there are as many backgrounds as there are individuals. There are parts of some measures of intelligence that do test some of the abilities we term elements of thinking so their tests cover an area that overlaps the elements of thinking but does not coincide with them. The validity of test scores is always a variable factor but we need not enlarge upon this. It is sufficient to say that the results of an intelligence test and the results of a test of thinking ability will correlate but not very highly.

In a similar way one can consider school marks. These are the results of tests that measure recall or memory. For the most part and in general, one can conclude that the pupils who get good marks are not always the ones who think well. Researchers have concluded that inference making ability and intelligence are not the same thing, although the person who makes inferences well often is one who rates high in intelligence. Others have spoken of a general problem solving ability which seems to be possessed in varying degrees by individuals and which does not depend entirely on the amount of information possessed by them. In other words, some people know many facts but are not able to organize and apply them to the solution of a problem. Some people can solve problems better than others. All, however, can be instructed in problem solving techniques and many can profit from such instruction. From this, a generalization can be drawn:

The Fifth Conclusion. The abilities measured by the intelligence tests are not the same which lead to efficient problem solving.

Marks and Memorization. Many teachers understand that the reason for learning involves the transfer of what is learned from one situation to another. It has been determined that when one understands a principle thoroughly through the process of establishing it inductively, then he is able to use it in his day-to-day life as he meets problems. When one has merely been told of a principle and lacks understanding of it, his use of it is limited. Even the people with high interest in a subject may gather many facts and be able to state principles pertaining to the subject and still be unable to see the application of the generalizations to their daily problems. As an illustration, one boy may be able to phrase the principles of electricity on which electro-magnetic motors operate and be entirely unable to locate trouble in a motor and repair it. Another boy who had learned the principles inductively through experimentation with simplified motors would probably have a more functional understanding. In another field, the student who has taken part in classroom and school elections understands the political framework of his community and his country better than he who has only read and been told about politics.

Unfortunately our appraisal systems in high schools test largely on the recall of facts and generalization and demand little of the student beyond an ability to give back the words received some time in the past.

The ability to gather facts is an important one. Beyond this ability lies that of applying them. This is also valuable and as one can improve the former through study and practice, so can he improve the ability to bring together facts in a logical relationship and to use the resulting concepts.

These ideas are summarized in two more conclusions:

The Sixth Conclusion. The ability to do reflective thinking is very likely to be accompanied by good academic marks but good marks do not necessarily indicate the presence of this ability.

The Seventh Conclusion. A good memorizer is not necessarily a good thinker.

Reflective Thinking Potential. Schools generally have failed to use the potential of the learner to best advantage. Courses have been built for the average student — meaning one of mediocre ability; textbooks have been written at low levels; and teachers have given their attention to the pupils who have demanded it. There is an abundance of evidence that boys and girls of high school age are able to think on a mature plane when the school stimulates them to do so. Generally, too, the schools have assumed that boys are strong in one field and girls in another. There is some evidence to substantiate this conclusion but not enough to be the basis of guidance into or out of subject matter areas.

Because of the misuse of such notions, we probably have lost some excellent minds in mathematics and science merely because their possessors were girls, and perhaps our lack of qualified men in diplomatic circles is due in part to the idea that boys are not proficient in learning languages.

From the foregoing two more concepts can be added:

The Eighth Conclusion. The ability to do reflective thinking is present in a child younger than one of junior high school age.

The Ninth Conclusion. No significant differences exist between the sexes as far as the ability to think reflectively is concerned.

Carl Purcell NEA

Thinking Reflectively

Organization of Material. One often is told of students who learn slowly but retain well. No doubt there are boys and girls who learn this way but the concept that slow learning and great retention correlate highly is the product of wishful thinking and is not supported by research. Lack of thinking ability certainly does not mean a compensatory share of retaining ability. Of course it must be remembered that if one learns thoroughly following good techniques, his retention will be better than if he works carelessly and only half learns.

It can be concluded:

The Tenth Conclusion. Pupils who learn quickly and organize their material well tend to retain what they learn better than do the pupils who learn slowly.

Self Expression. The term "self expression" has been used with many connotations. The connotation for this work has nothing to do with an undisciplined outpouring of emotional response. Rather it holds that a student does better work when he identifies himself with a task and can tell of his experience in his own words than when he is only told about or has read about something. A group of pupils were once stationed beside a highway so that they could estimate the velocity of the cars going through a speed zone. They then wrote a report of the behavior of the motorists driving through their town and wrote comments on the response to the law. The experience produced sounder learning than would equal time spent in a classroom talking about or reading about the speed laws in the various states.

The conclusion is:

The Eleventh Conclusion. The ability to think reflectively is increased when the learner is afforded the opportunity of self expression and uses the opportunity well.

Methodology and Reflective Thinking. Many of the high schools of our country do not accept reflective thinking as a valid and attainable goal of teaching. Much is said of teaching students how to think rather than what to think. This is laudable but few teachers have thought enough about thinking to produce the hoped-for result. Our great technical development demands men and women who can meet an ever-changing and ever more complex world technology. Beyond this consideration, the social aspects of our time with great national and international stress make a strong demand on men and women who can think. These people must come from our high schools.

The final idea deserves the utmost attention:

The Twelfth Conclusion. In general the teachers of American high schools have not yet learned to teach the elements of reflective thinking nor have these elements been widely realized as valid aims of teaching in the secondary school.

SUMMARY

The historical foundations dealt with in the first chapter are paralleled to a degree by the psychological foundations in the present chapter. Again the treatment has been minimal for the specific purpose of the work. The contribution of several of the better-known psychologies which seem to have influenced most the methodology of the high school have been described in brief.

In addition, twelve conclusions concerning methodology have been garnered from a great deal of research and have been presented as an empirical basis for methods. The concepts gained from these differing areas of study may well be used as guidelines in developing, or selecting, a methodology for the secondary schools.

SUGGESTED ACTIVITIES

1. Stage a short debate, as you suppose one might have been held just prior to 1900, between a Faculty psychologist and an Associationist. Relate the argument of each side to the methodology of the schools.
2. Compile a list of words which have come into the vocabulary of the American people during the last five years. What new concepts related to these words should be recognized and taught in the schools today?
3. Identify the methods used in the high school you attended and compare your experience with that of other students in the class.
4. Read on or more articles concerning method and in a current periodical. (Ex. *NEA Journal, The Clearing House, The High School Journal*) Present a summary, or summaries, to the class.
5. Draw identical simple patterns such as this —l—| |—l— on several sheets of paper. Have different students embellish each pattern by "doodling" and then try to relate the results to the backgrounds of each. It must be remembered that such projective devices are interesting to the untrained but not significant.

QUESTIONS FOR SELF EVALUATION

1. Explain briefly what you understand by Faculty psychology.
2. What practices can you remember from your own school days which apparently stemmed from Faculty psychology?
3. Indicate the fault William James found with Faculty psychology? How did he attempt to prove his point?
4. Outline briefly Thorndike's theory of learning.
5. Define the term "insight" as used by the Gestaltists. How is insight related to Associationism or Connectionism?

6. What do you understand by "scientific method"? Do you see why it is not always a good term to use for the thought process involved in this work? Indicate your reasons.
7. In your experience, has the pupil with the ability to memorize had the advantage over the poor memorizer in our school system? Indicate the reasons.
8. It has been reported that some great writers and inventors were not successful in school. What are the factors that work against some gifted individuals in our schools?

BIBLIOGRAPHY

1. BLACK, MAX. *Critical Thinking.* Englewood Cliffs, N. J.: Prentice-Hall, Inc., 1946.
2. BROWNELL, WILLIAM A., AND HENDRICKSON, GORDON. "How Children Learn Information, Concepts, and Generalizations." *Learning and Instruction.* Forty-Ninth Yearbook of the National Society for the Study of Education, Part I. Chicago: University of Chicago Press, 1950.
3. BURTON, WILLIAM H. *The Guidance of Learning Activities.* New York: Appleton-Century-Crofts, 1952.
4. BURTON, WILLIAM H., KIMBALL, ROLAND B., AND WING, RICHARD L. *Education For Effective Thinking.* New York: Appleton-Century-Crofts, 1960.
5. BURTT, E. A. *Right Thinking.* New York: Harper Brothers, 1946.
6. COHEN, MORRIS R., AND NAGEL, EARNEST. *Introduction to Logic and Scientific Method.* New York: Harcourt Brace, 1934.
7. DEWEY, JOHN. *How We Think.* Boston. Heath, 1933.
8. FAWCETT, HAROLD P. *The Nature of Proof.* Thirteenth Yearbook of the National Council of Teachers of Mathematics. New York: Bureau of Publications, Columbia University, 1938.
9. HUNT, MAURICE P., AND METCALFE, LAWRENCE E. *Teaching High School Social Studies: Problems in Reflective Thinking and Social Understanding.* New York: Harper and Brothers, 1955.
10. LARABEE, HAROLD A. *A Reliable Knowledge.* Boston: Houghton Mifflin, 1945.
11. MORRISON, HENRY C. *The Practice of Teaching in the Secondary Schools.* Chicago: The University of Chicago Press, 1926.
12. RUSSELL, DAVID H. *Children's Thinking.* Boston: Ginn and Company, 1956, Chapter 6.
13. WATKINS, RALPH. *Techniques of Secondary School Teaching.* New York: Ronald Press, 1958.

CHAPTER 3

Adolescent Behavior

OVERVIEW

The school's responsibility to society in regard to the behavior of young people is not well defined nor can it be. It exists, however, and presents those who teach questions which must be given sincere consideration. Some of these are: Is the school responsible for the driving habits of its pupils and graduates? To what extent is the school obligated toward the problem of young alcoholics? How far does the school go in the teaching of morality in sexual behavior? Can the school develop skills of thought and attitudes within the young people which will give them a sound basis on which to build solutions to life's problems? We may not be able to answer these questions but we can look squarely at the evidence from which they spring.

For the evidence bearing on these questions one must look at the influences beyond the school at work on our youth, the morality of our society and the lessons it teaches them, and their own concepts of what is right and what is wrong.

The thesis for this chapter holds that all of society's influences, good and bad, contribute to the learning of youth and so must be considered teachers of the young people.

SOCIAL SITUATION FACED BY YOUTH

"There just isn't any work in Chicago for a person like me. There are good jobs for a man who can weld or is a tool and diemaker but there are just too many guys for the unskilled jobs. I hate to go home to tell Mother and Dad that I can't make a go of it." So spoke a high school graduate returning to his home in Alabama. Going from town to town seeking work he had found his way to Chicago, where, eventually, he had to face the hard truth that the American economy has little room for the man or woman without some vocational preparation. It has even less room for the young person recently graduated from high school. The labor laws and insurance company policies force industry to be very cautious in employing the worker who is not yet twenty-one years of age.

One Killed — Six Injured!

So ran the headlines in a small town newspaper. Of great interest to the people involved, the story attracted little attention in other papers. Such accidents occur too frequently for any particular one to rate highly as a news item. The story behind the news in this case is appallingly similar to many many others. Three young couples about eighteen years old were out for an evening. Drinks, illegal for children of their age, were not hard to purchase. The car could do 120 miles per hour. "The kids weren't bad kids," the townspeople will say to each other after the funeral, "they didn't mean any harm." One is sure they didn't. But what lack in their education accounts for behavior with such tragic results?

"If you can take care of Gary and Susan from eight until four, I can take over then and feed them their supper and put them to bed." The

Southern Illinois University School
Herbert Smith

Cars Are Important In a Teenagers' World

young woman, daughter of the older one to whom she was speaking, spoke as one hoping for the best from circumstances from which little could be hoped. Married at sixteen, mother at seventeen, mother once more at eighteen and divorced at twenty, her young soul struggled for strength to carry a burden beyond her capacity. With no income from her ex-husband, who had nothing from which he could pay, she was now with her parents who could ill afford the great drain on their modest income. When one contemplates the numerous early marriages in our schools, knowing that many of them are not happy marriages, he is forced to question the society which yields such situations. The high school is a most important agency of society; it alone has most of the young people within its walls.

Incidence of problems small. The foregoing incidents are all from life; none is fiction. It is fortunate that only a small percentage of our high school youth run into tragedy but those who do illustrate a great principle of education. Everyone reacts to his needs. Moreover, he reacts to his needs as he perceives them and he acts in the manner which seems best to him at the time of decision. The more skillful he becomes at perception and decision making, the more likely are his needs to be met in a satisfying manner. What agency should offer more opportunity for growth in perception and decision making than the secondary school?

The great proportion of the high school boys and girls who progress normally through the various grades and whose social life is beset by no great troubles are not exceptions to the principle stated. It is true that their ability to meet life successfully at this early stage is predictive of happiness in later life; nonetheless greater decisions are ahead of all of them. Teachers cannot, as adults, prepare leaders for tomorrow for any particular decisions because the future holds too many new things in store. Youngsters must be provided with those skills which will aid them universally in determining what is right and what is wrong.

Traditions in a society. Every society builds for itself many traditions, attitudes, and rules of behavior which govern the actions of its members. Each of these rules is a generalization which has grown from a hypothesis through trial by experience to its present status. In our society stealing is wrong. Long ago man theorized that all men would be happier if one did not take another's belongings. After some generations of being tested, the hypothesis was stated as a law: "Thou shalt not steal." The generalization, as a law, has now stood for many more centuries. If one man is attempting to rob another, the victim may even kill his attacker and be declared innocent of any crime.

In a stable society, the traditions and rules of behavior do not change much from year to year or decade to decade. The members are secure in that they know what to expect in the way of reward and punishment.

In a society which changes rapidly the members lose a measure of their security. This loss leads to fear and a consequent change of behavior.

Rapid growth of knowledge. The boys and girls in the high schools have lived in a time of great change. Technological developments, especially in manufacturing, communications, and transportation, have greatly quickened the way of life. Great changes have come suddenly and, to use a teenager's phrase, "We've been shook!" All of the changes impinge on the high school to some extent but some beat on it more directly than others. Knowledge has expanded. The high school was not organized as an agency for terminal education only and the present increase in college attendance indicates it serves this purpose less and less. On the other hand, there are still thousands and thousands of boys and girls who will not go to college. This means that the secondary school must enlarge its curriculum for both general and vocational education. Of equal importance to the teacher in the classroom is the fact that pupils pick up a good deal of the new knowledge through the press and television. The teacher cannot hope to keep up with all the areas of knowledge open to his pupils but he must be prepared to cope with their questions. Whereas the school master was truly the master when one could become an expert by reading textbooks, today's increase of knowledge is so rapid that the teacher must understand how to guide the pupil to the attainment of sound generalizations from the flood of facts as they rush by.

Changes in loyalties. The loyalties of the American citizen have undergone a change in the last generation. Of course one still pledges allegiance to the flag and promises to support the government of the country. One may also remain loyal to a political party. Before 1939 loyalty to the United States meant simply what it says, but since World War II the country has had to declare itself on many issues. It has become the champion of one philosophy of government and this has led to the making of many decisions. The loyalty of any citizen, to be well-founded, demands some knowledge of the problems confronting the nation and insight leading to possible solutions. When this generality is applied to classroom teaching the result is that conventional teaching from a textbook is inadequate. Textbooks cannot keep up with world changes and no writer can encompass the field of international relationships. The teacher must develop techniques where the high school class is a research group in itself, a group which forms hypotheses, collects evidence, forms conclusions and evaluates them. An effort to achieve this in the classroom will be described in a later chapter.

Youthful Criminality

"This nation is hustling toward a frightful internal crisis. Ineed, I am convinced that we have already reached a crossroads we have been heading for since the beginning of World War II; and that if we fail to admit the deadly nature of this crisis and to meet it quickly and aggressively, we will pay with the life of our republic.

"The crisis manifests itself in what some call juvenile delinquency, and what I call youthful criminality, for that is what it is. I refer to vicious acts of vandalism, wanton brutality and mounting savagery which is typical of today's arrogant teen-age gangs."[1]

The above is the opinion of an expert, the Director of the Federal Bureau of Investigation. He identifies the change in the behavior of youth as a trend. We must reverse this trend, he declares, if we are to continue living in a free and decent society. If we are to survive, we must give our youngsters more chance to know and revere the spiritual concepts which are the real sinews of greatness, he declares.

The particular article quoted goes on to commend the work of organizations such as the Boys' Clubs of America but the teachers in America's classrooms play an even more important role in the social control of our teen-age group. The chance for them "to know and revere the spiritual concepts which are the real sinews of greatness" can come in the classroom under the guidance of a teacher who can bring the realization of such concepts from the lessons in history, literature, and other school subjects. It is to be noted that these concepts are reached through reflective thinking of a high order and cannot be instilled into the youngster's minds through declarative teaching. What the concepts are, moreover, must be determined from a study of the needs of our young people.

NEEDS OF YOUTH

"What can they be thinking of?" This question is often asked rhetorically by one who reads an account and sees news pictures of an accident such as referred to earlier. It may be that the driver was barely old enough to drive legally and was pushing his car to its limit of speed. The same question is asked when an item in the press deals with a gang war or tells of a raid in which young people are found using drugs. The question is rarely answered because the one who asks it generally feels there is no answer.

The truth is, of course, that there is an answer because any act is a result of a thought process. The classic experiments in learning all have one factor in mind — the learner is impelled by a need. The behavior which is studied as evidence of the learning taking place is the result

---

[1]J. Edgar Hoover, "These Fighters Against Youth Crime Need Your Help," *The Reader's Digest*, (April, 1961), pp. 145-52.

of the effect of the need on the nervous system of the learner. In Köhler's experiments for instance, the animals were hungry. Man, as other animals, is continuously striving to meet the demands of his needs. What do young people need?

In the first place, it must be pointed out that the needs of many of our youth are being met to a satisfactory extent as evidenced by the fact that most of our young citizens never get into serious trouble. The point made time and again in the results of one study was that delinquent youth total only a small percentage of the whole. In any city or rural area, this figure is seldom greater than six. Our youth is 95 per cent sound.[2]

There is no room for complacency, however, so we must try constantly to determine needs. Efforts have been made on a national scale several times. Perhaps as good a list as any is "The Ten Imperative Needs of Youth" as compiled by the Educational Policies Commission some years ago.[3]

The Imperative Needs

The first nine needs include those skills and abilities essential to vocational success, healthful living, good citizenship, and worthy use of leisure time. For our consideration, the tenth need should be stressed: "All youth need to grow in their ability to think rationally, to express their thoughts clearly, and to be able to read and listen with understanding." When we fail to provide the boy or girl with the experiences necessary to meet this need, the product is likely to be a "mixed-up kid," to use common parlance. The psychiatrists have longer terms, which are hardly more expressive, for the same condition.

In this part of our work, we are concerned with the needs of the adolescent as they affect the method of teaching in the classroom. The physical needs of the adolescent as well as the emotional and spiritual needs are fascinating and important areas of study, but are properly dealt with in books and courses concerned with the psychology of adolescence. The great principle of classroom teaching demands that all learning is an attempt to meet some need of which the learner is aware. The "deep-freeze" principle is not very effective. This principle is expressed by the teacher who admonishes the class: "You had better learn this now or you will be sorry when you go to college." The learning accomplished today is that motivated by the needs felt and recognized today.

[2]Robert C. Hendrickson and Fred G. Cook, *Youth in Danger,* (New York: Harcourt, Brace and Company, 1956), p. 298.
[3]Educational Policies Commission, *Education for All American Youth,* (Washington: National Education Association, 1944), pp. 118-19.

In attempting to answer his needs, the high school boy or girl is not particularly selective in the matter of agencies from which he learns. The school apparently is the most important education force but there are many other factors influencing him continuously.

Southern Illinois University School
Herbert Smith

Creative Ability Finds Many Channels in the Secondary School

MEDIA INVOLVED IN THE TEACHING OF YOUTH

The Book of Ecclesiastes tells of the shameful behavior and the poor attitudes of the young people of the time. Socrates wrote of the poor manners and the laziness of the boys of his day. It has always been this way even though philosophers know that change is constant and inevitable. Each generation is born into a new environment and must attain new learnings from it. This was strikingly illustrated recently by the eight-year-old child who came from the room where the family television was installed saying, "Well, they finally have that man in space."

To her it seemed only logical that men should succeed in an effort which, only a generation ago, would have been only the wildest fantasy. Discussion of life on other planets seems reasonable to the boys and girls in school today but such discussion was only nonsense in the opinions of most people thirty years ago. New learning modifies behavior which, in turn, modifies learning. Because of such modification, one generation behaves unlike another which is often disturbing to the older people but rarely to the younger.

Channels of Ideas

There are many new learnings attained by today's generation of school children through media of communication which have been recently developed and which are being exploited. The average child today, according to many studies, listens to and looks at television programs for about as many hours per week as he spends in school. Beyond that fact, he willingly takes many vacations each year from school but rarely, if ever, takes a vacation from television. The television is one of the new channels through which information and persuasive ideas are brought to the attention of most citizens. It is probably more powerful in its effect on the youngsters than the adults.

Many years ago the church and the school worked with the home to bring ideas approved by local tradition and opinion to the child's mind. The church and the school were the social centers of the early American community as well as the religious and educational agents. Even the few other institutions, such as the blacksmith shop and the tavern, upheld the local social structure in general. Thus established opinions and attitudes did not have a great many newcomers to contend with because there were few channels by which new ideas could enter the thinking of the people.

Radio and Television. As time went on, more channels to people's thinking were opened. The invention of the telegraph put the tiny hamlet in almost continuous contact with the rest of the country and with many other parts of the world. The telephone also made a great contribution to the spreading of opinions and attitudes. In a local sense, anyone who has had experience with a rural party line can substantiate this statement. In the 1920's the radio was established as a channel of thought into the American home. This was the beginning of a system in which an agency other than the parent or the child himself pays for bringing ideas to the family. The parent, as a member of a group, pays the minister and the school teacher. He also buys the newspaper and subscribes to the magazines. Of course he also buys the radio or the television set but the programming of these agencies is beyond his control. Beyond this, every newspaper and magazine is committed to publish certain types of articles and can be depended on to maintain the standards set by its policy. It does not have to please everyone but tries to satisfy a certain segment of the population. The radio has never successfully promoted any such policy. Most of the air time has, from the beginning, been sold to advertisers who can use one measuring stick only and often that seems untrustworthy. The only gauge which can be used is the popularity of the program as indicated by how many persons listen to it. There is little reward for quality on the part of the program in the way that a magazine or book of quality is supported by those who appreciate it. On the other hand, within a decade of its origin as a mass medium of culture, the radio had settled into a pattern of daytime serials, many comedy programs, of which some were good, and a great many programs of music. Liberally interspersed were the commercial messages which, in themselves, were popular. Teachers who taped programs often found children were disappointed if the familiar little jingles extolling soap, or stomach remedies, were omitted. Here, then, was a channel of ideas into the very home itself whose intake end was under the direct control of commercial agencies. Television practice has followed radio very closely and can be seen as a great expansion of the radio channel or as a parallel one. In any case, it is a far more effective channel than the radio and has come under the same control.

The Film. The motion picture film, generally produced as public entertainment, is well established as a channel of ideas into the minds of the public. The source of the idea in a particular motion picture is removed from the home but the child's attendance is more easily regulated than is his attention to a radio or television program. Of course the aim of a film is to make a profit and this means that the spectacular and the sensational are often exploited. For years many films were produced on small budgets and the quality, or even desirability, of some were questionable. In the last decade the number of films being produced has dropped and sincere efforts have been made to improve the quality in order to combat the inroads that television has made on theatre audiences. It should be pointed out the modern film has delved into questions carefully avoided until only a few years ago; although adultery, prostitution, incest, and perversion were taboo they now have become commonplace in American and foreign films. The motion picture film has always attracted the young people of high school as a major fraction of its audience and the increase of the numbers of drive-in theatres has done nothing to lessen the truth of this statement.

The Press. The newspaper, the book, and the magazine have long been channels of thought. Changes in printed material have been less spectacular than the development of communications through electronic devices but some changes are noteworthy. The great popularity of the paper covered books has put the classics within the financial reach of almost everyone. Along with this has to be accepted the fact that it has also made available a great deal of written material that is undesirable, by socially accepted standards, for anyone's entertainment and especially that of a high school pupil.

A change has occurred in the magazine industry, too, that has its good and bad points. The picture magazine has become popular and, at its best, brings the important happenings of the world to the reader with realistic photography and great impact. It creates much that is beautiful through photography and reproduces much of the beauty of the past in a very inexpensive form. At its worst it portrays crime and passion hideously. Somewhere between the extremes fall the magazines devoted to the publication of pictures of girls. Unfortunately the good fiction magazine has not flourished in recent years and several of the long-established publications have ceased to be because of lack of support.

MORALITY OF YOUTH

It has been shown above that there are many channels through which ideas are directed into the thinking of our children. Some of these channels are new within the present century. Because much, if not all, of the maturation of one's behavior springs from his thought, the dependence of behavior on learning is not questioned. Is the increase in channels to youngsters' minds producing a significant change in patterns of thought and hence in morality? Evidence can be found to support each side of the question. It is evident from the study of all reports that by far most children grow into decent, dependable adults. This is true in even the most deprived areas of the country and the worst slum areas of our cities. The small percentage of those branded as bad by our society demands our attention, however. Psychologists and sociologists can explain the delinquency of boys and girls in specific cases but generalization on human behavior is very dangerous. Some delinquent youngsters come from broken homes but it must also be remembered that some very good youngsters also come from broken homes. Poverty produces delinquency in some cases; in others it instills fortitude. Extreme affluence produces some great leaders. Pat answers are impossible but it is important to us to study some of the evidence offered to boys and girls of high school age and to discuss some of the generalizations which may be formed by them.

Adults as Teachers

If delinquency is thought of as being divided into definite criminal areas, it is seen that juvenile delinquency is comprised of theft, especially of automobiles, sex crimes, drunkenness and disorderliness, and traffic violations. When theft is linked with drug addiction, when prostitution and rape are included in sex crimes, when traffic violations are vicious disregard for the life of others, the list is a horrible and terrifying thing. The teacher can see one awful truth behind all of this degenerate behavior: the adults teach the children all of these things! The adults supply the hypotheses and the evidence the children use in their thinking which leads to conclusions resulting in such terribly bad behavior.

Where traffic violations are concerned, the automobile capable of giving more, much more, than the legal speed limit was designed by a highly educated adult, was built by other adults, and sold, probably in the driver's neighborhood, by a responsible citizen. The speedometer reading of 120 miles per hour is in itself an hypothesis that the car can make that speed. The horsepower claims are evidence to support the hypothesis. Reinforcement is supplied in bountiful amount by advertising. In short, adults lead the youngster to a conclusion that it is desirable to drive very fast and penalize him when he does so. The adults are the teachers since they have influenced the thinking of the youngster which led to the conclusion.

Attitudes toward Sexual Behavior. No aspect of our society is more confusing than its attitudes toward sexual behavior. Magazine and newspaper advertisements emphasize the feminine figure and exploit such emphasis to sell almost everything. Radio and television comics who have made national reputations would be left almost speechless if stories and jokes referring to female anatomy were cut from their scripts. Movies have made many famous figures in contemporary history and have made the figures famous. Their advertising stresses bosoms continually. The hypothesis that a person is good or bad according to his or her allure for the opposite sex is presented to us every day. Evidence is heaped upon evidence to support the hypothesis. The learner, however, must stop with viewing the evidence. Once all of its implications are brought to bear between any specific couple of high school pupils, society says, "Stop, what you are thinking is evil! What you might do is disastrous!" The adults print the magazines, make the films, and tell the jokes but impress upon the younger people that the whole train of thought is wrong.

Prudishness has no place in education. There is no excuse for bringing up children in ignorance of their own bodies and their functions.

The great advances made in bringing knowledge of sexual matters wisely into the education of our children are extremely beneficial. Nudity in itself cannot be evil, but the exploitation of nudity for monetary gain depending on the lust of the person who buys the magazine or pays to get into theatre is evil. Sex crimes have increased in our society since World War II. There are many explanations offered. One, by a leading policewoman, is based on the great amount of pornography available on the newsstands and through more covert channels. There is no doubt at all that some of the adults of our society furnish much evidence to young people to support the hypothesis that anatomy is to leer at and gloat over. This is a terrible perversion of truth.

Alcoholic Confusion. The consumption of alcoholic liquor is an old problem. Thousands of sermons have been preached and thousands of lessons have been taught trying to convince people that such consumption is undesirable. It is paradoxical that the adult society which lauds Alcoholics Anonymous as a noble institution and commends one who has broken away from the whiskey habit as a true hero, supports almost unlimited advertising of the cause of the trouble and, by and large, condones moderate consumption. First, the hypotheses offered are confusing. They are: (a) moderate consumption of alcoholic beverage is an adult and acceptable practice, (b) immoderate consumption is disgraceful and harmful, (c) moderate consumption can easily grow into immoderate consumption. Second, evidence supplied to our children comes through radio, TV, magazines, newspapers, and billboards extolling the qualities of this drink or that. Evidence from the home, in some cases, the school, and the church says that all are evil and none is good, but young people evidently feel that one has to try for oneself to find out. The point here is that adults brew the beer, distill the whiskey, write the advertising, preach the sermons, teach the lessons and even attempt to supply the conclusions through legislation. Whatever may be the case, the children learn; some learn one thing, some another.

Inevitability of Learning

Attempts have been made by publishers of comic books and manufacturers of toy guns to explain how children can use their products and yet not learn from the experience. A small boy with a gun, it has been claimed, is merely playing a role which he will later cast off. By this line of reasoning, the child who takes piano lessons will cast off his learning too. The boy in the little league baseball organization is also merely role playing. Many small boys leave the piano alone when adult supervision is removed, many may lose interest in baseball, but a small percentage of boys continue to play the piano and a larger percentage maintain a lively interest in baseball. These are good aspects of society and we accept the laws of learning as they operate in these activities. Is it reasonable to disregard the same laws when they tell us that some boys who carry toy guns for years and read gangster comics and see gangster films and TV programs will cast this all off? Some will; as a matter of fact, most will, but some will not but will apply this knowledge to a destructive end. If our way of teaching children produces only one Charles Starkweather, an adolescent boy who was convicted of 11 murders, the price is far too high. Children have needs and form hypotheses from the answers offered by society and support them with the evidence society makes available. The school cannot hope to reform society absolutely but it must see itself as but one of the agencies of society teaching the boys and girls. All that society offers the youngsters is part of the teaching force of that society.

CODES OF YOUTH

"I have cheated, but if I give you my word I won't cheat, I won't because I never go back on my word." The seventeen year old girl in the principal's office thus expressed her code of behavior. Dishonest practice had crept into the classroom and the principal was holding private conferences with all members of the class.

"I have looked at books to find answers but I never have involved another pupil," explained another. In his code, outsmarting the teacher was part of the game but to copy an answer from a classmate was wrong.

"I won't promise not to cheat because I won't be a liar. I'll probably cheat again when the pressure is on because I don't want to fall behind the others. I won't tell you a lie, so I can't promise not to cheat." So a girl expressed her code. These three illustrations are from the same small class following one incident. If one probes below the surface of any adolescent group, he will find something similar. The picture of the high school boy accepting blame and punishment because he refuses to implicate his fellow pupil is a very familiar one. For the most part, teachers have respected the codes of their pupils and have refused to violate them or take advantage of them.

Written and Unwritten Codes

The code governing much of the attitude of the high school pupil toward the teacher, the school, the parent and society in general is an unwritten one. This has not always been so. Just before the turn of the century when the nature of the high school was changing so rapidy, the secret society with a secret code grew to be a very strong influence in school. Jess B. Davis in his autobiography, "Saga of a School-master"[4] tells of the great hold such societies had on the schools. They dominated most aspects of the school excepting that part of the class-work directly under the control of the teacher. In many respects they were similar to the Greek letter societies found on so many of our college campuses. Social prestige and security came with membership in one of the socially powerful societies in the school. Failure and frustration was the lot of them not invited to join. The codes of these societies were written and members swore to uphold them. The ensuing division of loyalties within a school made the administration difficult and produced much friction and trouble; while administrators and legislators were attacking the problem from their side with measures which finally made such societies illegal, wise teachers made their own diagnosis and administered their own remedy. They saw that the societies were meeting needs not met otherwise by the school. For his own part, Mr. Davis organized an orchestra and channeled the pupils' energy and interests along an acceptable path. Literary groups and science clubs and other associations were formed and so the extracurricular program was started. The written codes, some highly artificial and some even harmful, were abolished. The unwritten code, which had existed through the ages, remained.

Today's Code. The code today is probably not greatly different from that in days gone by. It is based on the principle that one is loyal to the group to which he belongs. When he ceases to be loyal, he ceases to belong. When the child, in early adolescence, identifies himself with others making a similar effort, the laws which protect the group form the code. Hence a boy or girl will not betray another to authority. The authority of the leader of the group is recognized. In extreme cases, such as the gangs found in some areas, this authority overrides all others. In most situations, of course, the attitude is more moderate and the school and civic authority are obeyed.

The leadership of the group is exercised through permissible social channels. Dictators of the group are paramount in the usage of slang, styles of dress, and so on. Fads are explained as dictates of the same authority. Most fads are quite harmless. If tan shoes and pink shoelaces are to be worn for a few months, it satisfies the code and hurts no one. If, on the other hand, it is the going thing to tattoo the boy friend's or girl friend's initials on the left arm using an ordinary needle and ink,

---

[4]Jess B. Davis, *Saga of a Schoolmaster, an Autobiography,* (Boston: Boston University Press, 1956), p. 128.

infections are inevitable and school authority has an obligation to intervene. Very recently there have been several schools reporting marriage as a fad. In one school, a considerable number of couples were married within a week. One school actually demanded that the pupils file an intent to marry one week before the ceremony so that records would not be confused because of the changes of name involved.

The Teacher and the Student's Code. It is generally felt that the teacher has a fairly well defined role in the pupil's code. The wise teacher accepts the code and its dictates unless harm is done to the individual child or the school program. He has definite responsibilities, however, which sometimes involve going against the code. In one school the principal, with support of several teachers, was keeping a boy in detention daily until the boy would have his hair cut so as to eliminate the duck tail which he affected. The detention meant missing football practice and this made the boy ineligible for the team. Was the principal justified? It must be said in his defense that the ducktail hair fashion had become closely associated with lawlessness. With black leather jackets and high boots, it denoted one who was contemptuous of any authority In this case, both the school board and the parents supported the principal and eventually the boy, very literally, had to bow his head to the inevitable. Such cases have actually come to the attention of the courts and the general ruling is that the teacher has the right to deny entry to the class to anyone whose wearing apparel or personal adornment is such that it might be detrimental to the learning situation. Many high schools have successfully suggested to the student body that they, the pupils, write a code to cover this aspect of their school life. Invariably the code accepted by a whole school is acceptable to the administration and the public.

SUMMARY

Boys and girls learn not only from their teachers and through the experiences offered through the school but from all agencies of society with which they come into contact. Many of these agencies teach ideas and concepts without regard to the influence on the attitudes and morals of the adolescent. Yet, in his search for answers to his needs, the adolescent inevitably meets the evidence and forms his conclusions.

The powerful agencies of our society influencing our young people today include automobiles, television, radio, films, and the press. Few if any of these forces are controlled for the primary purpose of creating a desirable learning situation for boys and girls.

In their search for answers, young people look to their peers and the consequent interaction builds up a code which becomes a powerful agent contending for the loyalty of the adolescent.

Good high school methodology takes all these factors into account in dealing with both the behavior of the young people and the subject matter presented to them.

SUGGESTED ACTIVITIES

1. Seek an interview with the director of a "Teen Town" or other such organization and arrange for an evening or two there with the youngsters. Observe their attitudes towards each óther. Try to determine their opinions of the town in which they live.
2. If possible, arrange a class trip to a nearby state hospital for the mentally ill. Ask the doctors in charge to have a clinic planned for the visit and have questions concerning the incidence and severity of mental illness in children of high school age.
3. Determine how many pupils in your home town school are married. If the guidance director or other official will supply the data, discover what correlation there may be between marital status and rank in class. Compare the drop-out rate of the married pupils to that of the general school population.
4. Determine what percentage of the pages of some popular magazine is devoted to advertising and report on how some of this advertising might affect the attitudes of the high school pupil.
5. Search several high school handbooks for a code of behavior compiled by pupils and adopted by them. If several such codes can be found, compare them as to main principles. Compare them with the code found in Appendix B on page 251. Discuss the code as the culmination of a thought process.
6. From a nearby United States employment office, determine the job opportunities available to youth in the vicinity and the number of workers seeking these opportunities.
7. Attend one or more films which seem to be popular with teen-agers. Report on some of the concepts which boys and girls may derive from them.
8. From an informal survey of the college class, determine some magazines read by students when in high school. Get some copies of these magazines and analyze them for concepts which would be more attractive to teen-age boys and girls.

QUESTIONS FOR SELF EVALUATION

1. What does the law in your state demand in regard to the teaching of the effects of alcohol?
2. What is the legal minimum age for driving an automobile in your state? Does this age seem reasonable to you?

3. Identify one or two television programs you consider undesirable for viewing by high school pupils and explain your stand. If you consider none undesirable, identify two particularly good programs and indicate why you think they are good.
4. If your high school had a code composed by the pupils tell how it was developed. Was it effective? Does it seem reasonable to you today?
5. Consider any one theatre with which you are familiar. Is there any policy evident which determines the choice of films which it shows? How does the policy, or the lack of it, influence the thinking of the youth of the area?
6. Analyze and defend your own attitude toward the codes of behavior which exist in most high schools in this country.
7. What is the incidence of juvenile delinquency in your home town? How does this compare with the national average?

BIBLIOGRAPHY

1. ALBERTY, HAROLD, Reorganizing the High School Curriculum. New York: The MacMillan Company, 1953. Part I.
2. BOSSING, NELSON L., Principles of Secondary Education. Englewood Cliffs, N. J.: Prentice-Hall, 1955. Part III.
3. GRAMBS, JEAN D., IVERSON, WILLIAM J., and PATTERSON, FRANKLIN K., Modern Methods in Secondary Education. New York: The Dryden Press, 1958.
4. HANSEN, KENNETH H., High School Teaching. Englewood Cliffs, N. J.: Prentice-Hall, Inc., 1957. Part I.
5. JERSILD, ARTHUR T., The Psychology of Adolescence. New York: The MacMillan Company, 1957.
6. KLAUSMEIER, HERBERT J., Teaching in the Secondary Schools. New York: Harper and Brothers, 1958. Chapter II.
7. ROTHNEY, JOHN W., The High School Student: A Book of Cases. New York: The Dryden Press, 1953.
8. SCHORLING, RALEIGH, AND BATCHELDER, HOWARD T., Student Teaching in Secondary Schools. New York: McGraw-Hill Book Company, 1956, Appendix C.
9. TAYLOR, L. O., McMAHILL, DON R., AND TAYLOR, BOB L., The American Secondary School. New York: Appleton-Century-Crofts, Inc., 1960. Part I.
10. THAYER, V. T., The Role of the School in American Society. New York: Dodd, Mead and Company, 1960. Part II.
11. WATTENBERG, WILLIAM H., The Adolescent Years. New York: Harcourt, Brace and Company, 1955.
12. WIGGINS, SAMUEL P., Successful High School Teaching. Cambridge: Riverside Press, 1958. Part I.

CHAPTER 4

Methods of Teaching

OVERVIEW

The prospective teacher in search of a practicable method often finds very evasive answers. He is told that there is no one method—that one has to use pieces of one method and bits of another, that the method has to come from his own personality and so on. He is subjected to a great many names for methods and is confused by the addition of other names for techniques and procedures. Is there some classification of method which will get things into a neat package? Has there been a historical development of method through the ages? Above all, is there a method peculiarly suited to our country and its system of government? Is there a method which of itself can give children experience to strengthen a democratic form of government?

The reader will find in the present chapter a classification of methodology and definitions with which he can build his own concepts of what methods can be used and which approach seems most promising to him. The relationship of the curriculum to method and that of philosophy and psychology to method will also be dealt with in these pages.

CONTRASTS IN METHODS

A school existed about 500 B.C. in the southern part of what is now Italy in which the student was not permitted to speak in class for the first three years of his attendance. The great teacher of the school, Pythagoras, believed that it took that length of time for the learner to come to a conclusion worthy of expression.[1] A school existed in England in which the pupils were incredibly free to do as they wish. Smoking,

---

[1] "How We Learned to Think," *Richards' Topical Encyclopedia,* (New York: Richards Company, Inc., 1961), Vol. 13, p. 4.

swearing, skipping classes and other activities were permitted even though the children were as young as eight years of age. The great teacher of that school, Alexander S. Neill, believes that only faith in the child expressed by allowing him almost absolute freedom can determine the method by which he is taught.[2]

The picture of a grown man studying three years before he dares to contribute one idea to his field of knowledge contrasted to that of a dirty, swaggering child smoking a cigarette and swearing at the headmaster's wife would seem to indicate that there is nothing common to various methods of teaching, yet the concept of freedom as expressed by Neill holds the clue. Methods of teaching differ mainly in the degree to which the learner is free. The ancient scholar was anything but free; the pupil in the English school mentioned is as free as an individual can be in a society.

Methods can be classified, then, as to the degree to which they permit the learner to be free—free in action, free in thought. Although our illustration implies that there has been a continuous movement toward freedom in teaching, one would be hard pressed to defend this statement as a thesis. Comenius and Rousseau advocated more freedom than is allotted to many pupils today and Socrates may have been freer in his method than many a modern teacher. In general, however, in the last fifty years newer methods have emphasized a liberalizing approach to the learner.

CLASSIFICATION OF METHODS

Although many writers have dealt with methods of teaching there has been no standard classification accepted by the profession. One authority[3] does speak of the teacher-centric method which includes recitation and lecture and the pupil-centric method which includes group method, student-teacher sharing and group discussion. This division is based essentially on the transfer of some power of control from the teacher to the pupil or, in other words, the increase of freedom to the pupils in the pupil-centric method.

Other authorities refer to a legion of methods, some of which might better be described as procedures and techniques.

In this work are considered as they are identified and classified following:

---

[2]Alexander Sutherland Neill, *That Dreadful School,* (London: H. Jenkins Limited, 1937).

[3]C. B. Mendenhall and K. J. Arisman, *Secondary Education,* (New York: William Sloane Associates, Inc., 1951), p. 88.

1. The lecture method including the Socratic lecture technique.
2. The recitation method involving the textbook-assignment technique.
3. The socialized recitation method also involving the textbook assignment technique.
4. The unit method which includes what has been termed the problem-solving method, the project method, and the discovery method.

   The units within the unit method may be based on subject matter or on experience.

This classification omits many of the "methods" to be found in the literature of the field. It seems that titles such as "demonstration method," "laboratory method," and "project method" indicate procedures that are acceptable in one or more of the foregoing categories. As illustrative, the demonstration is valuable in the lecture and can be equally so in the study of a unit. The skill with which the demonstration is presented determines whether the technique is good. It can be good or poor in any method. In the lecture method the demonstration can be used as an introduction to a concept which the teacher develops and perhaps establishes as a theory. On the other hand, it can be used as verification, by the teacher, of a theory or concept which he has put forth. In a unit method based on experience the demonstration can be presented by the teacher or a pupil as an exploratory experience which will provide evidence for the class in their study of a hypothesis or it can be used as a verification of a generalization established by the class or some member of it.

The Laboratory Technique

The laboratory technique may consist of sending children into the laboratory to perform certain exercises with scientific equipment and materials. It may be that the teacher has already told them what to expect if they are doing the "right" things and what will happen if they do the "wrong." With a restricted deductive method, such a use of the laboratory technique is almost a certainty. If, however, the children go into the laboratory to further the development of their own hypotheses and are free to make mistakes, then the laboratory technique is functioning in a different manner entirely.

Some examples of the "project method" on close examination turn out to be merely application of the textbook-assignment method dressed up with a project technique. If a class undertakes a project at the teacher's command and is directed through it by him with little or no freedom of choice of subject matter or expression of opinion, little has been gained. Only when the learner has increased freedom of choice of activity, and freedom of expression, can we point to a beneficial change in method.

The Discovery Method

One sees today references to the "discovery" method. This is essentially an inductive method of teaching in which the learner is offered experiences through which he may discover concepts. The methodology based on reflective thinking—as that function is defined in the second chapter—contains the discovery method within it. The discovery method concentrates attention on the steps of reflective thinking which deal with the collection of evidence and the drawing of conclusions from it. The method is good to the extent that the process of reflective thinking is followed and the techniques involved are sound.

RELATIONSHIP OF METHOD TO REFLECTIVE THINKING

Reflective thinking is a process within the learner and is hoped for as the outcome of any method of teaching. The hope is fulfilled to a greater extent in some methods than in others. In the lecture method wherein the teacher presents all the ideas and the learner has no opportunity to contribute, the opportunity for reflective thinking on the part of the learner is limited. If the teacher and the textbook are not to be questioned, then the learner is challenged only to remember and to repeat. The college classroom is still the stronghold of many professors who never seek contributions from the class. Unfortunately many students of such professors tend to teach in the same way when they face high school pupils. There are reasons why lectures are acceptable to a great extent in college teaching but these reasons are not valid in high school teaching. The lecture as a device to be used occasionally is valuable to the high school teacher but, as a method, which implies constant use, it affords little freedom of thought to the pupil and is not desirable.

The Recitation

The term "recitation" used to mean exactly what it says. The teacher would call on a pupil to recite the lesson. If the lesson consisted of a chapter from a history book, the pupil would begin with the first paragraph and recite until told to stop. Then another pupil would have to take up the task and continue. The one who had recited could not then relax his attention because the teacher might recall him at any moment. Punishment for being unable to recite was often severe so the teacher had little trouble with motivation or maintaining attention. As implied, the textbook assignment was almost universally characteristic of the recitation method. The ability brought into action by this way of teaching, of course, was memorization. There was little freedom afforded the learner as he rarely was called on for any contribution to the lesson other than the parroting of what had been written in the textbook or spoken by the teacher. The star pupil in the schools using this method could run through Lamb's essays, Latin verbs, and Euclid's theorems with equal facility, but just how much became a part of his own functioning knowledge would be difficult to determine. Opportunities for the development of skills in reflective thinking was almost nonexistent.

The Socialized Recitation. In this century, the recitation method including the textbook assignment has been greatly modified and is often known as the socialized recitation. Most of us are familiar with this because we have been taught by it. In this method the teacher leads the discussion which very often is based on a textbook assignment made in the preceding lesson period. The modification is in the demands and questioning of the teacher. Instead of asking for a recitation of the written word he asks questions in order to probe the pupil's knowledge of the material. If the questioning stops there, little has been gained; if, however the questioning involves reasoning — if the "why" is added to the "what," "when," and "where" — then the pupil is afforded the opportunity to formulate and express ideas of his own and, to this extent, is free to learn. The socialized recitation based on textbook assignments is the link between methods in which freedom is denied and those in which it is granted.

Questioning. When we reach this point in the growth of method we see questioning as one of the essential skills of the effective teacher. Through wise questioning the teacher can lead the pupil through the process of reflective thinking and can build in him the skills essential to it. The socialized recitation is greatly enriched by the types of questions which Curtis devised for teachers of science. Because they are valuable to teachers in many fields they are listed following.[4]

1. Comparison or Contrast. This type of question involves the enumeration of likenesses or differences which can be arrived at through reflective thinking.
Example: What is the difference between weather and climate?
2. Decision For or Against. All questions involving a choice or an indication of preference. Questions are classified in this group if the answer requires a weighing or preference of factors or conditions involved. If the answer is arrived at without such weighing of factors or use of judgment, the question is classified as one of recall.

---

[4]Raleigh Schorling, *Student Teaching*, (New York: McGraw-Hill Book Company, 1949), pp. 242 ff.

Example: Do you think it is correct to call the Wright brothers the inventors of the airplane?

3. Application in New Situations. The employment of principles or other knowledge in a particular situation or problem with which the student has not heretofore been confronted.

Example: Suggest ways of correcting a bad case of reverberation in a hall or church.

4. Classification. This type of question involves comparison of two or more things in order to (a) place them in a predetermined group based on similarity, differences, or other relationships, or (b) define a group.

Example: What kind of change occurred in each of the following: ice melted, sugar dissolved in water, milk soured, warm pop foamed out of bottle, zinc dissolved in acid?

5. Relationships Including Cause and Effect. This type of question requires the student to perceive the interdependence or connection, either objectively or in the mind, between phenomena, conditions, or other data.

Example: What is the relation between friction and the efficiency of a machine?

6. Example or Illustration. A type of question wherein the learner is asked to give an example of a type or principle not found in context. This type is usually the converse of classification. Diagrams called for (if they are not a reproduction of an illustration in the text) are classed in this type.

Example: Describe a case that you have actually witnessed where inertia was a disadvantage.

7. Statement of Aim. Questions involving the author's aim or purpose in the selection or arrangement of materials.

Example: Why is the author interested in the history of elements?

8. Criticism. In this type of question the pupil must judge as the adequacy, correctness, or relevancy of a situation, statement, or diagram. He might also be requested to judge his own work or the work of another person.

Example: What are your main sources of error?

9. Inference. This type of question requires the student to draw inferences, or deduction from data, using as starting points previously learned facts, laws, principles, or other data.

Example: From the data presented, what do you think will happen to Niagara Falls in the next 500 years?

10. Discussion. This type of question involves consideration of controversial questions, and argument for the sake of arriving at truth or clearing up difficulties.

Example: Discuss the most important proposal before the United Nations during the past year.

11. Outline. This type of question requires that the pupil give a preliminary sketch or plan of some procedure that might be enacted or material that might be written.

Example: Outline the activities of the conservative program in your state.

12. Definition and Explanation. This type includes any question wherein the pupil is asked to give the exact meaning of some word, phrase, or statement, or to make the definition clear.

Example: How does a siphon work?

13. Recall. Any "recall" question will require an answer that depends chiefly on the use of memory. In this type of question the answer must have been given in the textbook, and the pupil is required to recollect only what is in the assigned reading. Questions often classified as simple, selective, and evaluative recall come under this classification. If additional mental processes are involved, such as drawing conclusions or making observations, they shall hold precedence over recall in determination of type.

Example: What do you consider the three most important inventions of the nineteenth century from the standpoint of the expansion and growth of transportation?

14. Summary. This type of question requires the student to make a résumé of principles of facts; i.e., a concise rewording of major or important ideas involved in any area of experience.

Example: What were the big ideas in Chapter 67?

15. Observation. This type of question requires the student to arrive at an answer as a result of direct observation at the time the question was asked.

Example: Examine the carrot. Where are the buds located?

16. Formulation of New Questions. This type of question includes those wherein the pupil is asked what question or problem comes to his mind or is asked to formulate a new question.

Example: What questions occurred to you while doing this experiment?

The socialized recitation is in wide use today in both the secondary school and the college and, because so many are being taught by this means, it will be strong for some time to come. It can be a very effective method when the teacher is skillful enough to stimulate the learner to "think for himself." On the other hand, when the teacher permits it to revert to immediate recall of facts from the textbook it must be considered as denying the pupil opportunity to think reflectively and hence it is not desirable.

THE UNIT METHOD

The unit method permits the teacher and pupils planning together to attack an essentially broad segment of knowledge. They may deal with it in a manner which promises them the greatest amount of benefit in light of the outcomes they deem most desirable. This concept encompasses so much in the way of procedures and techniques that Chapter 5 is devoted to it. The unit method has come to us with several names. The problem-solving method, the project method, the Dalton method, and others have contributed to it and, to some extent at least, have been absorbed by it. Those several efforts have been the result of attempts of the pioneers in method to give the learner his freedom to think, to develop the skills involved, to formulate ideas, and to be independent. Following the teachings of the great philosophers and psychologists, they have attempted to create a method suited to the demands of our time and effective in the American society.

THE RELATIONSHIP OF CURRICULUM TO METHOD

Curriculum has been defined as the total experience provided by the school for the child. It has also a more restricted meaning: it may mean a specific sequence of courses designed for a special purpose. The academic curriculum, for example, is a college preparatory sequence of courses in high school. For this discussion, let us hold to the more restrictive definition.

The curriculum does not determine the method. Two schools may offer a vocational home economics curriculum and meet all the specific demands of that sequence. One school may employ a teacher who uses a strict textbook-assignment method quite effectively. The other may have a teacher who employs a unit method with results as good as those of the first school. It would seem that an automotive repair curriculum in a vocational high school would be more inductive than a course in Latin in an academic school, but this is not so. The function of a carburetor can be taught in a rigid "do this — do that" manner and often is. On the other hand Caesar's Gallic Wars can be taught with great imagination and with much induction by the pupils. One can hardly say, it is granted, that this is often the case.

The Core Curriculum

The core curriculum more than any other, perhaps, has become associated with a method. Because of this confusion, definition is necessary. Alberty[5] has defined the core curriculum as being the group of subjects considered by the secondary schools as esesntial to their function. English and social studies are two such subjects and they are included in the core. Even though these subjects are taught in a subject-centered curriculum by a recitation method they are still part of the core.

Alberty pursues the term core through five steps. In the first, the several essential subjects are offered in a conventional compartmentalized fashion. In the next step, interrelations between two subjects are exploited and the separate courses are correlated. Moving on, two or more subjects are fused in a "block" program in which the compartmentalization is broken down. Class periods are much longer and, typically, one teacher presents subject matter from both areas as he sees fit. Beyond

---

[5]Harold Alberty, "Designing Programs to Meet the Common Needs of Youth," National Society for the Study of Education, Fifty-Second Yearbook, 1953. Part 1, Chap. VII, pp. 118-40.

that is more complete fusion with the evaluation of the pupils' work reported without regard to the specific subjects. At this point the single textbook is not used and the boundaries between subjects are not found. In the last degree, the classes meet for long periods of time, full half days perhaps, and are free to pursue almost any topic they and the teacher wish and may do it in almost any way. A class conceivably could enter upon a study of the causes of war and become involved in classic books on the subject, advanced experiments with rockets, difficult mathematical considerations as well as a great deal of sociology, psychology, and philosophy.

It can readily be seen that in the more advanced degrees of the core curriculum, the unit method is mandatory. Unfortunately, the concept involved and the method have become associated in the literature and popular opinion with a "laissez-faire" policy of school management. Neither a core curriculum nor the unit method calls for a "laissez faire" approach. In practice both demand strong organization and a large amount of self-discipline on the part of both teacher and pupil.

THE RELATIONSHIP OF PHILOSOPHY TO METHOD

The teacher's philosophy of education does not necessarily dictate to him the method of teaching to be used. The philosophy of Catholic education is well defined and the Roman Catholic teachers in parochial schools hold a great body of belief in common yet McGucken, a teacher in a university operated by the Catholic Church, states:[6]

"The Catholic as a Catholic is not concerned with curriculum. The Catholic as a Catholic is not concerned with method. He may advocate the outmoded method of drill; he may believe that the project method or the problem method has a place in his schools; he may employ the methods of 'progressive' education, while necessarily rejecting their underlying philosophy of naturalism; and there is none to say him nay."

In support of this viewpoint, one can imagine several teachers with similar backgrounds in philosophy teaching by different methods. Conversely, several teachers using similar methods might have differing philosophies. As a matter of fact, any of our public schools are illustrations of this situation. In general, a school may be characterized by a common methodology more easily than by a common philosophy.

On the other hand, there are some philosophies of education whose implementation demands a particular type of method. One could hardly claim to be a follower of Dewey and William H. Kilpatrick while

---

[6]William McGucken, "The Philosophy of Catholic Education," National Society for the Study of Education, Forty-First Yearbook, 1942. Part I, Chap. VI, p. 286.

utilizing an "outmoded method of drill." In practice, there is some confusion on this point as many teachers have liberal philosophies but feel
confined by their particular school systems to a rigid methodology.
This situation becomes a question of personal integrity and the teacher
must determine whether he can teach efficiently in spite of the conflict.
If he feels he cannot, then he should discontinue teaching in that school
system.

THE RELATIONSHIP OF PSYCHOLOGY TO METHOD

The psychology of education leads directly to method. If one accepts
the Laws of Learning as written by Thorndike, then one must provide
the learner with experience as demanded by these laws. If one is convinced that Gestaltism is psychologically sound, then he must provide
for the child according to these laws. The implementation of this principle is difficult because of conflicts among different schools of psychology and because of the lag in accepting the findings of the psychologists into our schools. The great reading controversy in our schools
is an illustration in point. Should the child read by understanding and
observing the function of each letter in the word "missile" or should he
recognize the word "missile"? There are articulate and vehement spokes-
men for each side of the question.

The schools today, to some degree, employ methodology based on
the old Faculty psychology and many critics would have this strengthened. Much of the present methodology stems from Connectionism with
an atomistic approach to the several fields of knowledge. One has only
to listen to the monotonous questioning demanding factual recall heard
in many classrooms to be convinced that this work of method is still
flourishing. The newer methodology, including that based on reflective
thinking, finds its basis in the newer psychologies which stress the integration of the factors of a problem by the learner. The newer method
demands a broader approach which will be delineated and described
in a later chapter.

SUMMARY

The thesis of this work dealing with methodology states that methods
can be classified as to the degree to which they permit the learner to be
free. It is implied that, in a free country, young people must exercise
the right to freedom wisely so that they can mature as people understanding the responsibilities and the privileges of the free.

A classification of methods is offered which traces a trend from the
restrictive to the liberalizing methodology in the schools. Although much
teaching still stems from older psychological concepts and some reac-

tionary force can be identified, the most liberalizing methods have their foundations in the philosophy and psychology of the twentieth century.

The curriculum, it has been stated, does not determine the method but as curricula grow and new demands of society are met by the school, so changes of methodology are called for.

Subsequent changes in methodology will be beneficial in a democracy to the extent that they afford the learner greater freedom of activity, of expression, and of thought.

SUGGESTED ACTIVITIES

1. With another member of the class as a partner, write and present orally a dialogue using the Socratic technique. The topic may be one concerning Greek culture or one of present day significance.
2. Through a role playing technique, organize the class in a recitation method lesson using selections of the first chapter of this book as lesson material.
3. If the core curriculum is offered in a high school accessible to you, visit a class for half a day or more. Discuss the methods used with the teacher and report the outcomes to the class.
4. State your own philosophy of teaching, to the extent you can, and determine whether this involves a method. If you think it does, which method is involved?
5. Analyze a workbook or textbook in your teaching field to determine the range of types of questions asked and the single type most often used.
6. Interview a college instructor who uses the lecture method effectively and discuss with him the advantages of this way of teaching at the college level.

QUESTIONS FOR SELF EVALUATION

1. In your opinion, what was Pythagoras' defense of his system of teaching?
2. From your reading and work in psychology, do you agree or disagree with Neill's work at Summerhill?
3. Have you had a class with a teacher who uses the Socratic technique? Did you find it satisfying or frustrating? Explain why.
4. Distinguish clearly between the recitation method and the socialized recitation method.
5. List as many as you can of the sixteen types of questions devised by Curtis. Devise new examples of each.
6. Define the term "experiment." To what degree did your experiments in high school and college classes meet this definition?
7. Illustrate what you understand by the "core curriculum" from your experience. or reading. Where does your concept fit into Alberty's five step gradation?
8. Relate the lecture method to reflective thinking as used by your college instructors.

9. List several titles used for the unit method and point out why each was adequate or inadequate to convey what was to be done. Is there a better title than "unit method"?
10. Was there uniformity in the high school you attended in regard to method? Was there uniformity of philosophy? Support answers by illustrations.

BIBLIOGRAPHY

1. BURTON, WILLIAM H., *The Guidance of Learning Activities.* New York: Appleton-Century-Crofts, Inc., 1952. Chapter II.
2. CANTOR, NATHANIEL, *The Teaching-Learning Process.* New York: The Dryden Press, Inc., 1953. Chapter III.
3. CLARK, LEONARD E. AND STARR, IRVING S., *Secondary School Teaching Methods,* 1959. Chapter VI.
4. GRAMBS, JEAN D., IVERSON, WILLIAM J., AND PATTERSON, FRANKLIN K., *Modern Methods in Secondary Education.* New York: The Dryden Press, 1958. Chapters IX-X.
5. HILGARD, EARNEST R., AND RUSSELL, DAVID H., *Motivation in School Learning: Learning and Instruction.* Forty-Ninth Yearbok, National Society of Education, Part I. Chicago: The University of Chicago Press, 1950.
6. KLAUSMEIER, HERBERT J., *Teaching in the Secondary School.* New York: Harper and Brothers, 1958. Chapter X.
7. MORSE, WILLLIAM C., AND WINGO G. MAX, *Psychology and Teaching.* Chicago: Scott Foresman and Company, 1955.
8. WIGGINS, SAMUEL P., *Successful High School Teaching.* Cambridge: Riverside Press, 1958. Part III.

CHAPTER 5

A Unit Method
Based On Reflective Thinking

OVERVIEW

If one is to learn to think reflectively, he must have the time and space to do so and the school teaching him is obligated to provide a good measure of freedom in each of these dimensions. Schools, however, have been niggardly with time, doling it out in short periods under rigorous regulation. The school has also tended to be penurious with space by drawing tight boundaries around small sections of subject matter. Efforts to liberalize the school allotments of time and space have not been successful so far although many attempts have been made. As a matter of fact, it is precisely in these considerations that the linkage between philosophy and psychology on one hand and practice on the other breaks down. The successful functioning of method is possible only when this union with theory is direct and strong. Of the methods identifiable in our schools today, the unit method offers more freedom in time and space than any other and hence affords the greatest opportunity for the reconciliation of theory and practice.

In the following pages, the unit method is described and illustrated. In other books, the reader may find definitions and descriptions of units that are not similar to those presented here. This is so because this work is an attempt to add both breadth and depth to the term "unit." The breadth is increased by the breaking down of subject matter barriers; the depth is increased by the establishing of skills of reflective thinking within this method.

BEGINNING AND DEVELOPMENT OF UNITS

The very word "unit" implies something that can stand by itself and has a definite beginning and ending. What we are reaching for in our teaching method has its start in the interests and needs of the learners

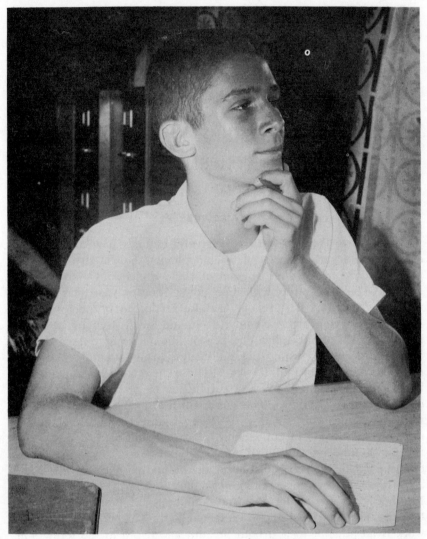

Southern Illinois University School
Herbert Smith

The Student is Given the Time and the Place to Study by Himself

and in the demands of present day society. Although the unit has a termination within the school curriculum it aims to give the learner concepts with which he can learn new facts and develop fresh ideas far beyond the limits imposed on him in the classroom.

The Unit Method

When one speaks of "the unit method" he immediately introduces a good deal of confusion. Years ago Curtis[1] told of the National Survey of Education's reporting ten plans in use characterized by the unit assignment. Although each "method" claimed a name and some distinction, in reality, Curtis stated, they were all pretty much the same thing and were different only in name. At the time, the use of unit method was making rapid advances in the secondary schools. Perhaps one can find firm ground more easily by tracing the roots of the general type of unit method. One root, certainly, would lead to the work of Herbart[2] who lived in Europe from 1776 until 1841. He developed a psychology of learning from which a purpose could be reached. The purpose was to prepare men to live happily in an organized society. This meant that each individual should be educated so that his personal character could contribute to a moral society. From this principle he went to method. As a matter of fact, Cubberley[3] identified Herbart as the first writer on education to place the great emphasis on proper instruction as opposed to mere knowledge or discipline. His first ingredient which must be present in good teaching is interest. His next ingredient is apperception — the comprehension of new knowledge in terms of the old. Herbart did not hold that all teaching should depend on these principles but left room for the memorizing of facts when such was called for. Even for rote learning, however, he felt that careful organization of the teaching process directed toward definite ends was essential. One cannot do Herbart, or any other great writer in education, justice in this type of book. The reader will find fuller treatments of his work both informative and fascinating.

Those who followed Herbart applied his principles to teaching method and brought forth the famous five steps: (1) Preparation, (2) Presentation, (3) Association, (4) Generalization and (5) Application. It is not difficult to see how the organization of the teaching of a segment of knowledge on these five steps would lead to a product clearly akin to a "unit."

In our country, an outstanding writer on secondary methods is Morrison[4] whose work was done in the first decades of the present century.

---

[1]Francis D. Curtis, "The Morrison Plan in Service," *Clearing House,* (May, 1935), pp. 547-54.

[2]See Chapter 2.

[3]Elwood C. Cubberley, *The History of Education,* (New York: Houghton Mifflin Company, 1920), p. 741.

[4]Henry C. Morrison, *The Practice of Teaching in the Secondary School,* (Chicago: University of Chicago Press, 1926).

He did not profess to have founded a method "but rather claimed to have done an analyses of teaching procedure." He offered five steps comparable to those developed from Herbart's work. They are (1) Exploration, (2) Presentation, (3) Assimilation, (4) Organization and (5) Recitation. Whether or not Morrison had Herbart's steps in mind is a matter of debate which is rather fruitless for our purposes. It is enough that we see in the work of these men an approach to the organization of teaching.

Definition. Since Morrison's work in the 1920's, the "unit method" has grown in many directions and under many guises. Authors in books on curriculum, compilors of state courses of study, and writers in the periodical field have put forth series of definitions and hundreds of illustrations. From this welter one must accept as a unit almost any treatment of a segment of subject matter content or any organized approach to a topic which cuts across subject matter lines.

With so many concepts of "unit" extant, one cannot identify any strong psychological framework common to all yet it seems most logical that a unit should begin with the elements of a thought process and progress through it logically until the outcomes desired are attained. The elements of a thought process are the ideas gained by the learner from his experience while the outcomes are generalizations, appreciations, or skills which will serve him far beyond the classroom.

In light of the foregoing, a unit is defined as a study of a segment of knowledge. In this study experiences are provided the learner who deals with them rationally so as to grasp concepts which become a part of his background for further experience. The concepts may be generalizations concerning phenomena or attitudes.

Since the presentation of this idea is difficult in the abstract, an illustrative unit is presented.

AN ILLUSTRATIVE UNIT

The great difference between the unit here presented and the conventional type lies in the presentation of experience prior to generalizations. As a matter of fact, the unit is taught most successfully when little, if any, generalization is presented to the learner by the teacher. It is hoped that the learner will grasp his own generalization as the result of reflecting upon his experiences. These experiences, real or contrived or even abstract, will be of value if they contribute to the reflection.

The Teacher as a Guide

Before the teacher can guide the learner along the path to any generalization he must know the way himself. He is like a mountain climber who can guide a neophyte to a particular mountain peak. In this activity he teaches his pupil not only to reach the one mountain peak but also instructs him generally in mountain climbing so that some time in the future he will attack and conquer other and higher peaks expertly. Even those who reached the top of Mount Everest were instructed by other famous mountaineers. So the teacher prepares his approach to leading a class to specific generalizations. He does not stand on the summit saying, "Here I am, come up to me." He goes down into the valley and joins his neophytes and climbs the path, familiar to him, with them.

The teacher carefully plans his work by listing the great principles involved in a unit. Under each of these major ideas he lists contributing but minor principles. Under each of these he ranks the experiences from which the ideas may spring and which he can provide for his pupils. This preparation can be likened to the mountain guide's familiarity with the ascents, slopes, and faces of the peak up which he is to lead his party.

With this preparation done, the teacher provides the learner first with experience. He offers the pupil the use of tools such as writing, reporting, evaluating as the guide instructs in the use of the rope and the pitons. The teacher questions the pupil to draw from him the results of his thinking upon the experience. He provides the students opportunity to compare their ideas so that each member of the class is assured of his progress. As the mountain climbers progress from easy to more difficult slopes, so the class is directed from minor given objectives to major. The teacher is with his boys and girls and may give them a boost occasionally but he does not carry them. Each must pull his own weight.

Let us come down now from the mountains and consider "A Unit on Housing." The generalizations cited first are part of the teacher's preparation. He will start his teaching with the experiences he has ready to offer his pupils.

A UNIT ON HOUSING

Major Generalizations:

1. The quality of the housing of an area is dependent on the resources of the area.
2. The housing of an area is a result of the demands of the climate.
3. The type of housing in any area is dependent on the building materials available in the area.
4. The quality of the housing of an area is dependent on the incomes of the people.

5. The quality of housing in an area correlates with the incidence of delinquency in the area.
6. The construction of homes is an important industry.
7. The financing of housing is a matter of national concern and of local importance.

Each of these major generalizations is built on minor generalizations. The following are illustrative rather than exhaustive in each case. It is impossible to indicate all the minor generalizations that might possibly lead to a major generalization.

Major Generalization:

1. The quality of the housing of an area is dependent on the resources of the area.

Minor Generalizations:
   a. Houses are built of many types of material.
   b. Material available locally is often cheaper than imported material.
   c. In any area, some materials are more expensive than others so many houses will be found built of the inexpensive and fewer of the expensive materials.

Major Generalization:

2. The housing of an area is a result of the demands of the climate.

Minor Generalizations:
   a. The colder the climate, the more insulation is needed.
   b. In cold climates, basements are often used to house a central heating plant.
   c. Storm windows (double windows) are used more frequently in cold climates than in warm climates.
   d. A gabled roof with a steep pitch will shed snow better than will a flat roof.
   e. In cold climates, house fires due to faulty heating apparatus are numerous and many deaths occur in such fires every year in our country.
   f. In some areas, tornado hazard makes the building of storm cellars advisable.

Major Generalization:

3. The type of housing in any area is dependent on the building materials available in the area.

Minor Generalizations:
   a. In our country, wood has always been a common building material.

    b. Bricks are used in and near areas where clay for making them is available.

    c. Stone has been used for centuries and is still used for large buildings but seldom for homes in our country.

    d. Local products, such as adobe, are sometimes used in house building in certain parts of the country.

Major Generalization:

4. The quality of the housing of an area is dependent on the incomes of the people.

Minor Generalizations:

    a. In farm areas, the fertile rich regions have good farmhouses and barns while in barren regions the houses and outbuildings are small and not well built.

    b. In towns and cities, the people with high salaries tend to live on the outskirts of the cities and in the suburbs while those with poor jobs, or none at all, tend to crowd into the congested central parts of the cities.

Major Generalization:

5. The quality of housing in an area correlates with the incidence of delinquency in the area.

Minor Generalizations:

    a. The crowded areas of cities have more taverns and places of ill repute than do the residential areas.

    b. The poor and transient classes contribute more than their share to delinquency. These people live in poor housing areas.

    c. In towns, the poor housing area is often found on one edge of town remote from better homes.

Major Generalization:

6. The construction of homes is an important industry.

Minor Generalizations:

    a. Much of the labor done by carpenters, plumbers, masons and others is on house construction.

    b. The lumber industry, as well as some lesser ones, depend largely on house construction.

    c. The government (United States of America) has passed much legislation to support and control the building of houses.

Major Generalization:

7. The financing of housing is a matter of national concern and of local importance.

Minor Generalizations:

   a. The federal government has assured several types of loans for house construction.
   b. Many banks and loan companies depend on house loans for a great share of their business.
   c. Many houses in the U.S.A. are not fully paid for but are security for debts called mortgages.

If a school is organized about a core, then it is possible that a unit such as the foregoing could be used in its entirety. If social studies and English formed a block of time, then the pertinent areas of the unit could be taught within this block while the science and business aspects might be used as integrating areas. If a high school is highly departmentalized, then the teachers of the various subject matter field can work together and present each aspect in the subject matter field to which it belongs.

The Teaching of a Major Generalization

Outlined here is the teaching of one major generalization that will serve to illustrate how each can be taught. The first is considered:

1. The quality of the housing of an area is dependent on the resources of the area.
   a. Houses are built of many types of material.
   b. Material available locally is often cheaper than imported material.
   c. In any area, some materials are more expensive than others so many houses will be found built of the inexpensive and fewer of the expensive materials.

The principles of teaching outlined previously indicate that experiences must be found through which the pupil can grasp the minor generalizations and from these the major generalization. The first minor generalization should prove fruitful. This states that houses are built of many types of material.

The Teaching of a Minor Generalization (Houses are built of many types of material.)

Of course, one could easily appeal to the class for contributions from their individual experiences and there is no doubt that wood, bricks, and stucco would be brought into the conversation. In one class, however, the teacher had teams go to various parts of the town in which the high school was located. Each team had at least one camera and took pictures with which they illustrated their report of the trip. Pictures were shown of houses with siding of clapboard, wooden shingles, asbestos shingles, brick, stucco, plywood, pressed wood, aluminum, corrugated iron, artificial brick siding, and old Coca-Cola signs. The school was in a fairly wealthy part of town and the pupils (ninth grade) were quite surprised to know that the other half of the population lived in some very miserable dwellings. Their concepts about what type of house many people in this country can afford were drastically changed. (It should be added that the pictures themselves were grist for an element on photography.) The reader can well believe that the class was convinced that houses are built of many types of materials.

After the scouting experience it was not difficult to foster the discussions about the correlation of quality of housing and cost. The local lumber yard was glad to quote prices on its materials and a local firm making a patented concrete facing (Brickcrete) was glad to supply samples of their product with prices indicated. The pupils studied the origin of the materials and indicated where each came from on maps. It was not difficult for them to comprehend the transportation problem involved in acquiring, in the Midwest, lumber grown near the West Coast. They could grasp the minor generalization dealing with the cost of transported materials with a minimum of help from the teacher.

The pictures of the houses presented facts leading to the third minor generalization. Whereas brick and stone were common to the houses of those people living in wealthier areas, artificial siding, corrugated iron, and old signs were found in the poorest district. Even in a wealthy town, the homes of the poor outnumbered those of the very rich.

When the class understood that a man's house often is the expression of his ability to earn, that some houses are cheaper than other houses and that a man's earning ability is determined, to some degree, by the vocational opportunities of the area, then they understood that the quality of housing is directly dependent on the resources of the area.

The class progresses through experiences which lead to other minor and major generalizations. In this progress thinking is both inductive and deductive. Established principles lead to further hypothesis until the class is able to unify their work into a comprehensive and significant body of knowledge to which each has contributed.

RECIPROCATION

The success of a method resting on the teaching of generalizations through experiences depends on the reciprocation by the learner of the interest and enthusiasm of the teacher. The reciprocation is not achieved by chance but has to be won by consistently sound procedure on the part of the teacher.

How is this done? The teacher is working with two variables: the material to be taught and the background of thinking of the learner. He adapts the first to the second if he is to be successful. Perhaps the greatest common mistake in teaching has been the reversal of this— that is, presenting material to the learner hoping that he will adapt himself to it. According to the Gestalt viewpoint of learning presented in Chapter 2, the integration of the background of the learner with the new situation (insight) may take place suddenly and the solution to a problem is revealed. The suddenness, however, is not the key factor in learning for the classroom teacher. While it is true that people experience such flashes of insight, a more systematic process may lead to a similar result.

If a learner is made aware of a problem and then, on his own motivation, formulates a hypothesis and diligently studies the evidence, he will form conclusions. These conclusions will be as sound as the judgment with which he evaluates the evidence. Careful teaching assures that the evidence presented will be within the powers of the learner to evaluate and hence his conclusions will be, in most cases, sound. As the learner is afforded success in formulating valid generalizations through proper methods of teaching, so will his ability as a thinker, as well as his confidence in himself, develop.

When this growth takes place in an individual who is a member of a group of students experiencing similar development it is strongly reinforced. As interaction occurs, there is brought about in the class an enthusiasm, an *esprit de corps*, which reciprocates the interest and the imagination of the teacher.

In following chapters will be found illustrations of the accomplishments of teachers in the ordinary academic subject matter areas, the esthetic and skills areas, and the possibilities in some neglected areas of our secondary curriculum.

The technique of involving the student in the conception and the development of a unit has become known as pupil-teacher planning.

PUPIL-TEACHER PLANNING

The learner more willingly identifies himself with tasks which he has helped plan than with those imposed upon him by authority. When the pupil is given some responsibility in the preparation of a unit he looks upon it as his own, in part at least, and wants to push the work along to a successful conclusion. Planning in which the student is involved also exploits the creative urge that lies within each of us and which is especially strong during the adolescent years. The process of including the boys and girls in the planning of the work which they will undertake to do as a class is termed pupil-teacher planning.

One authoritative work states:

A problem is always a personal affair, as teachers would do well to remember. The individual, whether in school or out, faces no problem until he stakes a claim to it. When he does this he acts as if he had shouted for all to hear, "This is mine! Let me get at it." The simple fact is that individuals become involved in only those problems they expect to solve. Invariably, therefore, their biases, knowledge, values — in short, their personalities — are vital factors in the reflection they carry on in problem situations.[5]

Pupil-Teacher Planning at the Secondary Level

Although the concept is simple, many secondary school teachers find it exceedingly difficult to allot any part of their teaching preparation to students. Perhaps this is because they have been taught by their education and their experience that preparation is the teacher's task. In addition to this possibility, the attitude of many boys and girls is not conducive to pupil-teacher planning. Because of puppet government student councils and other devices by which teachers have pretended to offer them responsibility, young people are convinced that any propositions made by teachers promising opportunities to work on their own are going to prove merely a sugar coating for bitter pills. When they do go along with the teacher, it is often with the philosophy that, if bitter pills have to be swallowed, sugar coating is a good thing.

In pupil-teacher planning the teacher must be ready to accept the guidance of the pupil to a great extent. If he has an outline for his unit well prepared and the planning with the children seems to be taking a direction not provided for by him, he must still let the children proceed. The particular effort may prove unsuccessful but they must learn by mistakes. The teacher can suggest that he should not coerce unless activities presume great risk to the safety and welfare of the class. In a rocketry unit, for example, a teacher should veto a dangerous experiment with powerful fuels. In a unit concerning consumption of alcohol, one could not permit the mixing and drinking of cocktails in the chemistry laboratory. The latter activity would be illegal although the manufacture of alcohol in a school might be permissible.

---

[5]H. Gordon Hullfish and Philip G. Smith, *Reflective Thinking: The Method of education*, (New York: Dodd, Mead and Company, 1961), p. 107.

Specific Skills Essential

For the teacher looking forward to pupil-teacher planning, the first duty is to teach the boys and girls how to participate. This is done most easily by giving to a selected small group the responsibility of preparing and presenting to the class a report on something they had experienced or studied. In a general science class on water pressure, for instance, two or three children could go to a local plumbing firm and get some estimate as to what it costs to install the plumbing in a typical home with one bathroom. The beginning might be as simple as having two or three pupils cooperate and report on encyclopedia accounts of the early use of lead pipes. After several groups have done such small tasks it would not be difficult to organize a section of subject matter in which each student had some definite responsibility to the rest of the class. Through these activities the pupils are taught the fundamentals of reading and practical research, the organization of material, and reporting. When several of the class have made some progress, the teacher can call upon them to lead small group studies in the next unit. After this degree has been reached, the class is ready to elect their own group leaders and, in most cases, the leaders are ready to meet with the teacher in planning new work. In practice, the procedure is often quite easy and simple at the high school level because the children have had similar experience at the elementary school level.

The Committee System

From observation it is apparent that the successful efforts at teacher-pupil planning often culminate in a committee system. The teacher meets with the whole class in a session devoted to assigning a class leader or president. Under the leadership of this child the class elects certain committees to deal with particular aspects of their studies. In this meeting, too, a timetable for the unit often is made up wih tentative dates for certain activities. In one meeting observed by the writer, the class leader requested respectfully that the teacher address the class on a certain day. A small group had come to a hurdle beyond their capacity and therefore called in the expert.

As the days go on, some are devoted to study and research, some to writing and some to reporting. The teacher always can ask for a general meeting in which to draw things together or to offer guidance if he thinks it is needed. Toward the end of the study, he pays close attention to the discussions of the class when they meet as one group and is strictly critical of their conclusions and applications. In the period devoted to the evaluation of the unit, it is his duty to ascertain that the pupils keep their feet on the ground and, while allowing themselves due credit, understand that their effort is not final but rather a preparation for further study.

The Use of Time

To one with textbook approach experience this procedure seems awkward and time consuming. It is, to the extent that the teaching of the skills of study and reporting takes time, but the hours so spent are returned manyfold when a class is organized so that each member is a contributor to motivation and the growth of knowledge. It must always be remembered that "covering" pages and chapters of textbooks is not at all synomymous with teaching children.

The Procedure Is Adaptable

Pupil-teacher planning is a procedure and not a method. The text assignment-recitation method has little room for it but most of the other methods are adaptable to it. It seems particularly well suited to the unit and experience type of method. It is a procedure which offers room for the lecture, the experiment, the socialized recitation, the report by a single member of the class, the film and similar instructional materials, and other techniques. With the advent of team teaching the pupil-teacher planning proecdure is more easily used than in conventional teaching because one of the team is available for planning during the school day.

PLANNING A UNIT — THE TEACHER'S TASK

The teacher must do a great deal of preparation to conduct a unit properly. Even though the pupils are planning it in part and are undertaking some research in it, the teacher is always the resource person whose duty it is to know where knowledge can be found or how it is to be acquired. If he has time to prepare before the students are involved he can organize the major and minor principles as described with the appropriate experiences. After this is done he immediately prepares a resource unit. In this he will have many references and the books and periodicals indicated on hand or will see that they are available. He will have studied the local community and will be familiar with the resources it offers. When he has these things ready, he weaves them into the unit as the boys and girls need them. Some few, no doubt, he himself will have to introduce. Of course a resource unit is rarely complete, as the teacher has to add to it continually as new generalizations develop and more materials accrue.

Inherent Dangers

There are pitfalls in all teaching. In the presentation of a unit, two of the familiar ones are ever present: the scarcity of material and the raising of controversial issues. A resource unit lessens the danger of the first pitfall and is as effective as it is thorough. The careful planning of teacher and pupils makes the second less threatening. This is not to say that all controversial issues are to be avoided but in some situations some are better left alone. In many cases, on the other hand, the only way to deal with a controversial issue is to present it to the class and expose it to a logical examination followed by a thorough discussion.[6]

TIME CONSIDERATIONS

"Do we have time to do it?" Perhaps the teacher asks himself and those working with him this question more than any other. It is important that he do so because he has a moral contract with every pupil to repay him amply for every hour invested in work denoted by the teacher. The hours of an adolescent are very precious even though he does not always act as though he knows it. In the conventional text assignment-recitation method, one has to assume that people learn at the same rate. This fallacious assumption wastes time at both ends of the ability scale. The poor students cannot keep up the pace, soon give up the effort and waste the rest of the time given to the task. On the other end of the scale, the bright child is bored at the slow pace and so he wastes his time too. All in all, the use of time is not efficient.

Once children have learned to work independently, the use of time becomes increasingly efficient. With guidance, the brilliant student attacks a problem which challenges him and works on it at his level. On the other hand, the less able pupil applies himself to a problem which he can encompass and pursues it with some success. Hence each learner is using his time beneficially.

No one can tell the teacher quite how much time should be spent on introducing the class to a unit, preparing the boys and girls in the specific skills essential to its pursuit, or any other aspect of the study. In general a brisk pace should be maintained and the wise teacher has deadlines to meet along the way to avoid the work's bogging down. It is often necessary to permit the fast learners to report what they have learned to the class or to smaller groups, and to move on. In this way, those who can learn the particular concepts inductively have done so. The less able have the opportunity to learn deductively from their fel-

---

[6]Controversial issues are dealt with in Chapter 8.

lows. This is a compromise, it is true, but the hard facts of individual differences within the class must be met.

SUMMARY

It has been the thesis of this chapter that a unit method of teaching based on reflective thinking is not only acceptable but also desirable in the American high school.

The unit is defined as a study of a segment of knowledge which transcends many of the barriers of subject matter and time found in some secondary schools. Because the definition is general, an illustrative unit is presented. The reciprocation of the teacher's enthusiasm by the student is considered a key factor in the use of this method. The planning of a unit is essentially a teacher's task but it is important that he involves his students in his planning.

It takes time to teach a class to work effectively in a unit such as described, but the skills developed in doing so make the immediate work of the students much more efficient and equip them to achieve more in the use of their time as they progress in school and in their vocational pursuits.

SUGGESTED ACTIVITIES

1. Choose a unit in your major field and express its desired outcomes, as far as possible, as generalizations.
2. From the foregoing, select one generalization, to be considered as a major one, and subdivide it into minor generalizations.
3. Select one of the minor generalizations from #2 and compile a list of experiences which would lead the learner to a grasp of this principle.
4. Devise a plan for the use of one of these experiences with a class.
5. Visit a nearby high school and study classes in your major field to determine which method, or methods, are used and the extent to which pupils participate in the planning of the class.

QUESTIONS FOR SELF EVALUATION

1. List Herbart's five steps and Morrison's five and relate one group to the other.
2. From your reading in this area, recall several definitions of "unit" indicating the wide latitude of definitions one can find.
3. Contrast "deductive" and inductive" teaching and indicate where each is desirable.
4. Define the word "experiment." To what extent does the "experiment" in the typical laboratory manual fit the definition?
5. What benefits do you see in the repetition of the great or classic experiments? (For example, Galileo's work with falling objects.)

6. Determine some aspects of your teaching field which lend themselves to pupil-teacher planning. What aspects, in your opinion, preclude such planning? Why?
7. Are there controversial issues in your academic area? If so, identify one or more and tell how you would deal with it in your class if it were introduced by a pupil.

BIBLIOGRAPHY

1. Anderson, Vernon E., *Principles and Procedures of Curriculum Improvement*. New York: Ronald Press Company, 1956. Chapter XV.
2. Bossing, Nelson L., *Teaching in Secondary Schools*. Englewood Cliffs: Prentice-Hall, Inc., 1952. Chapter III.
3. Bossing, Nelson L., *Principles of Secondary Education*. Englewood Cliffs, N. J.: Prentice-Hall Inc., 1955. Chapter XIII.
4. Burton, William H., *The Guidance of Learning Activities*. New York: Appleton-Century-Crofts Inc., 1952. Chapter XII.
5. Clark, Leonard H., and Starr, Irving S., *Secondary School Teaching Methods*. 1959. Chapter V.
6. Grambs, Jean D., Iverson, William J., and Patterson, Franklin K., *Modern Methods in Secondary Education*. New York: The Dryden Press, 1958. Chapter VI.
7. Hansen, Kenneth H., *High School Teaching*. Englewod Cliffs, N. J.: Prentice-Hall Inc., 1957. Chapter VII.
8. Jones, A. J. Grizzell, E. D., and Grinstead, W. J., *Principles of Unit Construction*. New York: McGraw-Hill Book Company Inc., 1939.
9. Klausmeier, Herbert J., *Teaching in the Secondary School*. Harper and Brothers, 1958. Chapters VI and VIII.
10. Risk, Thomas M., *Principles and Practices of Teaching in Secondary Schools*. New York: American Book Company, 1958. Chapters X and XIII.
11. Watkins, Ralph K., *Techniques of Secondary School Teaching*. New York: Ronald Press Company, 1958. Chapter XI.

CHAPTER 6

Approaches Within
Specific Fields of Study

OVERVIEW

It has been said, with wisdom, that the essence of teaching is illustration. This chapter is largely one of illustrations designed to teach the application of the principles stated in the foregoing chapters. It is not difficult to say that one should teach young people how to form hypotheses and so on, but is a much more difficult task to accomplish. How is it done in science, mathematics, social studies, and other areas of the high school curriculum?

In general, a teacher is prepared in one or two fields only. Some understanding of all curriculum areas is desirable, however, and a perusal of each field will prove rewarding. For this reason the present chapter is designed to give teachers and students a look into fields other than their own.

This work advocates a unified approach to the curriculum through the study of broad areas of knowledge transcending specific subject matter barriers. The consideration of separate subjects, therefore, may appear to be inconsistent but it must be remembered that in a unit with science content the methods of teaching science are effective and, in English literature aspects of a unit, the methods of English teaching are appropriate. In addition to such reasons, the fact must be faced that many of our high schools will continue to offer single courses which demand a knowledge of the specific fields' techniques.

SCIENCE

The boy standing before the biology class was not well dressed. In a school where most of the pupils were better dressed than he, his blue work shirt and his jeans seemed out of place. More important than his apparel was the long birth mark that ran from his hairline down to his

The Scientist Collects and Evaluates His Evidence

cheek line like an exclamation mark. Such a disfigurement might easily explain why a boy would be too shy to stand before a class and speak. But this boy was not shy. With great self-assurance he was describing to the class the results of some work he had been doing in the laboratory. In the same group, a written report had been prepared by a boy who, according to the school records, had an I. Q. of seventy. This boy had not been relegated to the back of the classroom where, according to routine methods, he could "do a minimum of damage to the rest of the class." He had taken upon himself the responsibility for a task within his limitations and had done well. At the other end of the scale, many students went from this classroom to college to pursue careers in medicine, science teaching, and other such vocational areas.

The foregoing situation is the result of very sound teaching in science. In this case, the class is organized into groups at the beginning of each unit. Each group has a leader and a secretary. At the organizational meeting of the class, the make-up of each group is determined by the class members, and a definite task is assigned to each committee.

Within the small groups, opportunity is provided for each person to have leadership experience. A good deal of emphasis is also placed on opportunities for self evaluation and group evaluation.

The first task at the beginning of each unit is to determine what problems exist within the unit and how each can be attacked. As a problem is identified, it is assigned to a committee. The first class session might be taken up by this preliminary work. In the second class period the committees might meet individually and establish a mode of procedure for the attack on their particular problem. The problem has to be well delineated and hypotheses have to be adopted. In some cases the collection of evidence can also be discussed. The next time the class meets as a whole the result of the committee work is presented and the ideas of each group are criticized by the whole class. As the need for laboratory work and other research becomes evident, time is allotted to each activity. The teacher is called upon to lead discussions or even to deliver lectures, if such are called for. Few teachers have their lesson plans outlined for them by the pupils they plan to teach, but the teacher of this class has. He, like other members of the class, has his assignment mapped out for him.

Most of the work, both in the laboratory and in the library, is based on a truly inductive procedure. Once a pupil has accepted responsibility for laboratory work, the task is to be done by him with guidance from the teacher when necessary. He has his problem clearly in mind; he forms his hypotheses, does the experimentation he feels necessary, considers his evidence, and makes his own conclusions. These conclusions are submitted to the class during a discussion period and are either accepted or rejected by the group. If accepted, a conclusion contributes to a generalization stated by the group. The case of a tenth grade girl may illustrate this procedure. The class was studying vertebrates and, of course, the subject of birds was brought into the preliminary discussion. One girl offered to mount a bird skeleton as her contribution. From somewhere she obtained a dead bird — it may be that she found it on the highway — cleaned the skeleton and mounted it. She presented a report of this work, together with the skeleton, as her part of the study.

It is plain to the reader, but must be emphasized, that this type of teaching takes care of many of the problems arising from the great span of intelligence and the various abilities met in the typical high school class. In the first place, the teacher is careful that no pupil is rushed into any position of leadership beyond his depth. Those who do not know how to lead are helped by observing others. No uniform assignments are made with deadlines to be met — each pupil determines what he can contribute and then is obligated to do so. Reading and library work are pursued by many boys and girls; they are not imposed on them. The classroom library contains books from the junior high school level to the college level. Many students of normal intelligence find it quite beneficial to do research in college level texts. The more intelligent scholars in some cases find the high school texts too shallow for their purposes.

Changing Purposes of Science Teaching

A defense for the introduction of science teaching into the high school curriculum involved the difficulty of the subject matter and hence its value for the intellectual development of the scholars. Those who still hold to Faculty psychology are able to point out this value, as science has never been known as one of the easiest areas of the secondary curriculum in which to achieve high marks. Among the newer critics of the high school, some have demanded more science teaching on this ground. Other purposes of science teaching have received support in the past. For a time nature study was highly acceptable because it taught an appreciation of living things and the wonders of the universe. Although nature study declined in favor of a group of biological sciences with a sounder scientific basis, the purpose still exists and is a very important one, although little has been said about it in the last few years.

Many authorities indicated two or three decades ago that the individual need of the pupil was the first obligation of the school and that science teaching was important because it met the needs of a growing curiosity and provided for vocational opportunity. These purposes have not been attacked and remain strong today, receiving a good deal of attention. Of late years a new note has been struck. Because of thrusts into outer space which, it seems to some, are very hazardous to our national security, it is the purpose of the high school science classes to prepare scientists for our national defense. This purpose of science teaching can be accepted only with modification in a democracy. If this national needs theory is to be followed, then the school must weed out all but the brilliant students in science and concentrate its resources on the development of these few. We do not believe it is wise to "teach the best and shoot the rest." We must cling to the belief that each child in our country is to be given the chance to develop to his fullest capacity even though his capacity is limited. Then our purpose in science teaching in the high school must be regarded as one of general education. The Harvard Committee has said:

> Science instruction in general education should be characterized mainly by broad integrative elements — the comparison of scientific with other modes of thought, the comparison and contract of the individual sciences with one another, the relations of science with its own past and with general human history, and of science with problems of human society. These are the areas in which science can make a lasting contribution to the general education of all students.[1]

The relationship of science to other subjects. Ideally science should be taught so that the specific lesson answers a problem, or helps to, in an area which includes the study of material beyond the limitations of science. In the "Illustrative Unit" found in the foregoing pages, the study of science is a considerable part of the unit which contributes to understanding of man's answer to one of his very basic needs—that of shelter. The illustration of the study reconstructing the skeleton of the bird is a good lesson in biology, but it can serve a fuller purpose as part of a study of man's struggle against death and disease. On the other hand, in science as well as in most areas of our curriculum there are lessons which are best taught in a subject matter-centered fashion. The bending and shaping of glass is an important skill to one who wishes to become proficient in the study of science. There is no need to integrate such an activity with any other teaching field; it is best to teach the skill simply as a lesson in science. In itself this lesson can be most complete as the steps go logically from identifying a need through a hypothesis to a conclusion and finally very real application.

---

[1]*General Education in a Free Society.* Cambridge, Mass.: Harvard University Press, 1945, p. 155.

To recapitulate, the purpose of science teaching in our society is one of general education. The student is to be taught scientific principles and facts; his appreciation of the universe is to be fostered; his curiosity and interests are to be developed. All boys and girls are to be offered the opportunity to explore in fields of science. Not all will become scholars in this discipline, but to those who can must be revealed their own precious potential.

The materials of science teaching. From the days when the alchemists were pictured working with vials and retorts and smoking mixtures, the scientist has been portrayed as a man working with things. Today's conquests of space have come about because of very complicated and costly things which scientists have devised. The teaching of science must involve materials and machines and their manipulation. It is not enough to teach about the reactions between substances nor the effect of forces on bodies. The child being introduced to science and the young person exploring its study must do some of the things a scientist does. What is necessary for such activity? A well-equipped laboratory and ample opportunity for field trips might be a comprehensive answer to the question, but these are not always available.

The science teacher is often fortunate enough to have a certain sum of money to spend each year on equipment. Of recent years, federal aid to schools for the purchase of scientific materials has brought about a considerable increase in funds available. In order to spend wisely, the teacher must know equipment and materials well and must organize his purchasing so that over a period of several years he has the selection he desires. A study of the catalogs of several reputable supply houses and the compilation of a master list of items are essential to success. Several comprehensive lists of equipment can be found in textbooks devoted solely to the teaching of science.

Materials purchased for individual work. If each student is to be given opportunity to do much of his own experimentation, then a great deal of material adaptable to the use of individual pupils is to be preferred over large and expensive installations suitable for demonstration. In one wealthy school there is a complete direct current electrical system with a motor-generator in the basement, cables to the classroom, and a very extensive switchboard in a supply room from which AC or DC can be directed to every station in the classroom. The installation would cost thousands of dollars today, and it cost hundreds when it was installed several decades ago. The study of electricity is only a part of the high school physics course, and effective teaching can be done in the area with ordinary AC outlets and with storage cells for DC experimentation. The money spent on the expensive system would have done more good if it had been spent on ammeters, voltmeters, model electromagnetic motor kits, radio components, and so on. The same school has an expensive apparatus to demonstrate lenses. The students could learn more efficiently if an adequate supply of small lenses were available for experimentation. The teacher of chemistry will do well to consider the use of micro equipment, which is less expensive than the ordinary glassware and which, of course, saves a good deal of money on chemicals used. In addition, the increased accuracy demanded in the use of this small equipment is conducive to thorough training in the manipulative skills of science.

Intensive use of materials. "I haven't enough equipment for everyone to do this experiment, so I do it as a demonstration." This excuse is heard time and again from science teachers. One does not have to use a set of equipment for each member of the class at one time. If the class is organized to seek evidence, various experiments will be designed to that end. If six experiments seem essential to the task, several students can work on one, several on another, and so on. The whole six experiments can be done at the same time. If the students wish, they can exchange equipment as experiments are finished and one group can repeat the work of another with modification. For illustration, in a study of light one group might be working with concave and convex lenses; another might be studying the refraction of light in water; another might be determining the focal length of lenses; and a fourth might be constructing a waterdrop microscope.

In a more conventional classroom — that is where the more common experiments are assigned by the teacher — experiment sheets can be designed and distributed to the students. Each one receives a complete set of sheets and works at his own rate as equipment becomes available to him. The teacher may assign certain pupils certain experiments to get the class started, but will find it wise to avoid any attempt to keep the class on a timetable. After several periods of such work, the class is called back together to discuss their findings. Some pupils will have done all the experiments, some will have done a moderate number, and some will have done few. In light of individual differences, this is to be expected.

Class control and glass breakage. "If our physics teacher had done things this way, we would have had water and broken glass all over the room." Thus spoke a student teacher to his supervisor, prior to a unit on mechanics, as they were setting out materials which included six small glass water pumps. There were thirty pupils in the class, and six would have these pumps to study while the rest were doing other things. The supervisor explained that this class too would react with playful violence if things were merely placed before them without preparation. When a group of boys and girls have identified themselves with a task and are anxious to find answers as opposed to being told answers, they will go about their business quietly and effectively. The teacher of the class used as an illustration had discussions of the purpose of the laboratory and its equipment. Before each unit the class determined to what extent and for what specific purpose they would use the lab. They adopted policies for its care and cleanliness. Because these determinations came from the students and because they had faith in the teacher's word that their decisions were important, they took care of their laboratory and their equipment jealously. Quite possibly youngsters who were driving mothers mad with untidy bedrooms were priding themselves on being careful and efficient workers in science, in which cleanliness is of great importance.

Particular methods of teaching in science. For many years it was assumed that the teaching of science also taught a scientific method of thinking. It was not until research in the early 1930's indicated that the high school pupils enrolled in science classes were taught no differently than those not enrolled. When the pioneer work done by Curtis[2] and Crowell[3] in identifying and listing skills in thinking and attitudes towards science was completed, it was determined that pupils learn what they are taught directly, or part of it, but learn very little beyond this. There are very few premiums in teaching as far as the learning process is concerned. In the last decades much has been written on teaching scientific method through science classes and some of this has worked its way into school practice, but there is still much to be done. The pattern set forth in the illustration has to be followed to some extent if pupils are to be afforded the opportunity to work inductively in science classes; and, although deductive work is quite essential, no great advance is to be made in a large problem in science without some inductive thought.

The particular methods of science teaching, however, do not lie in the skills of thinking area, as these skills are teachable through many, if not all, of the subject matter disciplines. The science class demands much experimentation, which demands many manipulative skills. In short, science methods differ from other methods only in the fact that students are to be given the chance to work like scientists with scientific apparatus. There is a right way and a wrong way to place a ther-

---

[2]Francis D. Curtis, "Teaching Scientific Method," *School Science and Mathematics,* 34: 816-19.

[3]Victor L. Crowell, "Attitudes and Skills Essential to the Scientific Method and Their Treatment in General-Science and Elementary-Biology Textbooks," *School Science and Mathematics,* 37: 525-31.

mometer on a table; the wrong way results in much breakage. Habits of cleanliness, accuracy, and other such concomitants can and should be taught in many courses. In short, the fine scholar in science has much in common with his counterpart in any other field of learning.

THE LANGUAGE ARTS

"I think that most of the stories in our literature which have become accepted as classic have set forth some generalization concerning people. The story is good or poor to the extent that it is successful in presenting and supporting the generalization." So spoke a girl in the tenth grade English class. As a group, the class had determined some time before that it would be beneficial to study portrayals of life in America as found in some of the better known books. Since the writings of Mark Twain seemed to loom so large, several pupils had cooperated in making a study of his works. In the presentation of their work to date, a member of the group had made the above statement. Some had read *Tom Sawyer;* some had read *Huckleberry Finn;* some had read some of the short stories; many had read quite widely of the great author's works.

"You have two ideas there," stated a boy who was not one of the smaller group. "First you say an accepted story sets forth a generalization; second you say that a good story presents its generalization well and supports it. What generalization is there in *Tom Sawyer?* I read it about five years ago and I just thought it was a good story."

"Well, the whole story is a generalization of what the American boy used to be, or what he thought he would like to be. Within this big generalization there are smaller ones. When Tom got the other kids to paint the fence for him, it was evidence for the principle that we would all like to have someone else do our work — especially if we were rewarded for letting them do it. When he was scared at night, it was evidence supporting the idea that most of us are afraid when we are alone at night or at least when we are alone in a graveyard."

"If someone says of a boy: 'He's a regular Tom Sawyer' does that mean he is using this generalization or stereotype?" another pupil asked.

"Yes. And when people speak of others as mean as Shylock or as wise as Solomon, they are doing the same thing. Sometimes they drop the comparison and use the simile 'He's a real Shylock.'" The teacher, sitting over toward the window, contributed to the conversation.

Other students quickly saw other parallels. Mrs. Malaprop was mentioned, as was Ichabod Crane. Paul Bunyan was seen as the archtype of all lumbermen, and then Davy Crockett as the idea of the backwoodsman.

"This is what Sinclair Lewis was after in *Main Street*. He generalized the small town," a thoughtful-looking girl said musingly.

"That's right," agreed one of her classmates, "and this is what Al Capp is doing in *L'il Abner* and what the cartoonist is doing with *Dagwood*. Storytelling, then, is mostly a matter of generalizing about people."

The teacher joined in once more, "You are right to a degree, Al, but remember the other idea Betty brought in at the beginning. How well the principle is supported counts. Many hillbilly heroes have been thought up and written about, but you know *L'il Abner* best. Why is that? Why is Tom Sawyer so accepted as a picture of the American boy?"

"Well, almost everybody knows something about *L'il Abner*. He has been in the comics for a long time and they had a play with the same title. So I suppose when he is mentioned, everyone has something to refer to. He is what you might call common knowledge."

"Why?" asked the teacher.

The girl making the report finally gained the floor again. "This is what I was getting after in my statements. Many people recognize their own ambitions and dreams in Tom Sawyer's escapades, because Mark Twain knew how people think and he made his evidence, as shown in Tom's actions, fit people's ideas. If they weren't true to life, at least they were true to dreams. Dagwood's troubles are just like those of a lot of men who like to think they are imposed upon by their wives and bosses, so we accept Dagwood as a good picture of what a henpecked man is."

The report went on to a discussion of the portrayal of the times in which Mark Twain lived and the part of the country in which he lived. We have seen enough to serve as an illustration.

Particular materials of English teaching.

One can distinguish the science rooms by the laboratory equipment; one might identify the social studies room by the maps in it, but many rooms in which English is taught have little to set them apart. Since the pupils read only the anthology assigned as a text, a dictionary on a stand, or, in more recent years, a small shelf of dictionaries, that is all there is to be seen. If, however, the teaching of English is to be done as teaching in reflective thinking, then the tools of research have to be available. Of course, these tools are books for the most part. Illustrations of many sorts are also desirable. These are useful in quantities greater than can be hung on the wall as permanent exhibits. A vertical filing system suitable for large pictures is convenient for keeping materials from year to year. The bulletin board is essential, as it is in every room. The current topic of study can be illustrated here to very good advantage. The idea that a student finds elusive in words can be grasped without difficulty through a graphic presentation.

Books are still the great tool of the English class. The English classroom should have ample reference material. At least one good encyclopedia, handbooks for current information (almanacs), and an authoritative atlas all serve good purpose. It might be that a group can emulate the elementary school in having a "reading corner" with a selection of books of interest to the class and several chairs more comfortable and conducive to relaxation than is the ordinary school chair.

Because oral reading is a skill to be fostered in all classes, but especially in the English class, a lectern is a very useful device. It does not have to be expensive. Although a handsome reading stand strikes a note of elegance, a neat table-top device made in the school shop is often acceptable. A very small stage in the front of the English classroom serves a very valuable purpose but, of course, is not always available. Where the speech offering of the school is considered a part of the English course, these last two items are to be considered essential.

Walcott[4] found that the committee approach offered a great deal of promise in teaching writing skills. In his technique, each paper was read and carefully edited by a committee of three. The writer is invariably one of the committee so that he has the chance to defend himself as well as to correct his own mistakes. As one might expect, some ten committees proofing and editing make for a lively class. The teacher is called on often for arbitration and hence has many opportunities to bring rules of grammar and points of style to the class. Nothing excites a writer more than seeing his work published. Once a class has written, proofed, and edited a number of essays, the publication of these in a classroom paper or magazine is a reward for the students and a spur to further efforts. With a class publication, eventually all the skills involved in producing a paper will have been taught to some extent. Beyond all this, the author adds: "But best of all the advantages is the demonstration of genuine human purpose as the motive for writing, the learning through personal satisfaction of what writing is for."

The teaching of literature is illustrated by the Mark Twain lesson. In a core curriculum approach, or in any integrated course involving

---

[4]Fred G. Walcott, "Some Needed Research in Composition," *School of Education Bulletin* (University of Michigan), December, 1961, pp. 33-6.

English, the reading of subject matter in another discipline is part of the grist of the English department assignment. In much of this a research method with stress on outlining, note taking, and reporting accurately can be used. The techniques which result in a good report in a science class are the same that make the report an acceptable piece of work in the English class.

The special purpose of teaching English. To readin' writin' and 'rithmetic, one writer adds,[5] as fundamental processes to be taught, speaking and listening and straight thinking. Later, dealing more closely with his field, he indicates that years ago a researcher identified 581 aims of teaching English. The author cited identifies one large and worthy aim of English teaching — the improvement of communication. He explains that the aim of improving communication is brought about through the betterment of writing, speaking, reading, and listening. Literature comes to us through reading and listening. The teacher, through these skills, increases each child's understanding to the highest point he can reach.

The value of the ability to communicate is not to be questioned, and the ability itself is certainly a fundamental aim of the teaching of English, but we must expand our comprehension of the term. Literature is communication, but this moves our question another step forward. What is the purpose of literature? Communication without something to communicate is meaningless, however highly skilled the writer and his reader may be. The function of literature is to develop, or contribute to the development, of generalizations concerning mankind and the world in which he lives. The attempt to build skills without an understanding of this turns out to be drudgery and leads to the many bitter and cynical stories of the terrible loads the English teachers have to bear. What could be worse than spending all evening correcting pointless themes written only for the sake of putting words on paper!

The special methods in teaching of English. The teaching of English divides itself into two major parts, interdependent, of course, but easily identifiable. The teaching of language skills comprises one division and the teaching of literature the second. Since the appreciation of literature depends as much on the first, it seems best to consider the language skills first. The high school pupil has already been taught much in the language arts in his elementary years. One cannot say how much because of the great diversity of elementary offerings. The high school teacher can assume, however, that further memorization of parts of speech and their function is not going to be reflected in

---

[5]*Ibid.*

great improvement in spoken or written speech. As one authority has pointed out, most experimental studies of composition have been conceived with a fundamental oversight: the need for children to do things for themselves.[6] This is the need toward which all work in language skills must be directed.

To teach students to do things for themselves, the teacher must stop doing them. To be more specific, as long as the teacher corrects and edits themes and essays, the pupil is going to let him do it. As a matter of fact, the student soon sees this as the function of the teacher

Carl Purcell, NEA

Ideas May be Conceived, Developed, and Presented in the Speech Class or Drama Club

---

[6]*Ibid.*

and feels little obligation to achieve anything near perfection in writing. Not only does this tend to produce poor work on the part of the young person; it also denies him the opportunity to learn editing and proofreading, which in themselves are valuable skills.

SOCIAL STUDIES

For our purpose, social studies is that group which includes history, geography, civics, government, sociology, economics, and combinations of these, such as "social living" and "problems in democracy" courses. The definition is not sharp because some studies, such as geography, are sometimes considered within social studies in one school and apart from it in another. Economics and sociology are taught as separate subjects in some systems. Psychology is taught as such in a few schools, but is included in various courses aimed at personal and social adjustment in a larger number. In general, social studies comprises a broad discipline which considers the development of our world's societies and their present modes of existence.

Illustration

"The war started because that Duke was killed at Sarajevo and the people of this country declared war on the other country and each had allies who had to fight, so pretty soon the whole world was at war." In these words a member of the world history class summed up his idea of the outbreak of the war in 1914.

"I don't think that that is really the whole story," spoke up another pupil. "Certainly a big war like that wouldn't necessarily follow an assassination. Many men in history have been assassinated, and up to that time there never had been such a war."

Several hands were up by this time, and the teacher hesitated a moment and then asked one of the boys to express his views. "I think that Jean is nearer right," he said, referring to the second speaker. "Last year we learned that the Boston Tea Party was really an incident in the Revolutionary War and not the cause of it. We found the causes went back a long way and were pretty complicated. I think we would find a lot of things brought about World War I."

By this time a girl has received permission to take over the discussion. "If what Charles says is right, it would be a good thing for us to study the whole situation in Europe in 1914 before making up our minds as to the why the war started or what started it. I suppose the Duke who was killed was the aggravation, and his death had some connection with the real causes. I think we should study this thor-

oughly, and perhaps we could understand more of what causes wars."
There was a chorus of assent at this suggestion, so the teacher followed
it. "George, you are the current chairman. Will you take over?" George
grinned amiably and took his place at the front desk. The teacher
retired to the back of the room. George called on Don to take notes.

"Jean," George said, "you had some ideas. Will you restate them so
we can use them."

"Yes, thank you," replied Jean; "we know that there was a terrible
war between 1914-18. Many nations were involved. We know that the
Duke was killed at Sarajevo, but we don't know if that was an important cause. I believe if we studied the causes of this war, we would
find factors that have been the causes of other wars." Don asked if
this stated a hypothesis on which to work, and the class felt it would.
Don wrote on the board:

Problem: Causes of World War I (1914-18).

Hypothesis I—The causes of the War were complicated and involved
many countries.

Hypothesis II—The causes of the War were in some degree similar
to the causes of other wars such as the Revolutionary War and the
Civil War.

This was readily accepted by the class. Now, however, a new question came up. Wes wanted to read a Hypothesis III. If Hypothesis II
verified these statements, we could proceed to another hypothesis.
This would be that, if the causes which brought about the wars the
world had experienced occur once more, it is probable that war will
break out anew.

"That's not a good hypothesis for us because we cannot verify it
without going through another war," was one argument.

"It is a good hypothesis just the same," was the defense, "because
knowing history is not any good if we can't use it for our problems.
Maybe we can't prove it, but we can state it and use it in our thinking."

The class assented to having the statement stand as a hypothesis
which could not be rejected or accepted on the grounds of any evidence
which could be studied. One girl summed up the attitude of the group
when she declared, "I hope this one remains unverifiable as long as
I am alive."

It seemed reasonable to the class that the next step was to read the
causes of World War I and to review the causes of the Revolutionary
War. It was pointed out that the Revolutionary War had been studied
and the causes of it were known by the class. Because of this and the
fact that two wars seemed to have a meager basis for comparison, it
was determined to study the causes of the Civil War and World War II.

By this time Charles had his hand up again. "Since we know something about all these wars and have studied the causes of two of them, couldn't we classify the various ways wars start and see how many types of reason apply in each case. We learned that in 1860 the Southern States were in trouble financially and the war was in part due to economic jealousy."

"Let us put down economic situation as cause number one," suggested the chairman. "Are there others?"

"Slavery was an issue," spoke one boy, "and I think differences in ideas are always a cause. Miss Horton, what word expresses the type?"

"I think 'ideology' is what you are looking for," said the teacher. "At present we have an ideology far different from that of other countries which are powerful. We have different sets of values and different ways of looking at things."

"Difference in ideology" was written as cause number two.

"We have read and heard about the balance of power existing in Europe and perhaps now the world," contributed a thoughtful-looking boy. "Could we suppose that jealousy in one nation because of lack of prestige would be a reason?" With general assent the desire for power was listed.

"I read once where Germany wanted 'to show her muscle to the world,'" said one of the boys. "Is this what we are talking about?" He was assured that it was. It was also recognized by the group that economic status and power are closely related.

"Personalities used to be involved in the causes of war," a girl suggested. "The attitude of George III was important. Napoleon was certainly related to the cause of the war of his time, and Hitler's influence was part of the cause of World War II. I think there are specific personalities in all these cases. Some one man has to give the first orders to fire." This statement was not accepted by the whole class, but all agreed that some dominant person, such as Hitler, might be causative. All agreed that under Genghis Khan and other leaders earlier in history, the person was extremely important. Finally specific personal ambition on the part of a leader was listed as a fourth type of cause. No other suggestions were made, and the class agreed that they would start their search for evidence using these four headings to the extent they could.

Since this sort of work involved individual reading, each member was expected to study the causes of one of the wars mentioned. The chairman asked for volunteer researchers for each of the four wars and, with some adjustment, about the same number of pupils was assigned to each. All were asked to have their research ready to report in three days' time.

The purposes of social studies teaching.

If one were to ask a group of social studies teachers to list the purposes of their teaching, the resultant statements would be numerous and divergent. High in order on the list of replies would be mentioned the importance of knowing the story of mankind, the lives of the national heroes, the results of the great struggles, and so on. Relatively few teachers would list the acquisition of great concepts or generalizations, and still fewer would stress habits of thinking within the social studies. Yet these are extremely important in this and other fields. Perhaps no teacher of the group would express anything like the following: "The foremost aim of instruction in high school social studies is to help students examine reflectively issues in the closed areas of American culture."[7] Yet this is the one purpose suggested by an authority in the teaching of social studies. The idea is expanded: "According to this statement of purpose, teaching materials should be drawn from a selection of conflicting propositions in such controversial areas as race and minority group relations, social class, economics, sex, courtship and marriage, religion and morality, and national and patriotic beliefs, plus a wide range of relevant data to be used in testing them. One might say, therefore, that in any given learning situation teaching materials should be drawn from (1) broadly social and highly controversial issues of the culture (2) knowledges, values, and attitudes of students and (3) relevant data of the social sciences."

It is not difficult to see that towards such a purpose only a flexible and adaptable method such as illustrated would be effective. It seems wise to point out that "relevant data" are mentioned twice. These data are the facts that many teachers see as the whole purpose of teaching. One cannot neglect the facts in teaching, but one must teach them and go far beyond them.

The materials of social studies teaching.

Some of the social studies areas such as history have been taught largely through the textbook, and there is no reason why the book should not receive a high place among social studies materials. The effective teacher, however, calls on many materials. There are many

---

[7]Maurice P. Hunt and Lawrence E. Metcalf, *Teaching High School Social Studies*, New York: Harper and Brothers, 1955, p. 228.

Southern Illinois University School
Herbert Smith

An Efficient Use of the Library Builds Many Scholarship Skills

good films and filmstrips available dealing with a multitude of topics in the social studies. It is not at all difficult for the teacher to gain access to catalogues of these aids, and their utilization should present no great problem. Their use is dealt with in the chapter of this book entitled "Instructional Materials." (9)

Let us look into a classroom such as that depicted in our illustration. The most notable feature is the colorful display on the bulletin board. Perhaps no teaching field is better supplied with material for this purpose. Posters from foreign countries, pictorial spreads from various state departments, charts and graphs from commercial enterprises are all available to the class interested enough to write to ask for them. The *National Education Association Journal* and other more specialized periodicals carry up-to-the-minute lists of sources from which to draw. The display area, which is really a teaching materials area, also bears evidence of the work of the class: maps, time line graphs, and charts all help the student to perceive ideas graphically presented.

A filing cabinet, or substitute, has a prominent place in the class-room and is readily accessible to the pupils. The wise teacher conserves the results of the work of one group of boys and girls and has it organized for other classes. There is little reason to have every class go through the same process to acquire the same materials.

Our particular classroom may have a display of reports visible. If the students are taught to record evidence carefully and to deal with it accurately, then the result will be some written product from each pupil or each group of pupils. It will be the most effective if it is bound in an attractive cover with some degree of permanency. A small magazine display rack is a striking and orderly device for making the booklets available to the whole class.

The social studies teachers never have too many maps and globes. In these days of rapid changes in national status, it is almost impossible to keep up with the face of the world through the use of commercial maps. Class-made materials serve the double purpose of engaging the students in profitable and interesting work and presenting up-to-date material. As well as the ordinary flat map, our classroom may have one or more three-dimensional maps composed of salt and flour, or papier-maché, and mounted on plywood.

In addition to pictorial material, there is a vast amount of printed matter available to the social studies teacher. If a class in American Government is studying an income tax unit, there seems no simpler or better procedure than to ask for income tax forms for the purpose and to fill them out with income reports. It matters little whether the incomes are real or hypothetical. Other government agencies will provide all sorts of reports and descriptive brochures at little or no cost. Most high school libraries have catalogs of such publications or one can write directly to the United States Printing Office.

The Methods of Social Studies Teaching

If one were to visit many social studies classes he would see a greatly divergent methodology. Many history courses are taught by the recitation method with little opportunity for discussion. Some teachers feel that the history class is best taught by the lecture method and point out that this prepares their students to listen effectively to lectures in college. The value of the skill is not questioned, but the effectiveness of the technique is. A few lessons directed particularly toward the teaching of the skill would be as effective as month after month of lecture without the special emphasis on outlining and notetaking. The spectrum would continue to a situation in which the teacher-pupil planning approach to broad problems is found. The foregoing chapters concerning methods in general and that directed toward reflective thinking supports this latter situation.

In the social studies, at least one textbook[8] is devoted to teaching as a process in reflective thinking. The same general purpose is served by two films[9,10] which offer good illustration and an excellent basis for interaction and discussion in a class or seminar dealing with teaching methods.

MATHEMATICS

The special purpose of teaching mathematics.

Mathematics has been considered by many teachers through the ages as the discipline most fitted for the teaching of accuracy and precision in thinking. This Faculty psychology viewpoint has not only persisted in our schools, but has gained some strength during the recent years. Let us consider what some modern teachers of mathematics say. In a statement of problems in mathematics teaching Fehr[11] identifies three educational goals:

a. Mathematics as liberal education — freedom of the mind
b. Mathematics as a basis for living and work — as the people's necessary tool
c. Mathematics as propaedeutics — as foundation for university study

There is little to elaborate on the third point made, as we expect many of our students in mathematics to continue their work at the college level, nor is there any difficulty in understanding the second point, as some mathematical skill is essential to getting along in society. The first point, however, needs much thought and perhaps some definition. "Freedom of the mind" most certainly means freedom to follow new paths, freedom to create, freedom to set up hypotheses and to draw conclusions. This is where the new parts with the old. To use the most obvious as illustration: Euclidean geometry has been taught as a highly deductive system based on axioms laid down by authority. This teaching has been done so thoroughly that many of us find it nearly impossible to wrench our minds from the patterns set and to accept newer approaches. Yet this is what teachers are called upon to do. Because they have been taught this way, when they are expected to teach in a newer manner they are sometimes at a loss.

---

[8]*Ibid.*
[9]"Near Home."
[10]"We Plan Together."
[11]H. F. Fehr, "New Thinking in Mathematics Education," *Mathematics Teacher,* 58: 424-9.

Rather than logical progress through a deductive system, as presented by many geometry courses, Cattegno[12] states that mathematicians create and struggle to repeat. After drawing a parallel in which the grammarian is held to be to the writer as the logician is to the mathematician, he goes on to say:

. . . . to teach mathematics would mean, then, to give experience in as many aspects of mathematics as possible, to let the learner find by doing, by struggling, and selecting which section of the wide fields correspond to his gifts, his powers, and his insights. Then the acquaintance with real challenges will bear their fruit and the learner will have the opportunity to become a mathematician who can trust himself to achieve something worthwhile at least for himself, if not for others.

The purposes of mathematics teaching include knowledge essential to living in our society — installment buying procedures, insurance programs, social security payments and so on are illustrative of topics dealt with under this heading. This knowledge is often drawn on in classes of practical or general mathematics. The purposes also include knowledge of the established systems of mathematics which are generally taught deductively. Neither of these commonly accepted purposes demands deduction only, but each is served well by inductive thinking, and the teacher must find ways to offer opportunity for this, even though it is as elemental as students discovering for themselves how to estimate the cost per cubic foot of space in a house, as illustrated in Chapter 5.

Beyond the elemental purposes lies the broadest and least defined of the objectives as identified by Fehr and Cattegno — Fehr's freedom of the mind and Cattegno's struggle to create. The attainment of this demands teaching of a highly inductive sort, because only by inductive thinking can the student see a vision of himself developing into a mathematician. Only thus can he see himself contributing to mathematical knowledge and going further than his teachers and textbook authors. From students who get a glimpse of this purpose come the men and women who willingly devote their lives to teaching mathematics and those who invent and develop the devices of automation and computing which are becoming so important to our way of life.

Special equipment for teaching mathematics.

The mathematics teacher has always made wide use of the chalkboard and simple measuring devices such as yardstick and protractor. The wooden or plastic triangles used for board work are also often in

---

[12]C. Cattegno, "Formalization and Sterilization," *Mathematics Teacher*, 59: 521-3

use. The large slide rule found in many classrooms has certainly won its place.

Beyond these elemental tools, however, many teachers are using several others. Some have set up mathematical laboratories in which students have adequate opportunity to measure, weigh, estimate, and verify many quantities. In many schools are found models exemplifying various mathematical functions. In general, many aids to teaching mathematics are improvised by the teacher. Such improvisation is extremely valuable and serves its own peculiar purpose. On the other hand, some supply houses offer standard materials for mathematical classes, and the catalogs of their firms offer considerable help to the experienced and inexperienced teacher.

Particular methods of teaching mathematics.

"So we turn the divisor upside down and multiply," concluded the seventh grade student at the chalkboard. Ordinarily the teacher shows the class that to divide by a fraction one "inverts it and multiplies." "It is a law," is often the explanation given. Let us see how this particular student reached the conclusion.

If a room is 22 feet long, how many 9-inch square tiles will make one course the length of the room? If the width of the room is 15 feet, how many tiles will be needed to cover the floor? This was the problem presented to the class from a discussion of kinds of floor coverings in the illustration unit on housing. Several students started working on it.

"We could work this with inches," was the first suggestion, "but that seems a lot of work. Let's stay with feet."

"We know that 9 inches is 3/4 of one foot, so we divide 22 feet by 3/4."

"We had a rule about that in the sixth grade, but I've forgotten it. So let's figure out how it is done."

"If we break the feet down into quarters and work with them, we might get some place. There are three quarters in each tile. How many quarters do we have altogether?"

"Well, in 22 feet we have 22 x 4 or 88 quarters."

"That's right. Now we have 88 quarter feet for the length of the room, and each tile will account for three quarters. So if we divided 88 by 3, we will have the number of tiles in one course."

"Eighty-eight divided by 3 is 29 1/3," concluded a boy keeping up with the others while recording the numbers.

"We'll have to check. We multiplied 22 by 4 and divided by 3. We turned the divisor upside down and multiplied."

"You figure out the width in the same way, and I'll try to do it by inverting."

"My answer is 20," came the almost instantaneous answer.

"So is mine. I guess we have figured out how to divide by a fraction. You multiply by the reciprocal — you multiplied by the denominator and divided by the numerator."

Let us consider another case at a higher level. Ordinarily the concept $(a+b)^2$ is taught by the teacher directing the students to multiply thus: $(a+b) \cdot (a+b)$, and, by simple algebra, $a^2+2\ ab+b^2$ is obtained. In many cases, this operation successfully progresses from one meaningless arrangement of symbols to another.

If a student were to approach this inductively, he might say, "$a+b$ is a sum, so I could draw a line so that one part represents a, the other b. Then I can draw a square on that line so the figure I have is $(a+b)^2$. I can account for part of that figure by constructing a square on a and another on b, as in the diagram. This leaves two rectangles, ab, or 2 ab, so $(a+b)^2 = a^2+2\ ab+b^2$. Since a can be any quantity and b can be any quantity, then I can generalize: the square of the sum of two quantities is equal to the sum of their squares and twice their product."

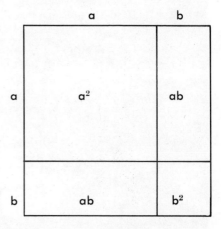

The difference to be noted is that one type of approach can produce a memorized fact and perhaps little more, while the other can improve the thinking skills and produce a functional generalization.

At present the teachers in the mathematics field are much concerned with method. Attempts are being made by several groups, such as Small and Kenner of Southern Illinois University, to perfect a method through which the student can see the functions of sets, the place of postulates and axioms, and the logical development of theorems. The writings of these groups deal largely with divisions of subject matter and introductions of concepts new to the high school field. Apparently little has been done to present methodology as such. Support for the approach illustrated is found in much of the literature. In one recent textbook,[13] the statement is made: "Although the deductive process provides the technique for drawing valid conclusions and deriving necessary consequences, the inductive process provides the means for imaginative inquiry and daring discovery. The investigations of specific cases and the observation of characteristic behavior can lead to conjectured generalizations. Such induction has played a very significant role in the history of mathematical research."

A conclusive statement is made later in the same work. It is asserted that "technical change can outmode in rapid and serious fashion mere manipulative procedures, but the basic structure of mathematical systems is anchored on the rocks of ageless endurance."

Carl Purcell, NEA

Graphic Presentation Aids the Development of Ideas in Mathematics

---

[13]Charles H. Butler and Lynwood F. Wren, *The Teaching of Secondary Mathematics*, New York: McGraw-Hill Book Company, 1960, pp. 80-2.

If mathematics is to be taught in this period of rapid change so that the manipulative procedures are not outmoded, then it is essential that our students comprehend basic structures and build from them. This can be done if induction, as well as deduction, is utilized in teaching. In other words, boys and girls are to receive instruction in reflective thinking in mathematics and to become proficient in the skills essential to this process.

SUMMARY

The fields of science, language arts, social studies, and mathematics have been discussed. These four areas form the nucleus of the academic offerings of the high schools of this country. Through illustrations, for the most part, the purposes, techniques, and materials peculiar to each of these areas are defined and explained. In this effort, emphasis is placed upon inductive teaching's making provision for reflective thinking on the part of the learner.

It is hoped that this chapter will answer for the academic type of subject matter field. The next chapter deals with the esthetic and skills areas while yet another considers the teaching of several rather unusual offerings of the secondary school.

SUGGESTED ACTIVITIES

1. Visit a science fair, if possible, and study the exhibits to determine to what extent each project demanded independent thought. If this is impossible, ask about projects under way in a nearby high school.
2. Obtain a science teaching materials catalog. From it compile a list of materials for a class of thirty for any one area, (chemistry, physics, etc.,) on which, if you were a teacher, you would spend your first two hundred dollars.
3. On a visit to a nearby high school, determine if the science schedule lists laboratory periods separate from instructional periods in science. Seek the reason for the arrangement used.
4. With various colored threads on cardboard, make curve stitchings of several geometrical designs.
5. Visit a high school mathematics class, paying special attention to the development of a thought process leading to the concept. If this is not discernible, determine how you would approach the task.
6. Analyze a chapter or a unit in a social studies textbook for the concepts taught and compile a list of experience you feel would be conducive to learning these concepts.
7. In a conference with a social studies teacher, determine which method of teaching he uses most of the time. Visit his class and consider the extent to which you think his method successful.

8. Select and view a film designed for teaching in the social studies. Consider whether the approach is primarily deductive or inductive. Suggest any improvements that could be made.

9. Select one well-known character from American or English literature. Have several members of the class list adjectives descriptive of this person. Discuss the unanimity, or lack of it, expressed.

10. From a visit to a high school play, or from memories of one in your experiences, devise a list of thinking skills involved in the learning of a part in a play.

QUESTIONS FOR SELF EVALUATION

1. Suppose you were teaching science in a school and were given the opportunity to remodel the science department. Would you recommend a lecture room and a laboratory or one room which could serve both functions? Support your answer.

2. Is the national need for scientists the best reason for upgrading our high school science programs? If not, what would you identify as the best reason?

3. To what extent and under what circumstances does the teaching of science lead to growth in scientific thinking?

4. What do you consider the most important function of mathematics teaching? Defend this answer.

5. Mathematical behavior relates to the ways in which the student perceives number and quantity. Indicate areas in other subjects in which high school pupils encounter quantities whose integration with mathematics is practicable.

6. It is a common practice to have many students working assigned problems in mathematics on the chalkboard simultaneously. Does this method support or detract from independent thinking?

7. State one major principle in the social studies and list briefly the experiences leading to it.

8. To what extent, in your opinion, does student government contribute to an understanding of the function of a democracy? Use a specific high school as an example if you wish.

9. Contrast a college lecture on the causes of the Civil War, or some such topic, with the approach to the same material for a high school class of American History.

10. From a unit on Mark Twain, what are one or two of the major generalizations you would attempt to teach? What approaches toward these would you utilize?

11. Outline the organization you would devise for the production of a small literary magazine in an English department or in a small high school.

12. In an introductory lesson to *Julius Caesar*, would you outline the play, read excerpts, or show a film of the play? If none of these appeals to you, what would you do? Support your answer.

BIBLIOGRAPHY

1. ANDERSON, HOWARD R., *Teaching Critical Thinking in the Social Studies.* Thirteenth Yearbook. Washington, D. C., National Council for the Social Studies, 1942.
2. BRANDWEIN, PAUL F., WATSON, FLETCHER G., AND BLACKWOOD, PAUL E. *Teaching High School Science.* New York: Harcourt Brace and Company, 1958.
3. BURNETT, R. WILL, *Teaching Science in the Secondary School.* New York: Rinehart and Company Inc., 1957.
4. BUTLER, CHARLES H., AND WREN, F. LYNWOOD, *The Teaching of Secondary Mathematics.* New York: McGraw-Hill Book Company, Inc., 1960.
5. HUNT, MAURICE P., AND METCALFE, LAWRENCE E., *Teaching High School Social Studies.* New York: Harper and Brothers Publishers, 1955.
6. REEVE, WILLIAM DAVID, *Mathematics for the Secondary School.* New York: Henry Holt and Company, 1954.
7. SAUER, EDWIN H., *English in the Secondary School.* New York: Holt, Rinehart, and Winston, 1961.
8. THURBER, WALTER A., *Teaching Science in Today's Secondary Schools.* Boston: Allyn and Bacon, Inc., 1959.
9. WASHTON, NATHAN S., *Science Teaching in the Secondary School.* New York: Harper and Brothers, 1961.
10. WELLS, HARRINGTON, *Secondary Science Education.* New York: McGraw-Hill Book Company, Inc., 1952.
11. WOLFE, DON M., *Creative Ways to Teach English.* New York: The Odyssey Press, 1958.

CHAPTER ⑦

Approaches In the
Esthetic and Skills Area

OVERVIEW

One can hardly question the importance of generalizations in subjects such as science, social studies, mathematics, and so. One is less likely to consider the significance of generalization in the learning of apparently simple acts such as sawing a board square or typing a sentence correctly. Yet authorities in the skills areas are unanimous in pointing out the thought processes essential to the performance of tasks of this nature and the importance of teaching skills through these processes.

Appreciations are often thought of as coming into being fully mature. Of course this idea is fallacious. Appreciations have their inceptions, their modifications, and their growth. The teachers in the fine arts subjects are cognizant of these beginnings and maturation and are concerned with teaching designed to foster appreciations.

For this discussion, the adjective "ideational" is used for subjects and for teaching dealing primarily with ideas. The term "skills and appreciation areas" is used to designate those aspects of education in which the development of skill and esthetic sensitivity assumes great importance. Of course subjects do not separate themselves clearly according to our criteria. Science is an ideational area in which the teaching of manipulative skills must be included. Industrial arts, on the other hand, is a subject in which skills are highly important but in which ideas are significant too. In this chapter an attempt is made to relate the development of skills and the growth of appreciations to the processes of reflective thinking. Since illustrations and considerations have been provided in the preceding chapters for the ideational subjects, this aspect of the esthetic and skill fields will not be pursued.

THE FINE ARTS

"I can't draw a straight line without a ruler." "I sing only in the shower."

These two clichés are heard so often that both are tiresome. Why do people feel it is necessary to belittle their own abilities in the fine arts? Does part of the answer lie in the experiences they have or have not had in their adolescent years as high school students? A renowned art teacher, Lowenfeld,[1] explains that at the onset of adolescence the creative approach of the child changes from one of unconscious creation to one of critical awareness. When the child becomes conscious of his efforts and critical of them, he often turns from this into activities supported by the group of which he is a member. To illustrate, many boys who are able to sing well will "act up" in music classes and refuse to sing in any choral group. The same boys may be found happily playing trumpets and trombones in the band at high school football games. One of the great functions of methods of teaching art and music is to bridge the change indicated by Lowenfeld and offer the student an opportunity for the creative drive to maintain itself through expression acceptable to the individual and his group.

The Desired Outcomes of Music Education.

A generation ago there was great concern by some educators that music teaching would dwindle in our schools because of the advance of radio. Young people, some thought, simply would not bother to learn to play instruments if an abundance of "canned" music were at hand. Fortunately their fears were ill-founded and today more high school boys and girls are playing in bands and singing in choruses than ever before. This is so because there are outcomes of music education fully as important as that of appreciative listening to the performance of others.

A Search for Truth. "Today there is .... a refusal to acknowledge truth and the laws that proceed therefrom — laws that we have called fundamental."[2]

The search for truth is within the domain of music. The writer quoted relates it to means of communication of our "individual expression of what truth means to us and what it has meant to others." In other words, through music we say what we ourselves feel, and also interpret what we think others have felt, is the meaning of truth.

[1]Viktor K. Lowenfeld, *Creative and Mental Growth,* New York: MacMillan and Company, 1951, p. 282.
[2]Justin Gray, "Music Education and Creativity," *Music Educators' Journal,* 46, (February, 1960), 58.

The outcome of the music class is not only excellence of performance, which is so important in itself, but also a growth on the part of the learner to express himself through music. This expression, of course, is greatly modified by his awareness of the expression of others. When we translate these principles of expression into classroom practice we realize that we must offer the student a great variety of experiences and some freedom of choice among them. This demand is met in part by the band teacher who lets the players choose, to some extent, the selections they are to play. It is also met by making available to the student a great many musical experiences. Some of these can be acquired through the media of recordings and tapes, some through timely television and radio programs, and some through attendance at concerts.

The Desired Outcome of Art Teaching

The outcomes of art teaching, especially with the recent emphases on self-expression, are sometimes rather vague. Some manipulative skills, an increase in the ability to perceive, and depth in appreciation are all laudable aims. Beyond these, however, is another consideration.

The Establishment of Freedom. "Methods that restrict the individual instead of making him free are poor. Methods having no relation to the individual needs of the student are rigid, and as such do not lead to the establishment of freedom."[3] This statement summarizes much of what is to be said for methods of teaching art. The teacher of art, perhaps more than his colleagues, has been told of freedom of expression. Some have accepted terms at face value and have felt that nothing short of absolute freedom is to be permitted in the classroom. The student must have freedom and opportunity to develop his own technical skills; he must have some freedom in his choice of subject matter and preliminary experience. That is to say, the high school art student needs time for study during which he can read about, view and analyze reproductions of the masterpieces in painting and sculpture. He deserves some freedom to choose whether he does much of his work in charcoal, oil, or stone. Once he has mastered some skills he may have his choice of subject. In all of these efforts, his freedom is to be tempered by the wise guidance of the teacher who has the knowledge and the experience which the student lacks.

Relationship of Learning in the Fine Arts to the Process of Reflective Thinking.

Let us review the steps of reflective thinking as outlined in a previous chapter. They are:

---

[3]Lowenfeld, *op. cit.*, 282.

1. A difficulty sensed by the thinker.
2. Recognition of the problem involved in the difficulty and delineation of it.
3. The formation of a hypothesis.
4. The gathering of facts to serve as evidence.
5. The use of the facts in forming a concept or generalization.
6. The application of the concept or generalization.

From an art teacher[4] we hear: ". . . .for an artistically significant
expression we need first observations then imitation to a certain extent,
digestion within ourselves, transformation, and at last a new giving of
shape."

These two statements, so different in terminology, are saying much
the same thing. The first steps are lacking in the second statement inasmuch as there is no expression of a need or feeling on the part of the
learner. The teacher of the fine arts, however, is quick to recognize that
boys and girls do have needs for artistic expression and that these needs
have to find their outlet in overt behavior. In other words, a child is
motivated from within to make music. To make music one must produce
a noise of some sort. The child may beat time with his ruler on a desk
or he may play skilfully on a violin.

When a child beats time with his ruler or sings, he is responding to
observations, internal or external, and most likely is imitating the object
of his observations. He is now in the fourth step of the reflective thinking pattern — his beats and his words are facts which he has gathered.
Whereas the learner of ideational material proceeds to inference, the
learner in the fine arts field "digests it within himself." It is important
here to bring in the ideas of the newer psychologies — the idea of the
learner integrating the factors of a problem situation by means of some
contribution of his own. We have called this "insight." This is the step
at which the person injects a part of himself into the product of his
thinking whether he is a scientist seeking a formula or an artist seeking
a form.

The application of the concept by the learner is quite parallel to the
transformation and giving of shape by the artist. The scientist may turn
up a factual thing such as a transistor as the answer to his problem while
the artist may produce a sonata. Each in his own way has applied his
own concept and by so doing gains satisfaction.

---

[4]W. Marcuse, "Art as an Ingredient of Education," *Educational Theory* 12,
(April, 1963), 117-23.

Implications for High School Methods

The authorities quoted from the fine arts fields and their colleagues are almost universally demanding teaching for creativity. A general understanding of the term is common knowledge but close identification of it is sometimes difficult. We have considered freedom for learning involving wide experience followed by individual contribution through thought as the essence of method in the ideational fields. In the fine arts, the same identification of creativity is to be made. The boys and girls need bountiful experience. Thanks to our many media of communication — both audio and visual — this wealth is readily available to almost every class which has an imaginative and persistent teacher. Most of the great music of our western civilization is now recorded along with much not as good that can be used for its own purpose. Many of our great paintings and sculptures can be viewed through opaque reproduction and slides as described in Chapter 9.

The contribution of the individual through thought process in the fine arts as well as in other fields, the "digesting within ourselves" as one author put it, can come only in an atmosphere conducive to its development. The band meeting three days per week in full session only and devoting itself to Sousa's marches may become expert at playing military music — but little else. The young musician must be able, after he has heard selections of many types, to attempt to play some of the pieces he wishes. He should have the privilege of inviting his friends to play along with him. It may well be that he will try his hand at arranging, orchestrating, and composing. All efforts such as these indicate a struggle to achieve and some may indicate growth. All of this means that time and space must be free to the learner. It is hoped that the teachers will find the time and the architects the space.

An illustration of teaching for creativity can be drawn from the field of art also. The freedom which very young children have in drawing and painting is relatively easy to provide in the early elementary years although even at this stage it may be lost. At the junior high school level, pupils often seem hesitant to use the freedom offered them in art class. They have lost their own creative freedom, according to Lowenfeld, because of their consciousness of self and have in its place a "critical awareness." In the art classroom this may bring about a sterile rigidity in which all the boys may copy each other in drawing pictures of space craft and the girls do the same with dress design.

The wise art teacher provides a great many experiences in art (facts to be observed) and many media for expression (things to be tried) and affords his students time to think and putter around (digest within themselves). As conclusions can be expected from boys and girls in the academic fields, so artistic results can be expected from thinking art students. The results of individualized teaching in the art class may appear weird to some observers but it must be remembered that Picasso and Dali are not accepted by everyone as accomplished artists.

From these considerations, creativity can be identified as a process going on within the learner. He is aware of needs to be met, can conceive a way of meeting them, can have available many relevant facts to digest, and can draw conclusions to offer for approval. Once verified adequately, the product of creativity is a contribution to knowledge.

Teaching Skills.

Does the approach outlined mean only "Give the pupil lots of material and let him mess around?" It certainly does not. Art and music demand highly technical skills which are developed through arduous work and strict self-discipline. The teacher spends some time demonstrating skills but he knows that he cannot convey them to his pupils. He can excite the student through experience in art or music; he can tap the motivating spirit present in many of our youth; then he can help them grow by supplying, along with their freedom to learn, technical aid when it is required.

THE PRACTICAL ARTS

The practical arts in the high school commonly embrace home economics and industrial arts. That these subjects have been considered of great importance in our country is indicated by the federal and state support granted them over the last half a century. That the labels applied to them imply a lower level of thinking than that needed in other areas of the curriculum is unfortunate.

There is a case, better not documented, in which a visitor to an industrial arts classroom expressed the opinion that little intelligence was called for in this part of the high school and that any high level of thinking was unlikely to be found. The teacher, an extremely clever man very proud of his craftsmanship, immediately seized a large wrench and chased the violator out of the shop. The visitor learned, it is hoped, that there are at least two sides to every consideration.

Introduction

The practical arts involve the teaching of ideas as well as the teaching of skills. Because of the emphasis on skills, however, they are often thought of as being concerned almost entirely with work done by the hands. Of course, the old term "manual training" implied just this. One well-known industrial arts teacher in his lectures on method used to say that it is impossible to train a hand. A hand, he declared, is a marvellous creation of bone, blood, and tissue but only the brain which directs the hand can learn.

In the ideational aspect of the practical arts, the method which leads to well-developed generalizations in other fields operates as successfully in industrial arts and home economics. In the development of a skill, there are also thought process involved, as a matter of fact, each skill is the culmination of a type of reflective thinking.

Industrial Arts. Several authorities have pointed out the importance of ideational learning in industrial arts classes. Ericson[5] states: "It is obvious, however, that more responsibility should be placed upon students in industrial arts classes for thinking out and solving a larger number of problems than is commonly the practice. To take the position, however, as some have done, that all assignments in the school shop should be solved by the discovrey of research method is obviously a short-sighted viewpoint. Later in the same work it is declared that the understanding of industry and of the industrial society basic to American life has come to be an accepted goal of industrial arts.[6] Another author follows a somewhat similar line:[7] "It is well for the teacher to appreciate that when his pupils are learning the theory of their trade they learn to analyze trade problems, to carry on reflective thinking, and to arrive at judgments which will determine how the skills are to be applied."

When one adds to the knowledge implied by the foregoing, the vocational aspect of the industrial arts program, he can conclude only that a great deal of thinking of a high order is called for. In few other courses in the high school are found more opportunities to discuss with boys their choices of career and to assist them in their efforts to make decisions. It is one of the few areas in which education at the high school level can be considered terminal. Indeed much industrial arts teaching is done in secondary schools which have a large proportion of their graduates going into, or at least seeking, industrial employment directly from school.

Teaching Skills. There have been many cartoons depicting a person sitting on a limb of a tree busily sawing off this means of support. His only excuse for such behavior, if he lives to need one, is "I didn't think." There are many little acts in our daily lives which we do "without thinking." Tying our shoelaces is a habitual act often used by psycholo-

[5]Emmanuel Ericson, *Teaching the Industrial Arts*, Peoria, Ill.: C. A. Bennett, 1960, p. 63.
[6]*Ibid.*, p. 174.
[7]Donald M. Kidd and Gerald B. Leighbody, *Methods of Teaching Shop and Related Subjects*, Albany, N. Y.: Delmar Publishers, Inc., 1955, p. 7.

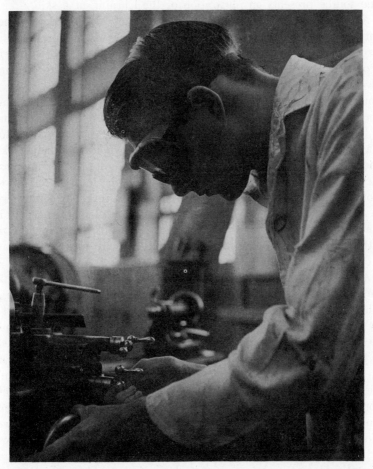

Carl Purcell, NEA

Foresight and Accuracy Are as Important as Skilfull Hands in the
Industrial Arts Classroom

gists as an illustration of a behavior that demands little in the way of
thought. One has only to watch a four-year-old attempt to tie his shoelaces, however, to appreciate how much mental effort goes into learning
skill which is eventually taken for granted.

Kidd[8] says that when skills are fully learned, they become fixed
muscular habits. He then defines a skill as a way of doing something

which does not require active thinking in order to do it. This definition may be oversimplified but for our consideration it will serve well. The same source presents an illustration of the learning of a skill.

A carpenter, in sawing to a line, does not have conscious mental control over each muscular movement as the sawing proceeds. The correct angle of the saw and correct pressures and length of stroke have become habitual through long practice. It is important to remember, however, that when the carpenter was first learning to saw, he consciously controlled each movement of hand and eye. After watching an experienced man perform the work he probably tried it himself and in his first attempts his mind told the fingers and arm muscles what to do. It appeared then, that some of the things we learn, namely skilled actions, are first attempted by having sight, sound, or other impressions reach the mind which in turn directs the muscles. Later, however, through practice and repetition the impressions result in actions which are automatic or habitual. The aim of the teacher of shopwork is to have manual skills become habitual as quickly as possible, leaving the mind of the learner free to deal with new skills or with ideas which cannot be converted into habits.

Analysis of Reflective Thinking. If we analyze this illustration for elements of reflective thinking we see immediately that there are generalizations to be reached and established. The "correct" grasp of the saw and the "correct" angle of the saw with the wood are determined only after some incorrect efforts have been made. The evidence used by the student is in some part the advice and demonstration of the teacher but it is also in part his own attempts to discover the right way. In the over-all activity, the conscious control of the hand and eye is a delineation of his problem and the factors involved watching an experienced man and his own tries are evidence — as is the resultant cut in the wood; by comparing his work with that of the experienced man, he infers that he has done well or otherwise. If he has done well he concludes that his method of sawing is correct and he applies this conclusion as he goes ahead cutting other boards and verifies his conclusion when he joins his various pieces and sees them fit well. If they do not fit well, his conclusion is not verified. That is, he does not saw well and must repeat the learning process.

Home Economics

"A good wife who can find?" (Proverbs 31.)

The question was probably asked before Old Testament times and certainly has been asked many times since. The good wife has many

---

[8]*Ibid.*, p. 5.

virtues, much knowledge, and a wide range of abilities. Moreover she must be prepared to be a good mother — which demands even more understanding and additional skills. The high schools of our country have tried, with success, to teach young girls to cook, to sew, and to do the many other things a good wife can do. Beyond these skills, however, they have attempted to impart to young women the understandings and appreciations which will help them establish happy homes.

From the beginning, home economics has had to enter the fields of science, social studies, psychology, and others. Often the lesson learned in home economics is one of application rather than comprehension. The student may have learned the principle of osmosis in the science classroom. In the home economics laboratory, she sees this process make possible the drying of fruit, pickling of vegetables, and the dehydration of certain other foods. Because of the frequency of application of principles, home economic teachers often think of themselves as a practical group. Bane has quoted an early leader in the field as saying:[9] "We must awaken a spirit of investigation in our girls, as is often awakened in our boys, but always, I think, *in spite* of school training. We must show the girls who are studying science in our schools that it has a very close relation to everyday life. We must train them by it to judge for themselves and not to do everything just as their grandmothers did, just because their grandmothers did it. But you are asking what all this has to do with domestic economy? Everything, I answer, because if you train the young housekeeper to *think*, to *reason*, from the known facts to the unknown results, she will not only make a better housekeeper, but she will be a more contented one; she will find a field almost unoccupied. The zest of intelligent experiment will add a great charm to the otherwise monotonous duties of housekeeping."

In amazingly close agreement with this are the ideas of a modern authority:[10] "Another challenge of the sixties is that we must, somehow, seek out the intellectual, liberal, esthetic, cultural, and general education values in home economics and give emphasis to them in future planning. In the realm of thinking, for example, no educational discipline offers any more opportunity for reasoning, drawing conclusions, making generalizations and applying principles than does the subject content of home economics."

There is no reason that the methodology of many ideational areas in home economics is any different from the methodology in other ideational fields. Even when a principle is dealt with in another disci-

---

[9]Lita Bane and Mildred R. Chapin, *Introduction to Home Economics,* New York: Houghton-Mifflin Company, 1945. pp. 144-45.
[10]C. Budwig, "Problems and Challenges of Home Economics Education," *American Vocational Journal* 37, (February, 1962), p. 19.

pline, such as osmosis in science, it can be taught, or its application can be taught, through the process of reflective thinking.

The teaching of skills in home economics is not unlike that in industrial arts which have been illustrated. In learning to make buttonholes, the girl sees the need, gathers evidence through instruction, and concludes that her way is or is not a good one for achieving the desired end.

An Opportunity for Problem Solving

Many teachers of home economics feel that the problem solving method, as it is often called, works best in their field. There are reasons to support this opinion. The problems are often close to the student's needs and are sometimes introduced by her. Many approaches to solutions are possible since the fields of science, art, and psychology are considered wide open to the students. The lay-out of the home economics classroom frequently lends itself readily to small group discussions. The evidence gathered is often tangible and adaptable to graphic presentation. There are frequently many conclusions of an esthetic type in the problems. The students' own preferences, though highly individual, may be readily acceptable. Above all, the principles gained in home economics classes in larger proportion are retained by the students because they become functional in the everyday activity of making a home.

BUSINESS EDUCATION

Business education, together with several major fields of study, embraces several distinct subjects. Of course methodology differs from one to the other. Business law, for example, could not be taught well by a specific plan worked out for a shorthand class. Business law deals with stated generalizations and these can be reached by the pupils in a manner similar to the generalizations of social studies or science. As a matter of fact, some authorities would consider any course in law a part of the social studies curriculum. Conversely, shorthand teaching is essentially the development of a skill or a pattern of skills. Learning to type and to operate office machines is also largely a matter of skill development.

In discussing the teaching of generalizations, one business educator says[11] that "when particular teaching problems are faced, it is found that every teacher must teach generalizations. The 'functional method'

---

[11]Herbert A. Tonne, *Principles of Business Education*, New York: Gregg Publishing Company, 1961, p. 224.

of teaching shorthand, for instance, is supposed to be a method of dealing with specifics and ignoring principles. Yet, unless the student acquires certain generalizations, he will never master shorthand. The disagreement does not involve the question of whether generalizations are to be learned but how they are to be learned." The author goes on to discuss the inductive and deductive approaches. He concludes that the question has to be resolved in light of the ability of the teacher and many other factors.

It is important to us that the inductive, as well as the deductive, approach is considered essential to good teaching. Of course, as Tonne points out, the emphasis in teaching skills is necessarily on pupil activity. "Too many teachers seem to think that they can develop skill for their pupils merely by talking to them." This, of course, reflects an absurdity in teaching, yet many teachers of various skills feel that instruction through verbal means will do the job. In skills above all, learning depends on the pupil's having much evidence and great opportunity for inferring from his evidence. In typing and shorthand the great part of the evidence must be the learner's own efforts to achieve. His judgment will be criticism of his own work and the identification of his mistakes. His conclusion will inevitably be his own standard of achievement. How ever high the school may set the standard, the student will function out of school at his own accepted level of accomplishment. This accepted level determines what he has "learned" from his course of study.

TEACHING FOR PHYSICAL FITNESS

Before the turn of the century, the Committee of Ten appointed by the National Education Association with President Charles W. Eliot as chairman, placed the teaching of health as the first obligation of the secondary school. Subsequent groups have reaffirmed this principle. Since the teaching of health is of great concern to the teachers of physical education as well as those engaged in instruction of classes entitled "health," we use the term physical fitness to include both areas. The purpose of all of the studies involved is to provide the student with the opportunity to gain the knowledge, appreciations, and skills which will help him preserve his own physical and mental health. Within this broad scope, some differentiation must be made between teaching and coaching. Very often the purpose of coaching is the winning of games. There are methods for "keying up" players and "firing up" teams which possibly do contribute to the gaining of yardage on the football field and the sinking of baskets on the basketball floor. Techniques directed to such ends hold little interest for us in this work. If they run counter to the best health of the player, they are to be deplored.

Ideational Learning. Much of the work done in the teaching of physical fitness is directed toward ideational learning. It follows that methodology which is successful in social studies and science also is successful in this area. As a matter of fact, the unit method is supported by many teachers in the field. The unit on grooming[12] found in one of the leading works on health education can be considered as an example. Later the same source presents a problem solving method which is essentially parallel to the unit illustration presented in Chapter 5 of this book. When one thinks of the great importance of the conclusions made by the student in his study of physical fitness — conclusions leading to eating and sleeping habits and other practices on which his very life depends — then it is apparent that skill in reflective thinking serves the young person extremely well in this area.

Principles in sports. "No matter how tired you are, tell yourself that your opponent is even more tired." This is one of the generalizations taught the wrestlers of an outstanding coach. Within most of the competitive games, there are patterns of thought not readily seen by the casual spectator. These patterns of thought lead to principles which are extremely important — some, it is true, for the sake of the game, but many for the sake of the players.

Wrestling is, of course, a matter of applying pressure to the opponent's body. While some pressures are relatively harmless, others can cause intense pain and permanent injury. One could teach high school boys to wrestle by letting them try everything on each other until they discovered that there are some very destructive holds. By this time, however, many boys would have been hurt. A wiser method would be to set up a learning unit with the avoidance of injury as the theme. Following the hypothesis that some holds cause injury and some do not, the boys could quickly gather evidence to throw light on their problem. It is quite probable that they would conclude that pressure against the natural direction of any joint can be injurious and thus should be avoided.

In games such as basketball, generalizations abound. Although the players, and sometimes even the teacher, may not always realize it, these generalizations are taught through a thought process. The difference between effective and ineffective teaching lies largely in the differences between the thought processes called upon. Repeated prac-

---

12Bernice R. Moss, Warren Southward, and John Lester Rhinehart, *Health Education*, Washington, D. C.: NEA, 1961, p. 237.

Carl Purcell. NEA

A Learning Situation in Which a Mistake Can Hurt

tice, with resulting awkwardness and errors of judgment, is actually evidence put before the player who has an opportunity to decide what is right and what is wrong. His conclusions from such problems governs his behavioral patterns which in turn establish habits.

The Growth of Fundamental Skills

The growth of the fundamental skills in games is not unlike the growth just outlined. A young boy is faced with a basketball and a hoop with a considerable distance between the two. His problem is delineated for him. His past experience of throwing balls of different sorts is part of his evidence. The instructions of his teachers also present to him facts and generalizations which contribute to his thinking. Each effort to send the ball through the hoop adds to this evidence. As he studies all this, he sees that one manner of shooting scores better than another. He tries and discards, concludes and repeats. His final conclusions are seen in the many little factors which all play an important part in his ability to score.

FOREIGN LANGUAGES

Although it may not seem so at first glance, the teaching of foreign languages is directed mainly toward the development of skills. The development of ideas and appreciations accomplished through language classes is important within itself but does not contribute directly to understanding, speaking, or writing the new tongue.

Terminology. Several terms have been used to indicate methods used in foreign language courses. The traditional way involving extensive translation and vocabulary study became known as the "indirect" method although the label was not used until the "direct" method utilizing conversation was developed in the early decades of this century. It is interesting to note, however, that early in the seventeenth century Comenius described and recommended such a method.

Newer terminology refers to the conventional system in which the student studies about the foreign language in English a good share of the time as "coordinate." This method is not generally favored as it does not meet the aims of foreign language study. The modern conversational approach, in which the use of English is avoided and which takes advantage of the abundant practice opportunities offered by the devices of the language laboratory, is termed the "audio-lingual" method.

The audio-lingual method follows the principles of learning which supported in this work. It offers the learner the chance to identify himself with the language because he attempts to use it from the very first; it provides him with abundant evidence through the pattern set by the teacher and the various recorded voices; it allows him to experiment by speaking back in the foreign tongue to the teacher or the tape recorder with knowledge of his own progress; and it permits him to reach a stage of proficiency at which he can verify his work by listening to recorded or television programs in the foreign language. This is in contrast to the atomistic, word-by-word memorization approach which was supported so well by Faculty psychology in vogue a century ago.

Description of a Class in French. The first and most important feature to notice in this lesson is that the teacher uses French exclusively. When one talks about a foreign language in English, he learns only to think about that language in English. He develops few, if any, habits of thought in the other tongue.

Let us visit the group studying French on Monday morning. The teacher greets the class cheerfully in French and, like friends will on Monday morning, inquires about the weekend activities of several of the students. Many of the class had attended a basketball game on Friday evening — one boy had participated. The school had lost this particular game and several Monday-morning coaches wanted to tell why. It was not easy to deal with idioms such as "lay-up" and "hook-shot" but, because French only was permissible, they managed. Some few had attended a movie and their reports on this were simple for them, as they had read many reviews and criticisms of films in the various French periodicals available in the room. Of course some were humorous. One boy had evidently eaten and slept and had done very little else. A girl described an attempt to copy a complicated hairdo. There was a good deal of laughter as there should be, because if one cannot laugh through the French language he understands neither the tongue nor the people very well.

Not every Monday morning is like this. The class always has a topic on which they are working and very often the conversational type of lesson is devoted to the topic, to small group activity, or to reporting findings and conclusions. On Tuesday the class presents a different phase. Divided into small groups, they are discussing French literature in French. Each group has selected and read a story and is now reviewing and criticising it. After some time has gone by, the class reorganizes as a whole and a reporter from each group offers a précis of the selected story to the others.

On a Wednesday the class meets somewhat formally. The grammatical errors of the past lessons, identified during these lessons, are referred to and corrections are indicated. A new lesson in grammar is presented by the teacher and time is allowed for written practice and exercises.

Thursday is devoted to a work period and members of the class can be observed at several activities. Some are reading stories; some are searching reference books; some are writing; some are occupied in the language laboratory.[13] This laboratory is in an adjoining room and glass panels between the two permit the teacher to supervise activity in both areas. He is directing the class in the truest sense of the word, as he has guided each pupil to interesting and constructive effort. This guidance, however, does not mean policing so he is available to any student who needs help.

From the work of the week each student submits a short written theme on Friday. It may be a book report or a research effort. It may be an original story or an essay. The period is devoted to the reading of some of this work and for each reading the whole class becomes a group of critics who readily say what they think of their friends' efforts. All the prepared papers are eventually submitted to the teacher who will read them and correct any errors made before he returns them.

Of course there is no need to set up a week's program with rigidity. The language laboratory can be used every day for part of the period or during the whole period by various students. The several techniques

---

[13]See Chapter 10.

described could be used in an infinite number of combinations and in almost any order.

The Aims of Foreign Language Teaching. The traditional method of foreign language teaching was directed toward translation of the written word. The high school or academy graduate in times past was prepared to read Caesar, Cicero, Ovid, and other authors if he had studied Latin and was expected to translate English into Latin. Today the aims of our language classes include much more than translation. Our students look forward to foreign travel; some hope for employment in foreign countries through government agencies; some look forward to entering vocational areas demanding foreign language knowledge in our own country. More important than all of these, we live in an intercultural world in which the understanding of our neighbor gained through a knowledge of his language is considered a part of general education.

The specific foreign language class has two quite different aims. The first of these is the learning of a language as a means of communication. Of course communication demands four skills: hearing, speaking, reading, and writing. One authority has said:[14] "There is in our country today a widely held view that the learning of a contemporary language must no longer be only in terms of books, translations, grammar exercises, and word lists — with reference made to English at every point. What should be learned instead is a use of the new language as its native speakers use it so that we may communicate directly with them as well as study their civilization and their literature. Such learning involves the ear and the tongue as well as the eye and the hand, and it involves meanings that are valid in the new country. At the beginning it is largely centered in those areas of language with which the native speaker is thoroughly familiar before he goes to school: the sounds of the language, the proper forms and right order of words, and a small but effective vocabulary for communication about everyday life." The same authority has said:[15] "The single paramount fact about language learning is that it concerns, not problem solving, but the formation and performance of habits."

Following this line of thought, we consider the teaching of foreign language a matter of teaching communication skills — hearing, speaking, reading, and writing — first, and the thinking skills, as outlined earlier, second.

In this second consideration we have support from authority inasmuch as it has been said:[16] "The foreign language teaching should be another

---

[14]Nelson Brooks, *Language and Language Learning*, New York: Harcourt, Brace, and Company, Inc., 1960, p. x.

[15]*Ibid.*, p. 47

[16]Charles N. Micarelli, "Aims of Foreign Language Study," *The Modern Language Journal* 45, (November, 1961), 296.

tool to be used in developing students' ability to analyze and reason. Of course, this tool must be perfected even as English must. One of the major goals of the reading selections used in a foreign language class should be the development of the thought processes." On the other side of the fence, it also has been stated:[17] "The acquisition of non-thoughtful responses is the very core of successful language learning."

It is fortunate indeed that the classroom teacher need not take sides in this apparent conflict. At the classroom level the answer is relatively simple: foreign language is a tool which depends on identifiable skills which can be taught. It is a tool to be used with other tools in the development of thought processes, or, in our words, in the development of further thinking skills. The wise teacher does not devote long periods of time to one aim and similar periods to another. He works toward each all the time and success is possible because the effort demanded by one aim complements that of another. Thus in the description presented advances were made on every front — conversation, reading, writing, and research.

Materials for Language Teaching. Perhaps there has been no area in the last decade in which progress has been more rapid than in modern language teaching materials. To the use of the textbook and, to a lesser extent, that of the disc and tape records, have been added workbooks, teaching machines, closed circuit television, and the language laboratory. The latter is essentially a highly developed tape recording system but its nature and use demand that we consider it a teaching aid in its own right. The utilization of the several machines is discussed in other chapters of this book. The prospective foreign language teacher will find the following source helpful: *Materials List for Use by Teachers of Modern Foreign Languages.* Modern Language Association, F. L. Program Research Center, 70 Fifth Ave., New York 11, New York. This list presents a brief description and evaluation of each item.

SUMMARY

The aims of education include undertakings and appreciations; the development of skills is often essential to the attaining of these goals. Some of our curriculum areas involve more teaching of skills and appreciations than do others. These have been identified as fine arts (music and art), the practical arts (industrial arts and home economics), business education, physical education and health, and foreign languages.

It has been shown that the ideas in these fields are to be taught in the same manner as the ideas in the other fields. In addition to this, the

[17]Brooks, *op. cit.*, p. 60.

learning of skills has been analysed and explained in an attempt to show that in such learning the thought process consists of skills which can be learned and which are not unlike the skills in the ideational areas. The teaching of these skills of thinking has been dealt with throughout this book.

The developing of appreciations also involves a logical process which can be followed by the teacher and the learner in the esthetic fields as well as in other curricular offerings.

SUGGESTED ACTIVITIES

1. Observe the choral groups in a local high school. Determine the number of boys participating as compared with that of girls. Is the proportion what you expected? Is so, why? If not, why not?
2. Discuss with a high school band director the repertoire of his students and their likes and dislikes. Search for reasons for their choices.
3. Have a music teacher, or a student in music education, discuss with the class the learning involved in playing an instrument such as the trumpet, where lip control and fingering must be mastered simultaneously.
4. In a high school class in art, observe the approaches taken to their work by individual students. Try to identify those children delineating their tasks, those experimenting, and those striving for a conclusion in a finished piece of work.
5. With a panel of class members, or led by a teacher of art, discuss the thought aspects of the teaching of art through free expression.
6. Arrange an observation of an industrial arts class in which a skill is being introduced. Try to perceive the steps of learning involved. If this is not possible, have an industrial arts teacher describe the planning of such a lesson.
7. Obtain some of the abundant display materials available for the teaching of home economics. Study and discuss the contribution of such material to the thinking process of the high school girl. In particular, note if there is a conclusion presented or implied in each display.
8. Identify several members of your class who have received typing instruction for two years or more and others who type but have had no formal instruction. Have each group illustrate their skills. Is there evidence of different learning principles involved? If so, are there differences in the results?
9. Have a member of the class who is in physical education illustrate the teaching of a fundamental skill in one game (ex. a tennis stroke). Discuss the steps of learning involved and the generalizations reached.
10. If possible, visit a language laboratory. From observation of others or from listening to a tape in a foreign language in which you had preparation, analyze the approach to learning, paying attention to the steps presented to the student.
11. Study one or more foreign language textbooks prepared for the high school. Determine, if possible, the method to be used by the teacher employing the textbook.

QUESTIONS FOR SELF EVALUATION

1. Analyze the thought process which concludes when a high school boy or girl says, "I like semiclassical music."
2. It has been said that free expression is the inductive approach in the teaching of art. Do you agree with this? Why or why not?
3. List several major generalizations which are desirable in learning to play a game of such as Golf. Outline a plan to teach one of these generalizations.
4. Identify a simple skill which you have mastered (ex. tying a necktie). Analyze this skill into steps by which it may be taught.
5. Compile a list of several major generalizations to be gained from a course in home economics. Indicate three or four minor generalizations supporting one of them.
6. Many school shops have safety slogans displayed on the walls. Do you believe that these contribute to the thinking of the learner? Defend your answer.
7. If you played in a school band, or sang in a chorus, identify any appreciation you gained from the experience and, if possible trace its development.
8. Compare your handwriting to that of another member of the class. Discuss with him any apparent difference in the quality of the examples so that you can compare the learning situation leading to both degrees of skill.
9. Shorthand symbols are essentially generalizations. Do you agree with this statement. Why or why not?
10. One much-used textbook for high school classes in French admonishes the pupils, "Remember. Think in French." This is written in English Is this consistent with effective thinking? Defend your answer.

BIBLIOGRAPHY

1. BANE, LITA, AND CHAPIN, MILDRED R., *Introduction to Home Economics.* New York: Houghton-Mifflin Company, 1945.
2. BROOKS, NELSON, *Language and Language Learning.* New York: Harcourt, Brace and Company, Inc., 1960.
3. DAVIS, ELWOOD CRAIG, *The Philosophic Process in Physical Education.* Philadelphia: Lea and Febiger, 1961.
4. ERICSON, EMMANUEL, *Teaching the Industrial Arts.* Peoria, Ill.: C. A. Bennett Co., 1960.
5. KIDD, DONALD M., AND LEIGHBODY, GERALD B., *Methods of Teaching Shop and Related Subjects.* Albany, N. Y.: Delmar Publications, 1955.
6. LOWENFELD, VIKTOR K., *Creative and Mental Growth.* New York: Macmillan and Company, 1951.
7. MOSS, BERNICE R., SOUTHWARD, WARREN R., AND REINHART, JOHN LESTER, *Health Education.* Washington, D. C.: National Education Association, 1961.
8. READ, HERBERT, *Education Through Art.* London: Faber and Faber, 1958.

9. REED, CARL, *Early Adolescent Art Education*. Peoria, Ill.: C. A. Bennett, Co., Inc. 1957.

10. SUR, WILLIAM RAYMOND, AND SCHULLER, CHARLES FRANCIS, *Music Education for Teen-Agers*. New York: Harper and Brothers, 1958.

11. TURNER, C. E., SELLERY, C. MORLEY, SMITH, SARAH LOUISE, *School Health and Health Education*. Washington, D. C.: National Education Association, 1961.

12. VANNIER, MARYHELEN, *Teaching Physical Education in the Secondary Schools*. Philadelphia: W. B. Saunders Company, 1957.

CHAPTER 8

Methodology and Some Neglected Areas
Of the High School Curriculum

OVERVIEW

There has been so much written about the needs of children and their education that more of the same is not really one of our major needs. On the other hand, our children are in a society which has much at stake in their education. The curricula of the schools are expressions of the concern of society that the school prepare the child for a happy and useful life. In the beginning of public education, the high school curriculum was not designed for our American society and has not yet succeeded in adapting itself completely to the needs of the great diversity of communities which constitute the country. Most of what is taught is firmly based on the needs of society and children, but inevitably there are fields of study about which there is some question. Although not ordinarily offered in high schools, do they offer knowledge which the young person can grasp and from which he may benefit? Philosophy, psychology, and anthropology may be considered such areas.

Our earliest schools were staffed by men and women with narrow academic backgrounds. That is, their preparation was in the language and history areas with emphasis on Latin, Greek and ancient history. Some mathematics was also included — almost all of it of the Euclidean and deductive type. The buildings used were most conventional, with typical rectangular rooms of a fairly common size. Equipment was limited to chairs and desks and books. This combination of narrow teacher preparation and restricting environment limited the offerings of the school. Whatever the theory demanded, and there were pleas for broader curriculum all through our educational history, limitations on methods kept teachers to a rather meager and uniform schedule of studies. There are fewer limitations today and, with a broader concept of method, considerations of the neglected aspects of our secondary curriculum are imperative. In this chapter the specific disciplines which might help remedy the neglect will be discussed.

INTRODUCTION

Traditionally the high school has accepted its curriculum and then devised methods to implement it. In the very beginning of education, the converse was true — the methods feasible determined what could be taught and then this became the curriculum. It may be wise to consider the possibility that methods may yet be a foundation of curriculum. We have stated that the essence of education in a democratic society lies in the freedom of the learner to ask questions and to search for the answer. Are the questions of our young people worthy of being used for curriculum building? This, of course, demands an identification of the questions our boys and girls ask.

Research in psychology shows that young people question their culture, including its religion and philosophy. They make inquiries about heterosexual relationships, possibilities of peace and war, and the logic behind these considerations. They wish to be informed on controversial issues. Many of our statesmen, as well as our educators, feel that the curiosity of young people should be satisfied to a wholesome extent by the school. If the secondary school meets this challenge, as it must, then one of two paths will be followed. In the first, the principles of philosophy, psychology, and anthropology will be introduced in the conventional subject matter areas. As a matter of fact, some of this has always been done and the amount is probably increasing. To follow the other path, which leads more directly to the destination, courses in philosophy, psychology, anthropology, and perhaps other disciplines will be added to the curriculum.

A study of its history would show us that curriculum revision is not accomplished by great changes surging through the country. Rather, it is achieved in small attempts made throughout the nation by teachers with foresight and devotion to a cause. We are now at this early stage in the introduction of several studies in what has been termed the "closed areas."[1] These closed areas have been identified as economics; race and minority relations; social class; sex, courtship, and marriage. For this work, we have chosen to consider these problems in their academic disciplines, i. e., anthropology, psychology, and philosophy. In some areas considerable work has been done on the high school level

---

[1]Maurice P. Hunt and Lawrence E. Metcalfe, *Teaching High School Social Studies*, New York: Harper and Brothers, 1955, pp. 233-9.

and in others attempts have been of a pioneer nature. We will study several examples of these efforts.

PHILOSOPHY

Dr. Willis Moore, Professor of Philosophy, Southern Illinois University, taught a course in philosophy in the University School in 1961-62. The first semester consisted of a study of ethics and the second a study of logic. The course in ethics will be discussed first.

Topical Outline for High School Ethics Course[2]
(Text: *Ethics for Today,* Titus)

1. The importance of ethics as a study.
   a. What ethics consists in.
   b. Need of ethical study today.
2. The origin and development of morality.
   a. Early moral codes, e.g., the code of Hammurabi.
   b. Pattern of development.
   c. Agencies in this development.
   d. Examples of this development.
3. Influence of heredity and environmental factors on conduct.
4. Theories of human nature.
5. Free will, determinism and moral responsibility.
6. Authoritarianism versus relativity.
7. Duty as the standard — the Stoics and Kant.
8. Hedonism
   a. Types
   b. Evaluation
9. Might is right theory.
   a. Types
   b. Evaluation
10. Self-realization as the standard.
11. A modified naturalism.
12. Experimentation in field of morals.
13. Health and morals.
14. Freedom of thought and expression.
15. Truthfulness.
16. Professional ethics.
    a. Medical ethics.
    b. Legal ethics.

---

[2]From materials provided by Dr. Willis Moore, Professor of Philosophy, Southern Illinois University, Carbondale, Illinois.

    c. Ethics in the educational situation.

    d. Business ethics.

    e. Ethics in the communication business.

    f. Marriage and sex.

    g. Ethics in race relations.

17. The ethics of war in the atomic age.

Since this class met for five days a week for periods of fifty-five minutes it was possible for the class to cover considerable material without having to rush through it, Moore reports. On the average about half the class time was given over to lecture and half to discussions and questions. Later he says that this was a difficult plan to follow because the high school pupils, being of one community, feel freer to discuss problems than do many university students. Consequently much time was spent in discussion. Although, as Moore points out, high school students go home every night and in some way or another relate their experiences to their parents, no objection was ever raised to the teaching in the ethics class. He feels that this was due to the fact that he was "reasonably successful in anticipating and preventing unfair interpretations."

It is of especial interest that the class, through working as committees much as in our illustrations, produced two documents. One is entitled *Ethics for the High School Student.* This follows the form and thought of other high school codes for the main part but one section, at least, is worth quoting: "A student should be courteous and respectful to members of the faculty. He should, however, have and exercise the right of free thought and open discussion in and out of the classroom."

The other work is headed: *A Code for High School Teachers.* This effort is a little more surprising and some statements are worthy of note: "Creativity — The teacher should foster, encourage, and demand creative thought and work on the part of his students. Only in this way can the student's personality be developed to the fullest. Furthermore the teacher should set the example by creative thought and activity of his own. *Controversial Issues* — B. The teacher should state his own opinion on all controversial issues pertinent to his course, preferably at the beginning of the term, so that the student can bear in mind the teacher's conscious or unconscious prejudices. Furthermore, the teacher should not be afraid to stand by his own opinion in open discussion."

Although we may not agree with these young people on all points, we see in their statements a demand for the freedom to learn. It must be pointed out that some of these boys and girls were the brighter students of the high school but there is reason to believe that one can expect results of a similar nature, if not of equal quality, from students of average ability.

Concerning this course, the administrators of the school stated: "....the philosophy course has admirably fitted into our school, especially among those students who are looking for a medium through which human values are studied.... Philosophy challenges the students who are capable thinkers."

Logic

The second semester of the philosophy course was devoted to a study of logic.

Topical Outline of the Logic Course
(Text: *The Art of Making Sense*, Ruby)

A. *Semantic Considerations.*
   1. Meaning of "being logical."
   2. Common forms of illogicality.
   3. Why study logic?
   4. Nature of semantics.
   5. Origin and nature of languages.
   6. Errors of symbolism.
   7. Types of ambiguity.
   8. Definition of words.
   9. Functions of language.
  10. Abuses of language.

B. *Deductive Procedures*
   1. Formal fallacies in thinking.
      a. Irrational appeals.
      b. Irrelevancies.
   2. The structure of argument.
   3. Logical versus illogical structure in argument.
   4. The syllogism.
   5. The hypothetical argument.
   6. Disjunctive discourse and argument.
   7. The nature of the dilemmatic situation and the dilemmatic argument.

C. *Inductive Procedures.*
   1. Partial and pseudomethods of solving problems.
      a. Omens and auguries.
      b. Spiritualism.
      c. Extrasensory perception.

    d. Random procedure.

    e. Inexpert authority.

2. Logical (scientific) problem-solving procedure.

3. The logic of observation.

4. The logic of reporting observation.

5. Formulating hypotheses.

6. Testing hypotheses.

7. Distorting effects of prejudice on thinking procedures.

As one studies this outline he is struck by the degree to which such a course is demanded by any system which claims to help people in learning how to think. Moore indicates that high school seniors seem little different from college freshmen in their ability to study logic formally. His classes contained some high school juniors and they seemed about as capable as the seniors. We are not going to push this progression further down the academic line but it does seem reasonable that some students in every high school age group would be able to grasp the principles involved in a course in philosophy. As things stand today, however, any inclusion of philosophy in the high school curriculum seems most defensible at the upper class level.

Logical Thinking

At least one high school, located in Lake Forest, Illinois, and there are undoubtedly others elsewhere, offers a course entitled "Logical Thinking."[3] It is in the English Department and is described as follows:

> This is a course in the principles of inductive and deductive reasoning, including the study of textbook models and the writing of papers demonstrating the use of various types of argument. Also included is a study of semantic principles: connotation, equivocation, figurative language, etc. Techniques of persuasion, editorials, magazine articles, and speeches, are also analyzed.

Thus we see the subject matter involved in the teaching of logic contained in the philosophy department of one school and the English department of another. Although the answers are different to a degree, it is apparent that each school has felt a need for the teaching of thought processes in the curriculum.

Bardsley's *Thinking Straight* is the textbook for the Lake Forest course. This is a college text which fits in fairly well but the teacher reports that there is a need for a high school text in the field.

An interesting note is found in the administrator's report on the course which calls for a greater concern on the part of the faculty for improving the thinking processes of students.

---

[3]*Curriculum Guide,* Lake Forest High School, Lake Forest, Illinois, p. 10.

ANTHROPOLOGY

If one visits elementary school classes just before Thanksgiving he sees some of them working on units concerning Indians. There are bulletin boards covered with tepees, arrows, headdresses, and other paraphenalia — some of it probably not recognizable by any Indian who might see it. In this work the elementary teachers are actually teaching anthropology and some of them are doing it very well. No one doubts the ability of the ten-year-old to grasp the concepts of pueblo living or of a society dependent on the hunt for food. The interest shown by children in foreign cultures, with the inevitable comparisons with their own, does not disappear with the onset of puberty but the high school has been slow on capitalizing on this fact.

One teacher, Mr. R. L. Dunlap[4], who introduced a course in anthropology to his high school students, sees in the study a most beneficial opportunity. He writes:

> The primary consideration in introducing the subject was that anthropology as a scientific discipline deals with man's social nature cutting across science and social sciences to give the student an overview of all that he has studied in those two areas in his entire program.

Another cogent argument in the defense of the offering pointed out that the area in which the high school was located was rich in archeological materials. Whereas uninformed persons would neglect or destroy valuable materials, a group of well-informed people would be a powerful agent for their conservation. Although one can readily agree with this, it must be pointed out that almost every corner of the United States, either through its heritage from the Indians or through more recent influences of one or the various migrant groups, offers a wealth of materials for a study of anthropology.

In the first six weeks of Dunlap's course sociology was studied formally. There need be no defense of this point or attack on it unless sociology were offered in its own right by the school involved. This work was followed by three units entitled (1) Race, (2) Ancient Civilization and (3) Archeological Methods. In conjunction with this last unit a site was acquired and everyone in the class was given a chance to dig. Some students made several "digs" although this activity was entirely voluntary. The site was opened so that a succession of classes would use it profitably. One can easily see in such teaching the abundant opportunities for students to detect problems, form hypotheses, literally dig out evidence, and form conclusions. From our viewpoint, an-

---

[4]R. L. Dunlap, "Teaching Anthropology in High School," *Education Digest,* 26: 52-3, April, 1961.

thropology lends itself very well to a free and inductive method of teaching.

As reported of the philosophy course by Moore, Dunlap had no opposition from the community even though the theory of evolution was studied — as it has to be, of course. As in philsophy, too, the course was rated high in interest by the boys and girls. Dunlap felt that his course was successful and this is borne out by the fact that the demand for it the following year necessitated the setting up of two sections.

There is other evidence to show that anthropology may be valuable because of its wide scope. Brameld[5] reports a class taught by Leeds to high school seniors who had failed to adjust to the conventional program. The teacher felt that there was therapeutic value evident from his efforts and also considered that there was a transfer to other subjects. We do not recommend any course for therapy particularly but this effort may indicate that boys and girls of low academic standing may be able to benefit from the study of these more unusual subjects.

An Introduction to Anthropology by Beals and Hojier[6] has been used at the high school level and found suitable.

PSYCHOLOGY

No other body of knowledge, perhaps, has been more maligned, misused, or misquoted than has psychology. The word is in almost everyone's vocabulary; it is used loosely in the popular press; and has been endlessly exploited by the advertiser. This situation alone would justify its consideration as part of the general education of our youth but there is far more powerful reason for its inclusion in the high school curriculum. To support this statement, let us look at the contents of one book designed for the secondary school.[7] The major units listed are:

1. Scientific Method and the Science of Psychology.
2. Personality and Popularity, Leadership and Intelligence.
3. Heredity and Environment.
4. Mental Health.
5. Friendship, Love, and Marriage.
6. The Citizen's Role

---

[5]Theodore Brameld and E. B. Sullivan, "Anthropology and Education: Anthropology in the Curriculum," *Review of Educational Research*, 31: 75-7, February, 1961.

[6]Ralph Leon Beals and Harry Hojier, An Introduction to Anthropology. New York: MacMillan, 1959.

[7]T. L. Engle, *Psychology: Its Principles and Applications*, Yonkers-on-Hudson: World Book Company, 1957.

It is not difficult to see in this outline the possibilities of answers to many of the questions young people ask. The mental health consideration is worthy of note by a member of a society which consumes tranquilizer pills by the thousands. Every other unit could be defended if such were necessary.

The method of teaching psychology is of great interest. The freedom for questioning can be abundant. The motivation for questioning is extremely strong in the study of psychology because the subject content is essentially the answers to those questions which one must ask himself — What am I going to do? How well can I compete? Who will I marry, if I do? Status among peers, courtship, marriage are all of great concern to students of high school age. As pointed out in Chapter 3, the movies, television, radio, and the press are constantly pouring evidence into the minds of these young people. Because this evidence is a hodgepodge and much of it prejudicial to the point of being propaganda, so much more is their need for the school to offer to the young boy or girl a framework within which he can deal with this great amount of grist for his thinking.

The world itself, or any part of it, can be the laboratory of psychology. Compare the following excerpt with the illustrative unit in Chapter 5 which was written prior to the present writer's knowledge of this passage.[8]

> If you live in a large city, or when you visit one, travel through one or more areas of homes of those obviously belonging to the higher socio-economic levels. Then travel through the poorer areas of the city. Contrast the homes, the schools, the churches, the stores, and the recreational facilities. Is there a difference in the personal appearance of the children and adults to be seen on the street? To what extent do you think the adult lives of the children will be influenced by these environments? You may wish to take some pictures to illustrate your report, but take care not to offend anyone, especially in the poorer districts.

If we are to teach through methods which offer freedom to question, which depend on the interests of children, and which utilize direct experiences, then psychology can fit effectively into the pattern of an ideal high school course.

TIME AND SCHEDULING

Very literally, many teachers are too busy to "give the students the time of day." The addition of other subjects to the curriculum is bound

---

[8]*Ibid.* 270.

to bring up serious questions. Can we add forever without some subtracting? Of course we cannot. Several avenues are open to the high school, however, to increase its offering. Following Conant's suggestion, it can operate a seven-period day. Some high schools are already doing this. The practice may result in slicing more varieties of academic fare a little thinner o., on the other hand, improved methods and the use of the many avai able educational aids may keep the quality high while increasing the quantity.

It may be wise to offer some subjects at an earlier grade level than is now the c ise. As the science teachers assign biology to the ninth year in some cases so that an advanced course can be offered in the twelfth year, so the high school might assign the United States history and the world history courses a year earlier and leave room for one of the courses we have considered. Many schools already have this time available for courses with titles such as Problems in Democracy. It may be that the time could be used better by a course entitled Anthropology. A closer articulation between the offerings of the junior and senior high schools would make possible more total offerings in many school systems. There is much to be said for considering the whole six-year secondary period as one continuous program.

A third possibility is the twelve month school year. In spite of the protests of those who claim to have disliked their years spent in high school, many informed educators consider the idea sound in many respects. Coupled with outdoor education and camping experiences it offers much to think about. A summer archeology course taught at a productive site through a camp organization could be both popular and effective. The maintenance of a summer school at Mesa Verde to which boys and girls of many areas could go would be an exceedingly interesting experiment. The presentation and defense of such a plan would need a volume in itself, but teachers, and especially prospective teachers, must have vision not limited by the boundaries built yesterday and upheld today.

CONTROVERSIAL ISSUES

The teaching of controversial issues has been limited in the history of the high school curriculum because the teachers were unable, rather than unwilling, to deal with them. While critics and educators have debated whether the teacher should face the thorny problems of our society in the classroom, the real point has often been overlooked, namely, that the teacher has not had the tools needed for the job. The tools are of two kinds: teaching aids and professional preparation. Up until the third decade of this century, the typical teacher used the single text-book in a high school course and was often severely limited in his own education.

The textbook was developed as an anthology of the best thought in its field of study. It was designed to be authoritative — the last word to be said on the topics it treated. The present day textbooks have moved somewhat from this base of organization but not far. The book must still limit itself to well documented material and to conclusions sup-ported by the majority of the scholars in the field. When the textbook has been the basis of method, as it has been so much of the time, then of necessity the learner must have in his hands both the evidence to be presented to him and the conclusions from this evidence. Hence no issue presented can properly be called controversial since some solution, or compromise, is presented. When the single textbook is used, as has frequently been the case, there seldom is much room for controversy. In addition to this, textbooks are rarely up-to-date. From the time an author composes a section dealing with an issue until the time the book reaches the student, the complexion of the issue may change radically.

Traditionally in the American school the teacher has not been an advanced and independent scholar. Various novels, such as *Rainbow County,* present the picture of the "professor" at the academy as being eccentric in his views and free in his presentation of them to his stu-dents. Such characters, if they existed in true life, were few and held short tenure in the school systems. In reality the teacher followed the desires of the community expressed by the school board — and liberal thinkers are not generally elected to school boards — or through the long standing mores of the society. No doubt some great intellects have been found in the secondary classroom but not all of them remained. School teaching has always, unfortunately, been used as a stepping stone to other professions and less frequently as a haven to those who failed in other professions. It is a national disgrace that the saying "Those who can do and those who can't teach" has become so well known to our people.

It is only in the last few decades that the teacher has had profes-sional preparation in the study of the child and his ability to learn. Both child development and educational psychology are relative new-comers to the college curriculum.

We have passed the time when any one textbook has to be the base of any course in the curriculum and when the teacher knows only enough to follow it slavishly. In many communities the school is open to those who wish to teach for the sake of truth itself. Leaders in our country, in which the school system was originally set up for the elite, today feel greatly concerned for the education of all of our youth. The words "poor" and "ignorant" are no longer synonymous and there is an understanding that the child in the slum must be cared for educationally as well as his suburban cousin. All this means that the many social issues which were kept with the skeletons in the closet can now be brought out and faced honestly. The great issue of the desegregation of our schools can be used as an illustration of a hidden problem brought to light.

Bearing these things in mind, one must conclude that facing controversial issues is not only the prerogative of the high school teacher but his duty. Both Moore and Dunlap introduced controversial issues into their classrooms and neither had any undesirable response from the community. The students in Moore's class stated that the teacher should deal with controversial issues, making clear his own stand in the beginning. We must disagree with this method if we are to be consistent. The teacher is to help the student delineate the problem and collect and weigh the evidence but the learner has the right to voice his own conclusion. It is quite probable that the conclusion will be modified because of class discussion or in the light of further evidence. The teacher's task is to guide the learner to a logical conclusion through a searching study of the problem.

SUMMARY

Following a hypothesis that method is a foundation of the curriculum and that the questions of the students may well be used in determining subject matter in the high schools, this chapter suggests the addition of philosophy, anthropology, and psychology to the offerings of the secondary school. Each of these disciplines is taught in some, but very few, schools; illustration is presented in each case followed by a discussion of the methodology suitable for the teaching of the specific subject.

Although there is no suggestion that controversial issues be taught as a course, it is urged that teachers, with better preparation and materials than those possessed by their predecessors, be unafraid to meet such issues in the classroom and teach them through a methodology leading to sound principles. As a matter of fact, the teacher is not granted the privilege of accepting or rejecting such issues but is duty bound to deal with each to the extent that he can within the limitations of his students' abilities.

SUGGESTED ACTIVITIES

1. Obtain class schedules of several high schools in your area and determine if some of the more unusual subjects are offered. Visit classes

in psychology or philosophy, if possible. Ask for course outlines and the names of textbooks used and compare them.

2. If possible, invite a teacher of one of these subjects to the class and interrogate him on methods and practices used in his teaching.

3. If a high school teacher is not available, invite a college professor to your class, preferably one who has had high school teaching experience, and discuss with him the offering of his field of knowledge at the high school level.

4. Analyze an outline of a general psychology course offered in your college and determine which units, or topics, would be feasible at a high school level.

5. Using the college class as high school students, stage a role-playing drama of a class in psychology discussing courtship or other topic.

6. Through a local museum or historical society, determine what anthropological evidence is available in your home town or college community. Organize a suitable section of this material into a unit of anthropology for a high school class.

7. From audio-visual materials catalogs, determine what films or other aids are available for the teaching of the subjects mentioned in this chapter.

8. Analyse several big city newspapers to determine what controversial issues are currently important. From the materials so found, identify the issues, or aspects of them, which would be suitable for a class in high school.

9. If possible, visit the current events lesson of a class in history or civics and indicate whether or not this was truly a class dealing with a controversial issue. Were the elements of the lesson controversial or factual?

10. Analyse a television program purporting to deal with a controversial issue. Indicate the degree to which this program would be suitable and beneficial to a high school class.

QUESTIONS FOR SELF EVALUATION

1. List some of the questions which are uppermost in the minds of high school boys and girls and the sources from which some of them could be answered.

2. Identify some of the closed areas of interest in high school teaching and indicate why they are closed. If possible, add to those listed in the text.

3. In which classes of the high school might one teach moral responsibility extensively? Can it be done without calling upon philosophy?

4. What reactions did Moore and Dunlap have from the communities in which they taught. Do you think your home town's reaction would be similar or different? Why?

5. To what degree does the outline of deductive and inductive procedures in reasoning presented by Moore differ from that presented in Chapter I?

6. To what extent was sociology taught in your own high school or other high schools you know? Can you differentiate between sociology and anthropology?

7. List several principles of anthropology which would be valuable in the high school. To what extent is the teaching of these principles feasible?
8. Select one principle from the foregoing and organize a teaching plan as described in Chapter IV.
9. List some of the topics suitable for a course in psychology. To what degree were these topics treated in any high school you know? To what extent are they feasible at the high school level?
10. Identify one currently controversial issue. Outline an attack for dealing with this issue in the secondary school.

BIBLIOGRAPHY

1. BEALS, RALPH LEON, AND HOJIER, HARRY, *An Introduction to Anthropology.* New York: Macmillan Company, 1959.
2. BEARDSLEY, MONROE, *Thinking Straight.* New York: Prentice-Hall, 1950.
3. ENGLE, T. L., *Psychology: Its Principles and Applications.* Yonkers-on-Hudson: World Book Company, 1957.
4. HUNT, MAURICE P., AND METCALF, LAWRENCE E., *Teaching High School Social Studies.* New York: Harper and Brothers, 1955.
5. PARKER J. CECIL, EDWARDS, T. BENTLEY, AND STEGMAN, WILLIAM H., *Curriculum in America.* New York: Thomas Y. Crowell Company, 1962, Chapters II and V.
6. PHILIPS, E. LAKIN, AND GIBSON, JAMES F., *Psychology and Personality.* Englewood Cliffs, N. J.: Prentice-Hall, 1957.
7. RUBY, LIONEL, *The Art of Making Sense.* Philadelphia: Lippincott Company, 1954.
8. TITUS, HAROLD HOPPER, *Ethics for Today.* New York: American Book Company, 1947.

CHAPTER 9

Instructional Materials

OVERVIEW

Teachers have always used instructional materials of one sort or another but for centuries little that was new was used beyond the textbook and basic scientific equipment. Even the blackboard or chalkboard has been in use for little more than a century. Today there are available numerous devices designed to help the teacher improve his work. What are some of the advantages of motion films and filmstrips? How can the teacher portray his own ideas by such graphic media? What instruments beyond the projector are available in today's high school? Above all, how does the school, the picture, or the sound produced by our machines serve to modify the thought processes of secondary school pupils?

As an attempt to answer these questions, the presentation of ideas through graphic and audio devices forms the central theme of this chapter. The use of pictures, from the textbook illustration to the motion film is discussed. Radio, television, tape, and other sound instruments are studied. It is pointed out that the great function of all of the teaching aids is to present evidence to the learner to aid him in the developing of ideas.

INTRODUCTION

Julian Bryan has produced a film entitled "Sampan Family." It is simply a record of the day-to-day activities of a family of China which lives on the River Min in a junk. A junk is a primitive type of boat about 14 feet long and 4 feet wide. Within the confines of these dimensions life is far different from that of an American family living in a typical western home. Words can hardly describe the adjustments made by the Chinese family, but the film can. Several years after viewing the film, the writer can remember vividly the lovable little Chinese boy as his mother washed his face before their breakfast. All the patience and forbearance conceivable are reflected in the small quiet features as they are given a quick once over with a cloth dipped in the river. What a contrast is revealed between the face washing of this little fellow and that of one of our children before the bathroom sink! Yet in each case the face is being cleaned — and probably on the mother's initiative too.

The small Chinese boy is still alive, we hope, and is now a young man. He is one of the millions of Chinese we read about in our newspapers and hear referred to on our newscasts, yet he is an individual and has evoked a response in thousands of viewers that only an individual can bring about. Many Americans have modified their concept of "Chinese" because of this picture. In other words, this tiny bit of humanity has been presented as evidence and the evidence has been applied to hypotheses concerning the Chinese people, very subtly perhaps, and decidedly has influenced conclusions concerning hundreds of millions of people.

Graphic Presentation of Ideas

Instructional materials are essentially devices to present ideas and evidence to the learner. It is recognized that some films and tapes, and even other teaching aids, present hypotheses to the learner; some present evaluations of evidence and conclusions. These last are in the minority, however; the great many maps, charts, models, pictures, etc. used in our schools are limited to presenting material to be used as evidence. In this they serve an extremely worthwhile function. The lesson to be learned in the use of instructional materials does not deal with the threading of a film through a machine — a very simple procedure that one can learn in a few minutes. The teacher learns rather to be alert always for ways in which to present graphically ideas or evidence as material for them. Such graphical presentation, when properly done, makes teaching more effective than it would be otherwise and learning faster. In this statement we can well include the acquiring or modifying of skills, appreciations, attitudes, and interests.

· VISUAL MATERIALS FOR INSTRUCTION

The picture was used as a teaching device long before the advent of the printed word — perhaps before the advent of the spoken word. About the time of Shakespeare, Comenius, who wrote a good deal about education, advocated the use of pictures in formal teaching. Teachers were not quick to adopt the practice but pictures have been used in increasing amounts from his time until the present. As classes became large, however, with no adequate enlarging or projecting device, the picture became somewhat ineffective. During their period of preparation, teachers were warned against holding up small pictures for the class to view when most of the pupils could see no details. Pictures handed from pupil to pupil, they were told, detracted attention from the lesson. Both admonitions are defensible today.

With present day techniques the teacher has bountiful opportunity to present almost any type of picture to a class of any size. As a matter of fact, television and film techniques make possible the presentation of relatively small pictures to groups of immense size. They also make possible the presentation of pictures of extremely small objects. For the classroom let us limit this discussion to projection and display devices. One elementary teacher started her collection of pictures for teaching when she was eight years of age. Her early decision to be a teacher never was changed and by the time she received her certificate she had a very large collection in the roomy attic of her parents' farm home. For years she spent a few hours each vacation period adding new material and taking out that which she needed for the coming term. This teacher has more than the ordinary amount of the two things essential to collecting materials: time and space.

Sources of Materials

For those of us who have a relatively late start in collecting materials, there is a great deal that can be done. Many agencies stand ready to send the teacher very fine pictures, charts, maps, pamphlets, and brochures. Each state has some sort of packet to send to the prospective tourist or settler and will gladly mail it to any teacher who asks. The railroads and bus companies have an abundance of advertising, most of an acceptable type. In every industry there are firms which are anxious to have children read their publicity materials. In almost all cases, these aids are free. The *National Education Association Journal* carries a list of sources each month. The booklet, *Free and Inexpensive Educational Aids*,[1] is very helpful. It must be remembered that looking at pictures is a pleasant pastime for children and that their use should be permitted only when it is directed toward some desirable outcome.

Unless a picture is enlarged to about 3' by 4', it is not wise to hold it before a class of thirty and expect it will teach every pupil something.

---

[1]Thomas J. Pepe, *Free and Inexpensive Educational Aids*, (New York: Dover Publications, 1960).

Materials handed around still disperse attention. Small pictures, but at least 5″ by 7″, can be displayed effectively on the bulletin board. The bulletin board is to be discussed later in this chapter. The opaque projector is a practical device and is now available to many teachers. Unfortunately the size of the picture the machine will accommodate is limited. Frye and MacMahon[2] have a process by which a picture can be taken from the paper on which it is printed and transferred to a piece of transparent plastic. The process is neither difficult nor expensive and the resulting picture is in actuality a slide which can be used in a slide projector or in an overhead projector if it is larger than a slide. The opaque projector is not available to all teachers and has limitations much like the overhead projector.

Carl Purcell, NEA

The Overhead Projector Permits the Teacher to Present the Written
Word Immediately

[2]Harvey Raymond Frye and Edward MacMahon, "Transparencies from the Printed Page," *Educational Screen*, (February, 1955), pp. 68-9.

Teacher-Made Slides

> By the rude bridge that arched the flood,
> Their flag to April's breeze unfurled,
> Here once the embattled farmer stood,
> And fired the shot heard around the world.
>
> Ralph Waldo Emerson (1803-1882)

A group of teachers from a midwestern state were on the bank of the river at Concord in the course of a tour of New England. "I have told hundreds of children about this bridge," one of the group stated, "but not until this minute have I been able to visualize the men on each side and the struggle they went through. With my slides, I will be able to bring my children right here!" This teacher had an inexpensive 35-mm. camera and was building a series of slides as she went along. Another teacher on the same trip was compiling a series for teaching social studies in the high school. He too could bring his pupils closer to concepts of American democracy through pictures he had taken. Staying much closer to home, another teacher made a study in slides of a local river and taught a unit of conservation on the basis of these slides. He designed his teaching procedure to make use of these pictures prior to field trips to several areas through which the river flowed. These experienced people knew that the more the teacher can express himself in his teaching the more effective his teaching will be.

The manufacturers of cameras and films have provided us with an abundance of materials for making our own pictures for projection. The 35-mm. camera is at present the most popular for slides but the 2 1/4" by 2 1/4" reflex camera, which offers a bigger film area for each picture and better opportunity for composition, is gaining support steadily. Cameras capable of doing fine work can be purchased at moderate prices. The competition in the camera field is intense with the result that the product of any one of the established firms can be relied on. Projection of 35-mm. slides is done through a projector which is adaptable to the use of the filmstrip and which is found in many schools. Projectors which accommodate the larger slides are found less frequently.

The Handmade Slide. Creative opportunity in the visual field is also offered by the handmade slide. This type is often 3 1/4" by 4 1/4" and requires, of course, a projector of the same dimensions. Materials are also available for handmade slides measuring 2" by 2" but many teachers find these dimensions too confining for their work. In either case, blank slides are available as etched glass, plain glass, and translucent plastic. On both the etched glass and plastic, one can use black pencil or special colored crayons. With these materials the slide can be cleaned easily and used again. Permanent slides can be made with ink.

The imaginative teacher can use these slides to present graphs of any sort. The use is not limited to his handiwork alone but offers opportunity for expression on the part of the student. Materials are available for making slides from the Keystone[3] firm and other sources.

The Instant Slide. The Polaroid Land Camera[4], which develops the film and produces prints in a matter of ten seconds, offers a very interesting chance for the teacher to work with slides. Special films are available which develop as slides. These have been available in black and white for some time and may soon be purchased in color. Each can be framed immediately after development in a plastic mount for insertion into a projector. Such slides are permanent. The camera is manufactured in several sizes each producing, of course, a picture of different dimensions.

The Filmstrip

The filmstrip provides a rich source of slides for projection. The filmstrip is simply a series of pictures on a strip of film. The use of this device is extremely simple and the projector itself is the same machine, with adaption, that projects 2″ by 2″ slides. On the strip the pictures are in sequence and are often accompanied by captions. The rate of projection is determined by the operator so the teacher can proceed at his own rate, can turn back to previous frames when he desires, or can omit any number of frames. The filmstrip generally consists of about fifty frames, is relatively inexpensive, and is durable. Whereas a school system is often better advised to rent sound films rather than to buy them, it may well be able to afford to own a good selection of filmstrips. As with any device, the teacher familiarizes himself with the filmstrip before using it and makes certain that it will advance the learning of the children toward desirable outcomes.

The Motion Picture Film

The moving picture approaches a live situation more closely than a still picture and to this degree it is more effective than the still picture. Perhaps no teaching device has been more abused than the motion picture. One still finds schools in which the whole pupil membership is sent into an auditorium to see films designed for particular class use. The film, to be meaningful, must relate to other approaches made to the area

---

[3]Keystone View Company, Meadville, Pennsylvania.
[4]Polaroid Corporation, Cambridge 39, Massachusetts.

of study, must be timely, and must contribute to the pupils' perception and understanding of what is being studied. This necessitates preparatory work on the part of the teacher which consists of studying the picture and determining just where and how it can properly be used.

In recent years series of films have been produced which are designed to teach whole high school courses. In these lie a promising approach to teaching the large numbers of boys and girls coming into our high schools. These films, of course, must be used under the guidance of teachers well prepared in the subject matter field and with minute attention to the progress of each pupil. The chance for misconcepts to occur in impersonal presentation of material is so great that it presents one of the great hazards of this type of teaching.

Sources of films. From the beginning the motion picture has been popular. It has been identified with entertainment and yet has proved itself to be a powerful medium of instruction. The film is not only informative; it has the power to create and change attitudes. Because of the fact that the picture is a very bright area in a darkened room, the film demands attention. Its use has made the control of children easier than has the use of some other devices. All of these considerations have produced a demand for films on every conceivable subject; not only schools, but industry and churches have asked for more and more of them. The result is a happy one for the teacher. Films are plentiful and most universities have a wide selection the high school teacher may use; many good pictures are available for purchase at a reasonable price; and many industrial firms lend them free of charge. The latter, of course, are for advertising purposes but the advertising is generally restrained, is in good taste, and offers no reason to make the films' use in school objectionable.

Maps

It may seem strange to us that an airplane enroute in a straight line from New York to England passes over Newfoundland. We may find it hard to believe that Montreal, on the St. Lawrence River which is ice-bound four months of the year, is at the same latitude as Venice where the canals rarely, if ever, freeze. The evidence which we have picked up here and there has led us to unsound conclusions. In the knowledge of geography possessed by some of us, misconcepts abound.

Maps and globes supply evidence we can present to pupils in their efforts to gain true concepts of the world. In light of the advances made in communication and transportation and with regard to political situations, it is exceedingly important that such sound ideas be imparted.

Wall maps are designed for many purposes. Political maps indicate countries and other divisions of the land area. Relief maps show where the mountains, valleys, and plains are found. Special maps are made to show the annual rainfall of certain areas, other maps indicate industrial and agricultural production, and still other maps are available for many purposes. It must be remembered that a map is essentially a picture and supplies evidence in a form less abstract than the spoken or written word.

Most of our maps are flat and the world is round, or almost so. This has always posed a problem for teachers and the only solution, since we cannot flatten the world, is to use a map in the form of sphere or globe. Although it has been used for centuries, there have been recent changes in the manufacturing of the globe. While the old familiar opaque globe is valuable and should be available to every teacher of the social studies, the transparent globe and the slated globe offer good opportunities for effective teaching. The slated globe has only the continent outlines drawn on it and the surface itself can be chalked to indicate what is desired for a particular lesson. After use, the lines can be erased and the globe is ready for another lesson.

Bulletin Boards

The good classroom carries a message to the learner. When a child enters the classroom in which English is taught well, it says to him, "See the treasures of literature." The good science room says, "These are some of the exciting things of science." Unfortunately some classrooms say, "I am only a poor colorless room. You'll probably be bored with me so sit down and amuse yourselves." The big difference in classrooms depends largely on the presence and use of the bulletin board. The bulletin board effectively used carries a message and delivers it with impact.

The Position. The bulletin board is often placed on the wall opposite the windows of the classroom and often in the front on each side of the chalkboard. The teacher is aware that the presence of large colorful areas in the front of the room distract much attention from a speaker, who normally is between these areas of the bulletin boards. Because of this, it seems wise to place the highly colorful and dramatic material in some other location. As a matter of fact, in the typical room the pupils enter from the front and while walking to their seats face the back wall. Here is the place, then, for the quick message presented with drama and color. The side wall can also be treated with imagination and vigor.

Improvised Bulletin Boards. The newer schools ordinarily have built-in bulletin boards. Many of the older schools do not. A problem often met by the teacher in old buildings is the great expanse of blackboard covering two or three complete walls. In some cases these old boards are camouflaged with paint and then the teacher is actually confronted with a slate bulletin board! This monstrosity can be covered with one of several types of fibrous wallboard which will accept paint and offers a satisfactory surface for the use of thumbtacks. At the worst the slate can be covered with stout plain wallpaper to which material can be pinned. The use of cellulose tape on a painted surface will soon produce an unsightly appearance.

The Up-to-Date Bulletin Board. The bulletin board must be kept up-to-date to be effective. It should be designed with some attempt at artistry but artiness is to be avoided. Materials should always be fresh and vigorous. Some authorities suggest keeping lettering and materials from year to year. It will be found that although some pictures do maintain their freshness when stored, most of them become discolored or faded with age. A good teacher is always watching for new materials and involves his pupils in the search. A lively bright bulletin board in which the pupils have a creator's interest helps to develop a lively bright atmosphere in the classroom.

The well-designed bulletin board says only one thing and says it clearly. The first glance of the pupil is rewarded with an interesting idea which is developed as he looks further. The bulletin board can plant an idea; it can state a hypothesis; it can present evidence or support a conclusion. Because of such versatility it can keep pace with the investigation of a problem and reinforce the daily lesson plans. It can make a room say almost anything the pupils and teacher want it to say.

The Chalkboard

The chalkboard is the "old reliable" of visual aids. It has served us for more than a century and still holds it own among our many newer devices. It is no longer properly called a blackboard because it comes in several colors. The teacher rarely has his choice of color as this is most often determined by the architects or designers. Where there is a choice, green is frequently preferred. The good teacher keeps his chalkboard clean so that the color of the chalk makes a strong contrast with the board itself. The use of colored chalk is extremely helpful in making scientific drawings and in delineating geometrical figures as well as in other fields. Many boards, however, are very hard to clean after the use of colored chalk and this has to be considered. The chalkboard lends itself to simple and straightforward work such as plain writing and schematic designs. It is not effective for artistic creation and flowery design. Most of the old slate boards have disappeared and in some cases the newer composition boards demand a certain breaking-in procedure. A teacher new to a school might well ask the administrator for any special directions in the proper maintenance of the chalkboards used in the system.

The Textbook

The textbook can be almost anything the teacher makes it. It can be a dreadful master demanding absolute obedience or it can be a useful servant. Properly used, it is an exceedingly important device to be used with consideration and skill.

Unfortunately the textbook is still the master in many of our school rooms. In some systems the administration determines which books are to be used in particular classes and holds the teacher responsible for the "covering" of the total number of pages. Even the adoption of specific textbooks by whole states is not yet a thing of the past. In more liberal areas the teachers are permitted, often as members of groups, to vote for one textbook or another but, once the book has been chosen, no deviation from its use is permitted. As in so many cases in which freedom is denied the teacher and the learner, restriction results in a stunting of the learning process.

The Selection of a Textbook. Some teachers are free to select their own textbooks and to change them when they think it is wise to do so. Others have no instructions concerning textbooks and are free to teach without them if they wish. Many effective teachers, however, feel that having a single textbook as one established authority is good practice. In all cases it is of utmost importance to the teacher that he know the textbooks in his field and that he be able to evaluate them according to certain criteria.

The good textbook is up-to-date. One can determine quite easily the date of the printing of a book but it is necessary to discover when the book was written as well as when it was printed. Many newly-printed books are revisions of older books and some are based on outdated study and are obsolete the day they arrive at the school.

The good textbook has many devices to aid the learner. Indices and glossaries are important for both good understanding and good reading habits. The definition and pronunciation at the foot of the page on which it appears introduces the new and difficult word to the reader. It goes without saying that good print and suitable illustration are indispensable. In many textbooks of science and other subjects, the use of plastic overplays has improved illustrations immeasurably. A schoolboy rarely treats his book with tender loving care, so good strong binding and durable stock are essential to stand up to the hard usage which he generally accords it.

The authorship is the number one consideration of any book. Because of this fact, many books are used even when new and better ones are available. The established author is often the safe author to select but the new author may have a better and more up-to-date presentation. Beyond everything, the author must show evidence of thorough knowledge of his field and sound scholarship.

The pupils in the biology and chemistry classes of one particular teacher choose their own textbooks. Although a popular book is considered the basic test for each class, early in the school year the boys and girls study the samples of the several high school and college books supplied by the teacher. From them they choose those they believe will be most helpful. Almost every year the choice goes to college texts because those designed for the high school are "too simple and repetitive."

The Relationship of Textbooks to Reflective Thinking. The term "textbook" came from the nature of the book itself. Originally the textbook had in it all the material which was to be conveyed to the learner in the specific academic discipline. It was authority absolute and final. The questions were raised; the hypotheses were stated; the evidence was presented and evaluated; and the conclusions were drawn and supported. The learner had only to master the text to be considered successful. The "text" portion of the word had some of the connotation of the today's "text" in a sermon. The teacher could "keep" school using such a device even he were neither a great scholar nor a good pedagog. His techniques consisted of assigning material, hearing recitations, and keeping the less ambitious pupils quiet.

The textbook today also presents evidence. To do so it also must raise questions and form some hypotheses. It does not, however, lead the pupil to believe that the conclusion drawn, sound in itself in light of the evidence available, is the final answer to the question raised. As a matter of fact, many books leave the learner to answer for himself the great questions involved. Much of the presentation, including the list of questions at the end of the chapter, in the textbook of today attempts to provoke independent thinking on the part of the teacher.

The Use of a Single Textbook. In the unit type of teaching described in Chapter 5 the class has the choice of using one textbook as the starting point in the exploration of a problem or surveying several for the purpose. The use of a single text has merit in that it affords a home base from which to operate. It gives the slower readers in the class something to hold to and thus offers them a measure of security. There is no reason why a class might not have such a basic book and supplement it by reading others in the field. If examination and choice of such supplementary material is allowed the boys and girls, the reading level and quality of the content chosen will be found to be relatively high.

Techniques. The typical high school class spans a range of six years in reading maturity. In other words, the pupils in an eighth grade will consist of some reading at the fifth grade level and some at the eleventh grade level with, of course, many at normal level. This span is greatly lessened only when the children are grouped according to reading ability. Because of the reading immaturity of some pupils, the teacher at the secondary level must have a mastery of some technique of teaching boys and girls to read a book. Some colleges offer courses to the high school teacher to aid him in this effort and there are several very fine books available. For our purpose, we will consider only a very simple approach.

The directed reading lesson is one technique which has been found helpful at the junior high school level and there is no reason why it should not prove as helpful in the senior high school. In this procedure the teacher directs the class to open their books at the beginning of a chapter. He requests them to read the title of the chapter and then ask questions such a title might raise. These questions are written on the chalkboard. He then suggests that each pupil read the first paragraph silently. After some time, he calls on one or more pupils to identify the idea of the paragraph. Very probably there is a relationship between this idea and one of the written questions. If there is, no doubt some child will point it out. After dealing thus with each paragraph of a section, he asks for volunteers who believe they can put the concept of the section into a sentence. The sentence, if it is sufficiently comprehensive, is written on the board. The relationship of the concept to the beginning questions, if one exists, is noted. By developing this technique through several lesson periods, not necessarily consecutive, the teacher will advance some of his pupils from sentence readers to paragraph readers and some will grow to the stature of section readers. Eventually some of his pupils will be able to read whole chapters quickly with good understanding. It must be emphasized that this process is designed to teach the skill of reading. It also teaches the lesson in the particular chapter fairly well but when the class has mastered the reading skill involved there is no need for the teacher to retain the procedure as a lesson plan to be repeated time and again. The teacher's aim is to develop in the reader the abilities to identify questions raised, to grasp hypotheses, to recognize and weigh evidence, and to judge conclusions shrewdly.

The Speed of Reading. Much has been written about the speed of reading and there are several methods which promise a great deal of improvement in this ability. In our consideration it is enough to say that the more the learner can read in the time available to him the more ideas are presented to him. The better he is able to read, the better is he able to make judgments. These skills contribute to his growth as an independent thinker.

Workbooks.

The workbook can be used well in teaching. To the beginning teacher especially it offers help as a reviewing and a testing device. Some workbooks are stimulating and thought provoking, affording the learner a structure for sound inductive thinking. Others do not measure up to this high standard but are merely series of exercises to be used as busy work.

The beginning teacher would do well to familiarize himself with the several workbooks in his field and to select the one which offers the most promising treatment of subject matter material for close study. He may or may not use it, but before he does he must make certain that the workbook can contribute to the outcomes he has set as beneficial for his class. If it cannot contribute, there is little reason for asking the children to buy it or to waste time on it. The decision not to use a workbook one year should not preclude its use the ensuing year as these instruments are constantly changing and being improved.

AUDIO MATERIALS FOR INSTRUCTION

A certain teacher of Spanish provides each of his pupils with a small reel of tape for a tape recorder at the beginning of the school year. Periodically each pupil records his efforts at speaking Spanish on this tape. If he is not satisfied with the result he can repeat his efforts time and time again. At the end of each marking period, however, he submits his tape to the teacher for evaluation. A good many recordings made by people who speak Spanish well are available in this class so that a guide to pronunciation and intonation is on hand at any time. This imaginative use of the tape recorder is illustrative of what can be done with this versatile machine. Recent expansion of its use in language laboratories is considered in the chapter dealing with teaching machines.

The Tape Recorder

The use of the tape recorder in music teaching and speech is fairly well advanced in our schools. The recording of radio programs and the audio part of television programs is quite simple on a tape recorder, and many schools have built up tape libraries of the more significant addresses and programs offered on commercial radio and television.

Some years ago the Minnesota State Department of Education organized a "Tapes for Teaching" program which has since grown beyond the borders of the state.[5] In this system a teacher submits a request of a recording of any one of many addresses, programs, or dramatic excerpts. He sends a tape with his request. After a few days he receives his tape or one like it back with the desired recording on it. When he has used this tape, he may keep it for repeated use, erase it for other use, or submit it once more with another request. This program offers teachers of many subject matter areas a vast source of teaching material. Other such systems can be found in other parts of the country.

Radio

The radio has proved to be a very practical means of communication and has served many useful purposes. In the school, however, it did not make the headway expected of it and is used in relatively few classrooms. The obvious reason, of course, is that the offerings of commercial radio during the school day have not been valuable in light of the desired outcomes of the curriculum. Many social studies classes, for example, meet at 10 o'clock in the morning. In any one locality the chance that a specific program will be available at that time is almost nil. Many teachers, however, have combined the radio with the tape recorder. With this combination, a radio program can be taped at any time and is then available when needed. There is very little technical difficulty involved in the procedure.

In many towns and cities the radio stations have made time available to the schools for broadcasts of a noncommercial type. This practice has afforded boys and girls wonderful opportunity to write and produce plays, to offer musical programs, and to do other creative work. Such programs can be used well as a public relations instrument. A word of caution is necessary. Some schools have eagerly accepted the responsibility of filling a half hour each week only to learn that they are not up to the demands of the allotted time. The teachers find the adventure turned to a chore, the pupils run out of good ideas, and what started as an asset turns out a liability.

Television

Early in television history a great comedian pointed out that we had something wonderful in the television set to use for the advancement of culture but that, without doubt, we woud sell our opportunity to those people who manufacture cigarettes and stomach medicines.

---

[5]*Educators' Guide to Free Tapes, Scripts, and Transcriptions, 1961* (Educators' Progress Service, Box 497, Randolph, Wisconsin.)

His prediction proved correct and commercial television offerings are open to severe criticisms. The daytime programs are often pointless and tiresome with no value as far as the school is concerned. During times of crisis, of course, presentations are often timely and of great worth and it may even be good school administration to have some arrangement whereby pupils interested can see part of the baseball world series. These peaks, however, do not change the essential picture. The many worthwhile offerings of television can be put on to video tape and used for projection on television circuits for schools equipped to receive them, but this is a highly technical procedure far beyond the ability of the teacher not trained in the field.

Some years ago the federal government allocated a certain number of channels of the television spectrum to educational puposes. The stations using these channels are noncommercial and must broadcast programs of an educational or cultural nature. These stations are owned, in most cases, by the great universities and their development is promising. In some areas, they are offering suitable programs to the elementary and secondary schools and are making possible a considerable expansion of the curriculum. Closed circuit television is being put into use in some schools. Combined with team teaching, such systems offer all sorts of possibilities and there is no doubt that there will be more experimentation and new techniques will be developed. A further consideration of this medium is to be found in the chapter dealing with teaching machines and team teaching.

COMMUNITY RESOURCES

The best study of mankind is man and every school has access to the study of man and his works. One movement in high school curriculum development was based on the hypothesis that the community is essentially the high school curriculum. This meant that the subject matter to be taught in the school should come directly from people in the community and their occupations. Of course the elementary school for decades has centered much of its study on the immediate locality.

The writer once observed a rather stout lady teaching a general science class. The period was devoted to supervised study. The teacher loomed over the small boy in front of her as she stood between him and the window. He glanced up at her covertly and with a frown as much as to say, "Please get out of my light!" In truth she was in his light in a more abstract but no less important manner of speaking. Here was a child reading about erosion when not more than ten feet away from him was the out-of-doors with a hundred discernible illustrations of the concept. Why does earth material settle on the walk? Is the sediment carried along in the gutter in a rainstorm subject to the same laws as the sediment in a river? The community — almost any community — contains the answers.

The Field Trip

One can take the class to the community or bring the community to the class. When one takes the class to the community he conducts a field trip. This may mean anything from taking a biology class around the schoolyard to study the plants and trees to conducting a tour entailing hundreds of miles of travelling to visit Washington, the capitol of the country. Each activity is a technique of teaching a lesson and is planned as such.

The field trip grows from the efforts of the teacher and the pupils to find an answer to a problem. If, in the growth of a unit, it becomes apparent that the class can pursue its goals best by leaving the school, if the evidence is best studied outside the classroom, then the field trip is necessary. The problem to be studied has been identified, the hypothesis has been formed, and evidence has been sought before a decision concerning a field trip can properly be made. Beyond this, the class has been prepared for close observation and accurate reporting while on the trip. Pages of books can be reread when necessary and experiments can sometimes be repeated but the field trip must be regarded as a "one-shot" opportunity.

Precautionary Measures. A note of caution must be injected. The slips of paper granting permission for children to be away from school ordinarily demanded by the administration are highly desirable. They indicate the parents' awareness of the activity and the teachers' intent to perform their duties in accord with regulations. In legal considerations, they are of less value than some teachers believe them to be. Nothing permits a teacher to be negligent of a child's welfare and if a mishap occurs on a trip and the parent of an injured child sues the school and teacher on the grounds of negligence a very difficult problem is presented. It is hardly possible to predict what the definition of "negligent" will be in any law suit. The teacher must be able to show that at all times the children under his care have adult supervision. Before embarking on any trip it is highly important that he have on file in the administrator's office a description of the activity and the precautions taken.[6]

---

[6]See chapter 13 for legal considerations.

The Community Resource Book

At the secondary level the local field trip is a device for the study of evidence bearing on the cultural or vocational aspects of the community. Although the individual teacher can do his own research and determine what is important for his class to see in the community, many school systems have available a source book listing the various institutions in the area which can be visited. Such sources indicate not only the nature of the experiences practical in the community but also the proper channels of approach to the various organizations. Of course the imaginative teacher will seldom be satisfied with an established list but will explore its possibilities in the interest of time.

Community Speakers

The people of a community are a valuable resource to the teacher. Citizens who have gone to distant parts of the world are often willing to show slides of their travels. Experts in fields such as medicine, law enforcement, and industry are glad to speak to young people about the aims of their vocations. The young teacher must be advised to "look every gift horse in the mouth." He is responsible for all spoken material directed toward his classes, hence it is best that he know the gist of what the speaker is to say before he says it. Denominational aspects of religion, personal aspects of local politics, and some topics in medicine have little place in the public school classroom.

Each speaker produces evidence on one question or another; some will put forth theories and try to support them; some will draw conclusions. It is the teacher's responsibility to see that the theories and evidence bear upon work being done by the class.

SUMMARY

The many visual aids designed for instruction present ideas to the learner or evidence for the support of ideas. In the case of books, the presentation is in the abstract. In the case of pictures, models, charts and so on, the idea or evidence is presented graphically and hence in a more concrete fashion. Specimens and other functional materials are evidence in themselves. Learning demands all available materials; the teacher understands that the less abstract the material the easier it is for children to learn from it.

Audio instructional materials often are merely transmissions of the spoken word and vulnerable to all its dangers. As much as we try, we still convey many misunderstandings to each other. Materials such as recordings of orchestras, bird songs and so on are direct presentation of evidence which can be judged.

The community of any school can be looked upon as a vast reservoir of instructional material. The things of nature, the institutions, and the people all have their stories to tell and their lessons to teach. It is up to the teacher to find good ways in which to use them.

SUGGESTED ACTIVITIES

1. Secure the catalog listing the films, filmstrips, and records available for rent from some nearby university and determine what films, etc. are available in your major field. Study the notations after the titles of films.
2. If your college has an instructional materials center, visit it and learn what you can of its operation. If materials are available for preview, ask for the films, etc. suitable for one unit in your major field, review them and use them in planning the unit.
3. If your local or college bookstore carries materials for making slides, obtain a kit and experiment in the making of slides which would be useful in teaching a unit in your major field.
4. If you have never taken any colored slides, determine at a photography shop whether your own camera is capable of such work. If it is not, borrow, buy, or rent one and buy a roll of colored film which can be processed as slides (transparencies is the word used in the trade). Suppose you were about to teach a unit on trees in biology or on dress design in home economics and take pictures to use in the teaching of such units.
5. If you have not had a course in instructional materials, ask a member of the department teaching these courses to afford you some experience with the film projector, the opaque projector, and the overhead projector.
6. Analyze one or more films used in your present college class or some other to determine whether it served to form a hypothesis, to defend an established theory or to offer evidence. Did it follow a thought process including all three of these functions?
7. Design a classroom for your teaching field indicating the extent and placement of chalkboards and bulletin boards. Indicate the type of seating you prefer.

QUESTIONS FOR SELF EVALUATION

1. List several principles to follow when presenting pictorial material to a class.
2. Compile a check list of steps essential to presenting a film to a class. One such step would be to be certain of the availability of the desired film.
3. What are the dimensions of the slides in ordinary use in our classrooms? What media are available to the teacher for making slides of this size?
4. Compare the advantages of the filmstrip as contrasted to the motion picture. What disadvantages must also be considered?

5. In what considerations is the bulletin board versatile? To what extent is it limited in its usefulness?
6. In your words, define the function of the textbook. Has its importance increased or decreased in the last twenty-five years? Defend your answer.
7. Are there widely used workbooks in your teaching field? Can you defend their use? Can you attack it?
8. What are the main precautions to be taken before taking a class on a field trip?

BIBLIOGRAPHY

1. ALEXANDER, WILLIAM H., AND HALVERSON, PAUL M., *Effective Teaching in the Secondary School.* New York: Rinehart and Company, 1956, Chapter 10.
2. BURTON, WILLIAM H., *The Guidance of Learning Activities.* New York: Appleton-Century-Crofts, Inc., 1952, Chapter 7.
3. CAMPBELL, RONALD, AND ROMSEYER, JOHN A., *The Dynamics of School Community Relationships.* New York: Allyn and Bacon, Inc., 1957.
4. CLARK, LEONARD E., AND STARR, IRVING S., *The Materials of Instruction.* 1959, Chapter 9.
5. CRONBACK, LEE J., *Text Materials in Modern Education*, Urbana, Illinois: University of Illinois Press, 1955.
6. CROSS, A. S. F., AND CYPHER, I. E., *Audio Visual Education.* New York: Thomas F. Crowell Publishing Co., 1961.
7. DALE, EDGAR, *Audio Visual Methods in Teaching.* New York: Dryden Press Inc., 1954.
8. DOUGLAS, HARL L., *The High School Curriculum.* New York: Ronald Press Company, 1956.
9. FINN, JAMES P., *The Audio-Visual Equipment Manual.* New York: The Dryden Press Inc., 1957.
10. FRANKS, JEAN D., *Human Relations and Audio-Visual Materials.* New York: National Conference of Christians and Jews, 1954.
11. GRAMBS, JEAN D., IVERSON, WILLIAM J., AND PATTERSON, FRANKLIN K., *Modern Methods in Secondary Education.* New York: the Dryden Press, 1958, Chapters 7 and 8.
12. HANSEN, KENNETH H., *High School Teaching.* Englewood Cliffs, N. J.: Prentice-Hall, Inc., 1957, Chapters 8, 9, 11.
13. KINDER, J. S., *Audio-Visual Materials and Techniques.* New York: American Book Company, 1958.
14. KLAUSMEIER, HERBERT J., *Teaching in the Secondary Schools.* New York: Harper and Brothers, 1958. Chapter 11.
15. *Mass Media and Education.* N.S.S.E. 53rd. Yearbook, Part II. Chicago: University of Chicago Press, 1954.
16. MICHAELIS, JOHN VOELL, AND DUMAES, ERICK, *The Student Teacher in the Elementary School.* Englewood Cliffs, N. J.: Prentice Hall, 1960. Chapter 10.
17. *National Tape Recording Catalog.* Washington, D. C.: Department of Audio-Visual Instruction, NEA.

18. NELSON, L. W., *Instructional Aids*. Dubuque, Iowa: Wm. C. Brown Publishing Company, 1958.

19. ROSAFF, MARTIN, *The Library in High School Teaching*. New York: The H. W. Wilson Company, 1955.

20. SPACHE, G. D., *Auditory and Visual Materials*. N.S.S.E. Yearbook 1960, Part I, 1961.

21. WALLINBERG, WILLIAM, *The Adolescent Years*. New York: Harcourt Brace and Company, 1955. Chapter 13.

22. WETTICH, WALTER ANCO, AND SCHULLER, CHARLES FRANCIS, *Audio-Visual Materials: Their Nature and Use*. New York: Harper, 1957.

CHAPTER 10

Some Recent Developments In Teaching

OVERVIEW

There are always new developments in teaching and today we can identify at least three: teaching machines and programed learning, language laboratories, and team teaching. None of these is really new as each has its roots in the past, with some experimentation done years ago. Nonetheless, these developments are being explored and exploited by many school systems today. Each innovation has its supporters who claim that it will help us a great deal and each has its critics who feel that mistakes are being made.

Teaching machines go back at least forty years; language laboratories have roots which can be traced back to the nineteenth century; team teaching probably is as old as the organized school. The resurgences of these devices are affecting most of our schools in one way or another. Administrators are considering purchases of teaching machines and many companies stand ready to provide both machines and programs. Perhaps no audio-visual instrument has spread more rapidly than the language laboratory in the last decade. Hardly a high school building is now being constructed or planned that does not provide for some degree of team teaching. The nature and use of these developments are discussed in this chapter.

TEACHING MACHINES
AND PROGRAMED INSTRUCTION

Teaching machines are devices of several types which have been designed to help with teaching. This definition is limited to those which present questions or items of information to the learner in a logical order. As the learner answers each question, either correctly or incorrectly, he is guided by the machine to the next logical question or is presented with information essential to his next step in learning.

Television, radio, the film projector, and the tape recorder are machines which help us teach but, since they present material only, they are not teaching machines as the term is used.

Development

Whether teaching machines do teach depends on one's use of words. Skinner, certainly one of the leading men in the development of the machine, states, "The machine itself, of course, does not teach."[1] On the other hand, an authority who has written a great deal on the subject, Galanter, states that the machine is a renaissance of the didactic and that it can teach.[2] Debate on this point of semantics is useless. It is certain that nothing can come out of a machine that a person has not put into it. The machine in each case is essentially a simple device and the material put into it comprises the important factor. The body of subject matter that is fed into the machine is termed the "program" and the author of it is known as the "programer."

The great upsurge in concern over teaching methods which followed Russia's first accomplishment in space brought new interest to bear on the teaching machine. Here, some felt, might lie an untried implement to make learning faster and more effective than it had been.

As early as 1915, Pressey[3] had developed a simple punch board testing device. To use this machine, the student read the question and answered it by selecting one of four responses presented to him. The punch board had a series of four holes after each question. The whole device was built like a sandwich with a hard board on each side and a card between them. The series of four holes for each question were punched through the upper board but only the hole for the right answer was drilled through the lower board. If the learner punched the right hole with a stylus provided, the stylus would go through the card and the hole in the board beneath it, but if the learner chose the wrong hole, the stylus was blocked by the second board. Pressey emphasized that this device gave the learner immediate knowledge of his results, redirected him to the right answer in each case, and made scoring simple and fast. The teacher could count the trials made by the marks on the card. This very simple apparatus was refined into a machine and a

---

[1] B. F. Skinner, "Teaching Machines," *Science* 128, pp. 969-77.
[2] E. Galanter, *Automatic Teaching*, New York: Wiley, 1959.
[3] S. L. Pressey, "Development and Application of Devices Providing Immediate Automatic Scoring of Objective Tests and Concomitant Self-Instruction," *Journal of Psychology*, 29: 417-447.

counter was added but the principle has remained essentially the same in the Pressey type of teaching machine.

The Teaching Machine Gives the Student a Chance to
Advance by Himself

Skinner's first work was done only a few years after that of Pressey and his machine differed basically from the punch board. The learner using Skinner's machine was presented with a question and, in a space provided in the machine, wrote an answer. He then turned a handle which advanced his answer under a sheet of glass where it could be seen but not altered and at the same time brought the programmed answer into view. The learner judged then whether the answer he had written was satisfactory. If it were, he could manipulate the machine so that the question would not arise again. If it were not, then the machine would present it to him again. The teacher, of course, has access to the program after the answers have been recorded.

These two men have designed the basic machines and variations of them are marketed by several companies. It is inevitable that other inventions and refinements will be made. Some of the machines are a push-button device with questions made for a five-choice answer. Machines are being perfected to make use of slides and films. They, of course, are doing the same work but through a different medium.

Crowder[4] has devised the "scrambled book." This device poses questions to the learner and then directs him to certain pages of the book according to his answer. If his answer is correct he proceeds to the next question but if it is incorrect then his attention is drawn to the particular part of the book which will establish a better understanding for him.

Description. There are several teaching machines available from various firms each with its own advantages and disadvantages. Several have been designed for use on the student's desk and are light enough to be readily portable. Typically this type of machine is about 10 inches wide and 18 inches long. These dimensions accommodate teaching programs which are on 8 1/2" x 11" paper, which is the standard size for business stationery. Because of this, it is extremely easy to adapt teacher-made programs to the machine. Loading the machine is very simple. One simply lifts the top, which is hinged, and places the program sheets on a platform. To unload one lifts the top once more and slides the used pages from under the platform. If one wishes to make sure the programs are not disturbed while in the machine, a wire can be passed through two small openings provided and then sealed. The first model of this particular machine provided for the answers to be written on the pages of the program. This, of course, meant that each program could be used only once. The second model has an attachment, available at a very reasonable price, which permits the answer to be written on a spool of paper such as used in adding machines. This paper is advanced with the program sheet and can be kept as a record of the responses.

Use. The operation of the machine is accomplished by turning either of two knurled knows which are found on each side. The tape for the answers is at the right which poses some difficulty for left-handed children. The learner advances the program at his own speed but is unable to reverse the action.

Disadvantage. The early model of this machine was of metal and very durable. The new model is very light but one must question the strength of the material. The body seems fragile for high school use and the top swings on two small plastic hinges which do not seem substantial. The older type presented the material to the reader at a convenient

---

[4]Galanter, *op. cit.,* Chapter V.

angle while the newer one presents it parallel to the desk surface and almost four inches above it. Unless the desk top is lowered, this forces the reader into an uncomfortable position which, for any length of time, would cause fatigue.

Improvisation. The machinery of a teaching machine is simple and one can improvise devices which will illustrate the principle and give him the "feel" of working with programs. It might be as simple as a 12″ by 18″ sheet of construction paper folded so as to make a cover for the program sheets. In the face of the cover, an opening is cut which is eight inches across and one inch deep at the left side and two inches deep at the right as in Figure 1.

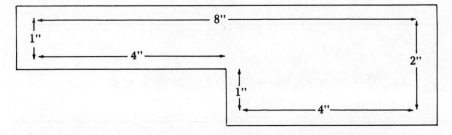

This opening should be made 1 1/2″ below the upper edge of the cover.

FIGURE 1. Shape and Dimensions of Opening in Cover of Teaching Machine.

The programer writes the question across the paper so that the learner reads it through the upper part of the opening and can write his response in the lower right part of the opening. As the sheet is advanced, the correct answer comes into view beside the learner's answer so that he can see if he is right or wrong. The program sheet is illustrated in Figure 2. The sheet can be advanced by pushing on its surface with the eraser on the end of a pencil. The writer has seen several other more substantial teacher-made machines constructed from a similar pattern but from "masonite" or plywood. One hesitates to recommend these amateur devices for classroom use because one is better off with professional accuracy and design. The reader must also be aware of the fact that commercial machines are patented and any attempt to copy one for financial gain would constitute a serious legal offense.

Programer writes and student reads question here.	
Programer writes answer here.	Student writes answer here.
Ex. What countries share the St. Lawrence Seaway?	
United States and Canada	*Canada and the United States*

FIGURE 2. Illustration of a Program Page.

As we have seen, the cost of teaching machines runs from almost nothing for improvised devices up to thousands of dollars for electronic complexes as used by the armed services. It is highly probable that the manufacturers' representatives will have evidence to show that teaching machines are a sound investment which will save money for the taxpayer. One must be careful to avoid complexity for its own sake. Since the lesson is the heart of the machine, the emphasis must be put on this rather than the mechanical device which manipulates the material. The machine, however, must be foolproof and tamper proof and these are not small requirements when the devices are to be put into school children's hands.

Programs. The material inserted into a machine has been termed the program. There is no reason why the teacher should not compose and print, or type, his own program. Many programs are made this way. On the other hand, there are numerous firms which print programs and their total offering covers almost all of the high school curriculum. Writing one's own program is not much more practical than writing one's own textbook. The companies offering programs advertise widely in several of the professional periodicals including *The Journal of Programed Instruction.* Many of the programs have been devised to accompany textboks or series of textbooks written for the secondary schools. The person who makes the program is the real teacher when a teaching machine is used. The marketing of programs has become a business venture and the competition is intense so the programer has come to be to the producing company what the author is to the textbook publisher. The various firms struggling for supremacy in the field are putting great pressure on teachers as consumers. From this picture we see that the program of any one firm will be standardized for use all over the country and will be aimed at the average pupil excepting in those cases in which the students are grouped according to intelligence. It may well be that separate programs will be available for the gifted, the normal, and the dull in some areas.

The programer is, very likely, a subject matter specialist. This statement is especially true at the high school level as opposed to the elementary level. The successful writer of programs is a deductive teacher although some claims are made that one with an inductive approach can be successful. The basis for some of these claims may not be sound. Royalties are paid on programs and various gimmicks appear to stimulate sales and increase royalty checks. In opposition to this, some teachers will attempt to make their own programs but as growth in the area continues, the "do-it-yourself" program will lose out.

The programs which have come to the writer's attention to date have dealt largely with science, social studies, English, and mathematics. These areas lend themselves readily to programing. Whether the fine and applied arts areas will make wide use of teaching machines is doubtful. It may be that their use will be limited to the factual and concepted aspects of this work and will not include performance.

RELATIONSHIP OF TEACHING MACHINES TO REFLECTIVE THINKING

Skinner has said that the machine does not depend on any established school of psychology but that it is a theory of learning in itself. If this statement is true it clears the deck of any theoretical impediments. The machine has at least some of its roots in the old "memory-drum" of Ebbinghaus' time. This was used in the attacks on Faculty psychology and the work involved supported Associationism and Connectionism in the United States. Taking a different approach, Galanter insists that the learner perceives a plan and hence learns according to Gestaltism. The teaching, he says, must produce a concept. This is hardly in line with the consensus concerning Gestaltism because the learner does not formulate his own concept but of necessity must reach one which the programer has already conceived and has inserted in the machine.

Both Skinner and Pressey lived and worked in the Thorndike era of educational psychology, and it seems that the Associationist theories of learning necessity will be called on in the defense of the learning machine. Those who compare programs speak of many little steps depending one on the other. This seems to be purely Associationism. There is no need to attack any or all programs on this point, but it will aid our understanding if we can relate the program to some theory of which we know the strengths and weaknesses.

One authority has stated that the individual who makes a program for a teaching machine must be an extrovertive person and a deductive thinker. The introvertive person who is an inductive thinker is frustrated by the need for preparing many little steps which lead inexorably to a generalization. Such a device cannot permit the learner's thinking to influence the outcome of the study. It will permit him no contribution. The same authority advises those who plan to use the machine, "Don't expect much independent thought." An educator who is presently devising a machine remarked to the writer, "Of course, in this age we have no time for the Socratic method." This is indeed a sad commentary on teaching in a day when more leisure than ever before is available to more people.

A brief discussion of several psychologies of learning was presented in the second chapter of this book. Among them was Gestaltism and other planetary theories. It was shown that insight is a prime consideration in these theories. Insight is defined as the integration by the learner of the several factors in a problem situation and the relating of them to his experiential background. If the machine takes insight into account, it must be predictable with absolute certainty since the conclusion already written into the program is reached inevitably. The misuse of such inflexibility is terrifying to one who holds precious the right of the individual to think. Of course, if the program is limited to factual and undebatable material which the learner can use as a basis for reflective thought, there need be little concern for his independence.

It is now possible, as far as invention goes, to have a child enter our schools in the first grade and proceed to graduation, doing all of his learning by means of teaching machines. This is a terrible thought and a long way, we hope, from reality.

To summarize, it can be said that the teaching machine is a good reviewing device in situations where factual recall is important. Programs can be, and are, composed which guide the learner through a deductive train of thought as in some of the courses in mathematics. Fewer programs are found which are inductive in nature and even in these the thought of the learner must follow that of the programer. As in so many other aspects of our teaching program, the teaching machine program starts with the advanced steps of the thinking process as we have outlined it because it is impossible to give the learner his freedom to sense a problem and identify it through a machine. He can gather evidence by this means and can follow the thinking process of a teacher to logical conclusions. His freedom to infer is limited as is his freedom to make applications of generalizations. The teaching machine has a place in our schools but it is a tool to be used by the teacher who understands its real limitations.

THE LANGUAGE LABORATORY

As time has gone on, communication has become more and more important to mankind. Yet mankind has developed not one but many languages and, as the Biblical story showed long ago, has brought about a great deal of confusion. The alleviation of the condition lies in teaching the young people of one nationality to understand and to speak the language of another. This is partially a function of the schools and the search for methods to fulfill it in our country has brought into being the language laboratory.

Southern Illinois University School
Herbert Smith

The Language Laboratory Improves Skills and Can Be a
Gold Mine of Ideas

Introduction

Once upon a time there was a college student who thought to himself, "In this class I am only a note-taking machine and not a very good
one. I will buy a machine to take notes for me." So he brought a tape
recorder and set it on his chair just before class started, set it in operation, and went about other business. After class he returned for his
machine which now had a record of what had been said by the professor. Other students saw his recorder and bought themselves similar devices until the professor faced only machines. "Well," he said to himself, "I can get into this movement, too." So he bought a recorder and
taped his lectures in the comfort of his home. At class time one recorder
then talked to several other recorders. The professor and the students,
of course, went to the coffee room in the union and talked to each other
about interesting things.

This expedient use of the tape recorder indicates the versatility of the machine but is not to be taken as good teaching technique. It does illustrate, however, the essential structure of the language laboratory. Each student could take his machine and tape home and play the recording over to himself as many times as he liked, and in any sequence of parts that he wished, until he was satisfied that he knew it. He could ask himself questions, answer them, and then evaluate his responses from the tape.

A big university has a laboratory with 450 listening stations with thousands of tapes available much like a library open to all students. Each one can come in, dial a number from a catalog, and listen to the program on earphones. To make it even easier for the student to do homework, a series of stations have been installed in a dormitory so that the listener has only to go into the particular room, dial the appropriate number, and listen to the lesson desired.

Development

If one were to pursue the origins of the language laboratory he would ultimately end up with the first record made for the purpose of teaching a lesson in a foreign language. The date would be just prior to the turn of the century. Of course, the records of the time were expensive, fragile, and lacking in tonal quality. In spite of their drawbacks, records were used and, as they improved, became more and more helpful. Until the advent of World War II, the record was the essential tool of the foreign language teaching program. Several innovations came about at this time. Records were made with stretches of silence allowing the listener time to repeat the message he had heard. At this time, too, the commercial long-play record was produced. It is interesting to note that some schools had laboratories containing recording and listening equipment of the day and called them "phonetic laboratories."

Immediately after the war, the wire recorder was made available for commercial use. This device was very similar to the magnetic tape recorder which superseded it. The recording was done on a thin wire which went from one spool to another. On one spool of wire, hours of recording could be made as opposed to the few minutes possible on a disc. The wire was much cheaper than the older materials. Soon after the perfection of the recorder, magnetic tape replaced the wire because it was technically superior. Thus was developed the main tool of the language laboratory. Of course, it is often wise to add a good radio and a turntable so that one can use timely radio programs and desirable disc records.

Definition. The language laboratory has been defined as a place devoted to specific linguistic activities by means of permanently installed equipment.

Purpose. In teaching a foreign language the beginning effort should be on understanding and speaking. There are several good reasons for this. Among them is the fact that written skills do not help much in the development of oral skills, but the oral skills are extremely helpful in learning to read and write. With the textbook alone, the emphasis in the earliest lessons of a foreign language was on reading and writing — often merely the repetitious copying of single words which, having no context, were next to meaningless. Almost every one of us has had some experience with the memorization of verb forms and other linguistic drudgery. Yet the teacher with thirty or more students had little opportunity to give each boy and girl much chance to speak the new language. His own fluency, in many cases, left much to be desired and he retreated into English whenever possible. As a consequence of these factors, most foreign language lessons turned out to be sessions in which the students and teacher talked about the foreign language in English. Pupils frequently picked up a good deal of grammar and knowledge of syntax in the course of their foreign language study, but this often was the greatest gain.

The language laboratory brought great opportunities to foreign language learning. The pupil can listen to a spoken message many times and become accustomed to the rhythms and intonations of the speaker who may well be an extremely well-qualified reader. He can record his own efforts at speaking the new tongue and compare these attempts to the speech of the expert. Of great importance, perhaps, is the fact that there is no embarrassment involved when a pupil tapes his own words, listens to them, compares them with a model, and then erases them. In the conventional situation a teacher could listen to each student only a few minutes per day at the very best. With a language laboratory, the students can record their speaking on tape and the teacher can study the efforts of each at his convenience and can add, if he so desires, comments to guide the learner to better pronunciation or accent. The laboratory also brings to the most remote school some of the best possible readings in any foreign language.

Description. The language laboratory is a room in which there is a console which has a control panel, at least one tape recorder, and at least one microphone. The teacher or other person using the console can speak into the microphone, play the recorder, or both. If he wishes, he also can record what is being said into the microphone. The other component of the device is a listening station or a series of stations,

Many language laboratories are set up with thirty stations, but theoretically this number is virtually unlimited. The listening station consists of a pair of earphones and a microphone. The listener can hear whatever is being sent to him from the console and can speak into his microphone so that the teacher can hear him and, if so desired, record what he says. Because of the flexibility provided by the control panel on the console, the teacher can direct messages to one or all or any combination of listening stations. He can also listen to any station or any combination of stations. On this basic pattern can be built many variations so that listeners can select programs through electronic devices, record their own voices and then play back the tape or converse with the teacher. A language laboratory has been installed on a do-it-yourself basis merely by connecting a series of pairs of earphones to the output jack on a tape recorder. From this humble device, laboratories range upward to complicated installations costing many thousands of dollars.

THE TEACHING OF REFLECTIVE THINKING THROUGH THE LANGUAGE LABORATORY

The language laboratory is a very efficient device with which to present evidence to the learner. If one includes the communication between the teacher and the learner among the uses of the laboratory, then it will serve any purpose such as conversation would serve without the electronic channel. If we limit the uses to what is recorded on tape, then we must understand that the learner can get from the machine only what the teacher has put into it. In other words, the machine cannot truly take into account all the inferences and conclusions that students might reach from the use of the recorded material. In foreign language learning, however, one is greatly limited in his freedom to make his own decisions. As shown in Chapter 7, learning a foreign language is essentially the acquiring of habits. One does not infer that in French the word for "day" is "jour" and that it is preceded by "le." He is to learn these facts so that he can incorporate them into a language with which ideas can be expressed.

Within this limited scope, the language laboratory can be of great help in learning a foreign language. The evidence can be presented many times to the learner and this drill is important in learning a skill. The model presented is an acceptable standard while some classroom teachers of foreign languages, realizing some inadequacy in their preparations, do not consider their abilities to be up to high standards. The student using the laboratory is able to listen to and imitate the recorded model many times and reinforce his learning much more than he can under a more conventional system. In addition to all this, the pupil can listen to himself through the playback and modify his pronunciations accordingly. This is an extremely important point in regard to intonation. Without mechanical aids, we hear our own voices from inside ourselves. The conduction of the sound, of course, is entirely different from that through which we hear others. Some people can hardly believe a recorder when they first hear their own voices played back to them. The language laboratory presents the student's voice to him as others hear it — or almost so. Because of this, he is able to modulate his own voice to match the model more closely than he could without the playback opportunity.

The language laboratory presents a great diversity of material. Readings of the classics, poems, comedy skits, news reports, famous speeches, and a great many other things can be acquired on recordings. Related to learning theory, this means that the evidence available appeals to a very wide range of interests. A boy seeking a diplomatic career might spend hours listening to men like DeGaulle speaking to the French people while another would forego this opportunity to hear Fernandel being ridiculous. Each is learning to use the French language in an area which he considers worthwhile and thus meaning is added to his study.

In recent years, there has been increasing attention to the value of individual study. The language laboratory is a good answer as a technique of utilizing time spent in individual work. Although group instruction is feasible and important in this area, it is apparent that much time can very profitably be spent by the student listening to recordings he finds interesting and in imitating models whom he feels are beneficial to him.

To summarize, we can say that the language laboratory is a skill-building device and, because the learnin of a foreign language consists of building skills, is an extremely helpful instrument. In regard to reflective thinking, the language laboratory does not lead the student through a complete thought process but acts as an evidence-presenting device. Although some attempts will be made to construct programs on an inductive basis, basically the instrument will be used in deductive learning.

TEAM TEACHING

The great teachers of the world such as Jesus, Moses, and Aristotle have been individuals who stood so far ahead of their fellows that they simply had to face their task alone. Among the lesser teachers, the ordinary people, often an assignment seems too formidable to be faced by one person. In other situations it appears that several teachers might work better in unison than alone. To some administrators it occurred that a qualified teacher might be used to better advantage if he were given assistance. From these several considerations came the various rational bases for team teaching.

Introduction

Before the year 1800, instruction in the schools of this country, and others, was largely individual. Rousseau's assumption that Emile could have a tutor during his childhood and adolescence was not the fallacy in his day that it appears to be now. As the Industrial Revolution progressed and people swarmed to the factories, as humanitarian idealists strove to get small children out of these factories, as religious idealists struggled to have every child literate, so increased the enrollment of the public schools. To meet the demands, classrooms were made tremendously big so that one teacher could oversee the work of several hundred children. Because the teacher was really the overseer and advanced pupils, called monitors, did most of the instruction, the pattern became known as the monitorial system.

What was wrong with the monitorial system? The monitorial system had a lifetime spanning a generation in the first half of the nineteenth century. It died because of real weaknesses. The methodology depended far too much on rote learning in light of newer psychology. The monitor memorized a lesson step by step and assigned it to his charges who also learned it step by step if they were able. There was little if any regard for the individual and very small consideration of differences in ability. Control of behavior was of necessity extremely rigid and there is reason to believe that punishment was harsh. Although written theory as evidenced in the works of Rousseau, Pestalozzi, and Herbart had made great advances, in practice the thinking of these men was held to be highly idealistic or, in the case of Herbart, was warped and misinterpreted. It is probably safe to say that Dickens' concept of public school education in England in which learning was meager and punishment was abundant was far nearer reality than was the writing of the theorists. In our day, in some schools *The Black Board Jungle* picture is closer to reality than the writings of Kilpatrick. In practice a century ago Faculty psychology and Associationism were dominant.

Pressure of Numbers

The advantage of the monitorial system was evident. It was cheap. One teacher was employed to care for scores of children. The disadvantages became evident. It might be best for us if we could relegate the whole question to the department of ancient history but the demands of the time will not have it so. The great rise in the birth rate in our country began just after 1940. The vanguard of the children involved is now in college. They taxed our schools' capacity and those following have added to the burden. Now schools are faced with the inevitable fact that these children have attained adulthood and are having children. Because of social and technological advance, our society is committed to afford every child the education by which he can benefit most. Paradoxically, teachers have been denied rewards for their efforts to the point where far too few young people desire to teach. As a result of the ensuing pressures, and not only as the result of study and theory, support has developed for some modification of the old monitorial system. "Put the children into big groups and have one good teacher take care of them," is the cry heard. The plans for every high school building now on the drawing boards will not escape the question of rooms big enough to contain several times the number of pupils assigned to the conventional classroom. The modification of the idea that a high school class should contain from twenty to thirty pupils has been imperative. It has been a standard pattern for fifty years and our very recent history has made us question old standard patterns although we readily accept some new standard patterns. As illustration, we are not willing to accept the speed attained by the horse, but we are willing to accept a highly standardized car to attain a great new velocity.

Description. Although the term "team teaching" is self-explanatory inasmuch as it indicates teaching done by a team rather than by an individual, there are many sorts of team teaching. This is because many schools throughout the country have set up teams to answer their specific problems. No authority has said, "This is the way, the only way" to organize a team. Consequently, we can find examples of many types of teams. There are certain characteristics, however, that are somewhat common. The members of a team may run from two to ten, but four or five seems to be a common size. Inevitably, there is a leader — a teacher of ability and experience — and one or more other teachers called simply "members" who may be less experienced than the leader. In addition to these essentials, there may be "paraprofessional" workers. These people have some qualification, but do not have certificates. A housewife with a college degree but no professional training might be employed as a paraprofessional. Many teams also have a clerical member, full or part time, to do the typing, multigraphing, and other such work.

Three approaches to subject matter to be taught by teams are possible and several examples of each can be found in our high schools.

In the most common approach, several teachers of one subject pool their resources. Their conventional classes are replaced by large classes so that one may teach while the others prepare materials, correct papers, or help individual students. Two biology teachers, for instance, might put their classes together for lecture periods and to view films. One might do all the lecturing and the other do all the laboratory work, or they might share each aspect of teaching. In the second approach, the teachers of allied subjects might work together. There are science and mathematics teams who teach common elements of their subjects to large classes and work in the specific areas of their disciplines in small groups. English and social studies teams also work in this manner. Finally, there is the cross-discipline approach in which teachers of many subjects are on one team and work at times with very large groups. This last arrangement is very adaptable to the core curriculum. As a matter of fact, most core programs have been using it, essentially, for many years.

The Extent of Team Teaching. It is impossible to state how many high schools have one or more teaching teams. One publication[5] lists scores of them and it is certain that there are many not reported. The National Association of Secondary School Principals, under the Guidance of Dr. J. Lloyd Trump and with support from the Ford Foundation, has done much work on the utilization of staff in the high schools. Team teaching emerged as a very promising answer to wiser utilization of our teachers and was tried out in many schools cooperating in the study. In each case, the effort was directed toward a need of the particular school, but, at the same time, was considered an experimental procedure. This means that any particular plan could be abandoned after a year or two. On the other hand, the publication of the results of the experimental work brought it to the attention of other high schools with staff problems who formed teams of their own. It is certain that many administrators in older buildings are looking for ways of implementing teams while those building schools are considering modifications of conventional planning to provide the space allocations desirable for team teaching.

Space for Team Teaching

In the present literature of team teaching, one reads of the larger groups meeting in auditoriums, field houses, cafeterias, and other such places. Some schools have knocked out partitions between rooms and

---

[5]Table of Contents, "The Bulletin of the National Association of Secondary School Principals," 46: 270, pp. v-vi.

replaced them with folding doors. Many new schools are ready for team teaching as far as space is concerned. Typical is the Holland (Michigan) High School which provides four common areas seating 150 students each. In addition to this, in the smaller wings of the school, all but one of the classrooms are paired with operable, sound-retardant walls dividing each pair. (See illustration.) The single classrooms hold 30 students and the double classrooms 70. In addition to this, there are small seminar rooms which hold fifteen students each and can be combined in pairs so that each can accommodate 36.[6] Few schools make efforts to house

Courtesy of Dr. Donald Leo
Baltazar Korab

New Ideas in the Use of Space May Help in the Utilization
of the High School Staff

[6]Donald J. Leu, *Profiles of Significant Schools*, New York: Educational Facilities Laboratory, Inc., 1962, p. 10.

more than 150 students in a classroom although it is apparent that some use their auditoriums for exceedingly large groups.

Personalities in Team Teaching

The key person of a teaching team is the leader who must have certain abilities to an extraordinary degree. The leader is responsible for the organization of all the subject matter taught by the team and this demands a broad and deep understanding of his field. He directs the work of others so personal warmth and the faculty of leadership are called for. He is the final authority, within the team, on matters of student response and this demands a working knowledge of adolescent and educational psychology. His status as leader must be accepted by his members so, typically, he is a person of some maturity and experience. The question of whether a leader should be paid more than a member has not been answered. In general, his greater experience would put him above the younger member or a team on a salary schedule. If he is also the head of a department in the high school, he may receive compensation for this responsibility. There is some danger that the leader will be considered somewhat above the member teacher in status and will be paid accordingly. The high school staff will then be divided somewhat like a university faculty with its professors and lesser ranks. It seems this is a step away from democracy in education.

The member of a team can be termed "just an ordinary teacher" but he has to be capable of certain things not demanded of the ordinary teacher. He must sacrifice his own authority to a degree and some teachers find this very difficult. As a matter of fact, it is because of this that it is considered easier for a young teacher to become a team member than an older one who has been captain in his own classroom for some years. The team member takes direction in the organization of his subject matter from his superior and perhaps is expected to modify his methodology to suit that of the older person. He is also expected to be able to follow his leader in the development of concepts within the class and the development of skills and appreciations. This means that he may be striving for goals not his own, although, of course, all goals should be acceptable to all members of a team.

Some administrators see the team situation as an apprenticeship for the younger teacher. There is no doubt at all that the older teacher with great ability can make the youngster's introduction to the profession a pleasant and easier one than otherwise might be the case. Some colleges and universities see the team organization a fitting place to assign student teachers. Students retain their status as learners rather than assuming that of professionals, of course, but can gain a wealth of experience from the use of the several devices often found in ttam teaching, from the large number of boys and girls whom they meet, and, above all, from the guidance of the several professional members of the team.

The paraprofessional and the clerical worker follow directions closely. The paraprofessional corrects papers, marks standardized tests, administers examinations, engages in library research, and supervises study halls, if such exist. The clerical member is responsible, of course, only for mechanical aspects of the program and cannot be considered a substitute for the teacher.

Many teams also bring in outside personnel for special purposes. Inviting speakers into a school classroom involves many considerations which are dealt with in detail in Chapter 9.

The administrator of the school properly is not considered a member of a teaching team. If a team is to succeed, however, it is necessary that their administrator can be depended on for support at every turn. The old concept of supervision is negated by team teaching because the leader is responsible for supervision within the group. The administrator's function is to clear the path of such obstacles as inadequate space and materials.

Time Allocations for Team Teaching. "And No Bells Ring" is the title of the motion picture which illustrates the theory of team teaching as seen by Trump.[7] It is so named because the time allocations under a team teaching organization are not necessarily similar to those of the conventional program. Large classes may use a lecture period of conventional length but it is probable that they will not. Small group seminars may be lengthy or rather short. Above all, the program as outlined calls for a great deal of free time for the individual student to do independent work. Figure 3 shows the distribution of time suggested by the Commission of the NASSP on team teaching.[8] It will be noted that about 40 per cent of the time is given to large-group instruction, 20 per cent to small-group instruction, and 40 per cent to individual study. This division is only suggested but many schools attempt to follow it in practice. We are directly concerned with the relationship of this division to reflective thinking and will discuss it further.

The Devices Used in Team Teaching. From Trump's work and that of others, it is apparent' that the team teaching approach implies the use of all sorts of teaching aids. The use of television, tape recorders,

[7]To order this film write to: National Association of Secondary-School Principles, 1201 Sixteenth St., N. W., Washington 6, D. C.

[8]J. Lloyd Trump, *Images of the Future*, Washington, D. C.: National Association of Secondary School Principals, NEA, 1959, p. 9.

ORGANIZATION OF INSTRUCTION

Teaching-Learning Experiences:

Large-Group Instruction	Small-Group Discussion	Individual Study
Introduction Motivation Explanation Planning Group Study Enrichment Generalization Evaluation	Group examination of terms and concepts and solution of problems Reach areas of agreement and disagreement Improve inter-personal relations	Read Listen to records and tapes View, Question, Analyze, Think Experiment, Examine, Investigate, Consider Evidence Write, Create, Memorize, Record, Make Visit Self-appraise
PLACE Auditorium, little theater, cafeteria, study hall, classrooms joined via television or remodeling, other large room about 40 per cent	**PLACE** Conference room, classroom about 20 per cent	**PLACE** Library, laboratories, workshops, project and materials centers, museums—inside or outside the school plant about 40 per cent

With approval of Dr. J. Lloyd Trump

FIGURE 3

films, and all other devices is involved in the team's techniques of teaching. If students are organized into large groups, it is feasible to equip the auditorium of a high school with a battery of projectors of different types and with extensive audio machinery; such an investment would not be justifiable on basis of cost under a conventional single-class system. Similarly more efficient use of the language laboratory and teaching machines may be possible under the team teaching system than under the conventional. A member of a team, moreover, may well have more time to prepare materials than the ordinary teacher. The efficacy of team teaching, as outlined by some writers, depends largely on the wise use of teaching aids. The use of these instructional materials, however, is not dependent on team teaching.

THE RELATIONSHIP OF TEAM TEACHING TO REFLECTIVE THINKING

From the many reports of team teaching, the general practice is to introduce a topic or a unit by means of a lecture to a large group. The lecture is followed by small-group seminars and by individual study. To many this seems a plan used for years in colleges and universities. Such an organization implies that the authority on the subject lectures and sets forth the principles to be accepted and built on. The leader of the seminar, typically, clarifies the lecturer's remarks and follows up suggestions of illustrations and side issues. Individual study then verifies principles and looks into their application. This is a highly deductive process throughout and allows the student little freedom to identify and delineate problems or to form hypotheses. As in conventional teaching, great opportunity is provided for the presentation of evidence.

In the single discipline approach, the leader will be a specialist in his field and in cross-discipline approaches the members may well be specialists in their particular fields. This may or may not be conducive to the teaching of the thinking skills. The supporters of the core curriculum have been attempting for years to establish a wide approach to the curriculum areas with much interaction between the disciplines. It is quite possible that a teaching team consisting of several members who regard themselves as specialists might teach in very rigid compartmental units. It is disturbing to note that only half as much time is allocated to small-group work as to large-group work in the plan presented. Such a division of time seriously limits student opportunity to discuss problems within the group.

The team teaching approach can be adapted to teaching reflective thinking. We have stated before that such teaching demands that the school provide experiences for the learner from which he can infer generalizations, the time and place for such inferences, the right to reach his own conclusions and then to verify or modify them. If large or small group work is devoted to group identification of problems and formation of hypotheses, and then individual study time limit permits the student to gather evidence and form generalizations after which group techniques are used to verify and modify the conclusions, a measure of inductive learning might take place. It must be remembered that while we strive for some balance of deductive and inductive learning and while deductive learning is desirable in many situations, inductive learning is an essential part of the whole learning process.

Conclusions

The discussion of teaching machines, the language laboratory, and team teaching leads one to conclude that our answers to problems carry further problems with them. The teaching machine can do its job well — it presents pieces of information to the learner in precise order and offers him the chance to respond. His response is corrected if he is wrong. The teacher, including the programer as a teacher, faces many decisions as to how to use the machine for the best learning possible. He also has to determine and pay attention to the limits of the machine. The language laboratory extends the power of the teacher tremendously but he has to study the results of his use of the device to find out its weaknesses and failures.

Team teaching is apparently very significant in the great question of staff utilization in the secondary school. It can make use of space and instructional materials, perhaps better than can the conventional system, yet the dangers of rigidity and specialization may be very real. Every teacher, including the prospective teacher, owes it to himself to study such innovations and to determine their potential good. These three are currently in the limelight; others will come and go with time. The teacher searches unceasingly to explore every avenue which may lead to the effective guidance of the learner.

SUMMARY

This chapter has dealt with three of the important aspects of education which are currently in a growing stage, namely the teaching machine, the language laboratory, and team teaching.

The teaching machine has been developed in this century following the pioneering of Pressey and Skinner. The most important part of the machine is the program which is put into it. The program essentially breaks the material to be mastered into small steps, which are put into logical order. These steps are presented to the learner who advances when he has submitted the right answer to a question or is corrected if he has put forth a wrong answer.

The language laboratory is an extension of the tape recorder which permits a versatile use of microphones, tapes, and receivers. It enables the foreign language teacher to present to the class many spoken messages prepared by experts in the tongue. It also provides a means by which the learner can listen to his own efforts and make necessary modifications.

Team teaching has been used in times past, particularly on the college level. In today's pattern, one master teacher is aided by one or more professional workers and one or more clerical assistants. Typically the master teacher lectures, probably with discussion, to a large group of boys and girls who later meet in small groups led by the other teachers. Some economy of time and effort is realized in such an organization and some supporters feel it is a wiser use of teaching talent.

These three innovations have been discussed with the understanding that such efforts to improve teaching methods have followed one another throughout the history of education. As did seeds spoken of in the Bible, some have fallen on rocky ground and perished but others have taken root in good ground and have proved very beneficial.

SUGGESTED ACTIVITIES

1. Acquire a program for a unit or course in your field of study. Read it carefully, noting the development of concepts by easy steps. If possible, go through it on a teaching machine.
2. From various periodicals (ex., *The Journal of Programed Instruction*) compile a list of programs in your teaching field.
3. Visit a high school in which teaching machines are being used and observe a class working with them. Seek a conference with the teacher and discuss several aspects of teaching through machines.
4. Build a teaching machine of construction paper or masonite. Write a short program on a chapter of this book and teach a fellow student by means of it.
5. Determine what tapes are available for teaching on your campus through the instructional materials department. List those which might help you in your own teaching.
6. Visit a language laboratory in your home high school or one near by. Ask permission to study the console and to listen to a recording in a language you can understand. If you have no foreign language ability, ask to have a tape used as a beginning lesson in a foreign language.
7. If you have some training in a foreign language, bring a tape recorder and a tape for language teaching to class and illustrate how it might be used with high school pupils.
8. Invite a foreign language teacher who uses a language laboratory to class for a discussion of its advantages and disadvantages.

9. Visit a school which has a team teaching in it. Observe their work for several hours. Discuss time and space allocations with one of the teachers. If permissible, ask some of the students for their reactions to the organization.

10. Form a group with several other students which will parallel in preparation and interest a team of teachers. As a team, organize a unit of subject matter as the group would teach it.

11. From the office of student teaching on your campus, determine what opportunity, if any, is available to do student teaching with a team rather than an individual teacher.

12. Acquire from the National Association of Secondary School Principals up-to-date reports of the Commission on the Experimental Study of the Utilization of the Staff. (Some of these are available without charge.)

QUESTIONS FOR SELF EVALUATION

1. Define in a sentence or two what is meant by a teaching machine.

2. Is a "reviewing machine" a better trem for the device than a "teaching machine"? Explain why you answered as you did.

3. How new is the teaching machine? In your opinion, why did the work of Pressey and Skinner lie dormant so long?

4. Where is the nearest school using teaching machines? What type do they have? How many students are using them? Why was the particular type chosen? What are the teachers' reactions?

5. List several reasons why the language laboratory might add to the efficiency of a language teacher.

6. Relate the use of a language laboratory to the principle of learning that a knowledge of progress is beneficial. What other laws of learning may be involved in this teaching technique?

7. If you were teaching in your home town high school, where would be the nearest source of materials for language laboratory tapes? In other words, what would be the most convenient way to procure them?

8. Have you had a college course taught by several faculty members? If you have, contrast the efficiency of this system with that of the individual professor system.

9. List the three types of organization of curriculum for team teaching and indicate what you consider to be the strengths and weaknesses of each.

10. Acquire the plans for a school designed for team teaching through periodicals (ex., *Overview*). If this fails, draw a simple sketch of a high school floor plan with several provisions for team teaching. In either case, explain why the plans follow the pattern indicated.

11. If you were being interviewed for a position and the possibility arose that you would be the younger teacher of a team, what would be your reaction? Why?

BIBLIOGRAPHY

1. CLINCHY, EVANS, *Schools for Team Teaching*. New York: Educational Facilities Laboratories, Inc., 1961.

2. DETERLINE, WILLIAM E., *An Introduction to Programed Instruction.* Englewood Cliffs, New Jersey: Prentice-Hall, 1962.

3. FINE, BENJAMIN, *Teaching Machines.* New York: Sterling, 1962.

4. GALANTER, E., *Automatic Teaching.* New York: Wiley, 1959.

5. LUMSDAINE, ARTHUR A., AND GLASER, ROBERT, *Teaching Machines and Programed Learning.* Washington, D. C.: Department of Audio-Visual Instruction, NEA, 1960.

6. MALLENY, DAVID, *A Study of Experimental Programs in Independent Schools,* Berton, Mass.: Council of Independent Schools, 1961.

7. STACK, E. M., *Language Laboratory and Modern Language Teaching.* New York: Oxford University Press, 1960.

8. STOLUROW, LAWRENCE M., *Teaching by Machine,* Washington, D. C., U. S. Government Printing Office, 1961.

9. TRUMP, J. LLOYD, *Images of the Future,* Washington, D. C.: National Association of Secondary Principals, NEA, 1959.

10. TRUMP, J. LLOYD, *Focus on Change,* Chicago: Rand McNally and Company, 1962.

11. *The Journal of Programed Instruction,* (This periodical is devoted entirely to programed instruction.)

CHAPTER 11

The Evaluation of Learning

OVERVIEW

To evaluate his progress, one must know in which direction he is going and must be able to measure the distance he has traveled. An airplane pilot has his course plotted and instruments tell him how fast he is going. According to his situation, he also can spot landmarks or fix his position by the study of celestial bodies. The teacher's task of evaluating the progress of his charges, and hence his own success, is much more intangible than that of the pilot. The course is not well and carefully plotted for the educator, nor are the landmarks as permanent. No one has yet devised a way to obtain "absolute position" on the progress of one teen-age youngster, to say nothing of a classroom full of them.

On the other hand, the growth of knowledge, skills, attitudes, and interests can be measured to a degree. In this list can be included the skills of thinking. How are examinations, or tests, to measure such growth composed? What do the measurements yielded by them mean? How can they be used more beneficially?

The purpose and nature of evaluation is described in this chapter which includes sections of standardized examinations and teacher-made tests. A consideration of trends in appraising pupils' progress and reporting it completes the discussion.

PURPOSES OF EVALUATION

"How am I doing?" is a most important question. It is in the mind of every learner, and every teacher must find some answer to it. In the high school situation, the parents of the pupil, the administrator of his school, and the colleges which he may attend echo his question: "How is he doing?" The teacher perforce will make some judgment, and it is very important that this judgment be reasonably correct, for a mistake can prove extremely costly to both the student and the teacher.

What Is Evaluated?

In their many efforts to produce defensible reports to pupils, parents, and administrators, teachers essentially are evaluating growth. It is easier to speak of measuring growth than to speak of evaluating it, but the term is not sufficient because measurement is only a part of evaluation. To illustrate: two boys might each advance 30 points on a reading comprehension scale over a period of time. To one boy this might represent only what could logically be expected, while to the other it might mean a real victory over a reading problem. The teacher has first to measure the growth, and then he has to evaluate it.

The Basis of Evaluation

Measurement, and hence evaluation, has to be judged on evidence of growth. To the extent that teaching young people to think is a purpose of the high school, then some of the growth to be measured is that in the thinking skills. Of course, this is only a part of the picture. Since we must expect the student to develop desirable attitudes and skill in social relationships, we expect growth in these areas too. We instruct in areas where particular motor skills are essential, so we also measure the advance of the learner in this respect. The evidence of progress of these latter skills may be relatively simple. In some of the subject matter areas many devices are available to the teacher; in the more intangible aspects of pupil growth, measurement and evaluation are difficult. It is fairly easy to collect evidence to show that a girl has progressed from 30 to 50 words a minute on the typewriter; it is more difficult to determine the extent to which she has gone forward in the appreciation of literature and still harder to indicate her growth as a participating member of her group.

Self-Evaluation

"Know thyself" has come down to us from Socrates. The changes which have occurred in the world in the 25 centuries since his time have not made the precept easier to follow. If a young person is to think for himself, it is apparent that he should consider his own abilities, aspirations, and limitations. It is the duty of his teachers, furthermore, to make him aware of these things. Beyond this, there is much research reported which indicates that a knowledge of one's progress not only permits him to capitalize on his mistakes, but also acts as a true incentive. Most schools and school systems have left the once-a-year examination far behind and not only provide the student with frequent evaluations of his progress, but also afford him a great deal of guidance. As a matter of fact, the improvement of the guidance programs in our schools has done much to help the pupil become aware of his strengths and his weaknesses. The wise use of this knowledge gleaned from tests of intelligence, personality and other facets gives the student opportunities to look clearly and objectively at himself.

Evaluation an Intrinsic Procedure

"You had better study this because I will give you a test soon." Words to this effect are spoken daily by hundreds of teachers in this country. This is an indication that they use the evaluation system as a club with which they drive their pupils to work. Such a device generates extrinsic interest, or interest which lies outside the subject matter itself. The wise teacher uses the evaluative techniques for intrinsic interest. In this case, because he understands what he is doing, knows his purposes and is deeply involved in his progress towards them, the pupil is intrinsically interested in his work. If the learner is to have such interest, he has to feel himself a part of the team studying the problem at all stages from planning to evaluation.

TYPES OF EVALUATION

Behavior Evaluation

As long as high school pupils are kept sitting in rows with little to do but listen to the teacher, read the textbook, and answer a question when called upon, then the closer they can come to doing nothing, the better is their behavior considered to be. The judgment of behavior, as a matter of fact, has followed such a close pattern that a boy or girl is said to be good or bad to the extent he does or does not do what he is told. If the pupil is to be taught to think and act independently, then his behavior must be something more than subservient. The staunch virtues of courtesy, orderliness, honesty and obedience have lost none of their importance, but there are other considerations. A check list for behavior rating might contain items such as these:

1. The student has volunteered frequently to participate in discussions.
2. He has worked well independently both in class and in other situations.
3. He has shown initiative in designing attacks on problems.
4. He has been cooperative in attending committee meetings and has contributed to them,

5. He has assumed leadership when necessary and has been conscientious as a follower.
6. He has been considerate of others — both teachers and fellow pupils.
7. He has submitted written work which has been thoroughly prepared.

Although the evaluation of behavior traditionally has been reflected in a mark purporting to indicate the quality of deportment or "citizenship" exhibited by the pupil, there is no reason why this should continue to be the case. The teacher is quite justified in evaluating the student's behavior as just described in relation to a subject matter area and to report his findings on the report card. Of course the results of such behavior will correlate well with those of more conventional measures of proficiency.

It may seem strange that the considerations of the evaluation of behavior has contained no mention of misbehavior. As cold is the absence of heat and darkness of light, so misbehavior is the lack of desirable behavior. The skillful teacher can guide a class to act in desirable ways and, because their time is thus occupied it cannot be devoted to undesirable activities. An aspect of the art of teaching is the establishing of standards acceptable to both the school and the student.

Skills

A youngster was having trouble with a problem in mathematics. Even the numbers with which he had been helped by the teacher were wrong. "Are you hard of hearing?" asked the teacher, not sarcastically. "No," sighed the boy, "I am just hard of thinking."

Only recently have we as teachers made a direct effort to evaluate the skills of thinking. Yet it is not difficult to measure, to some degree at least, the sklils of thinking which have been identified in this work. In everyday class discussion the teacher can spot pupils who are skilful at discovering and delineating problems, those who can formulate sound hypotheses and go on down to the evaluation of generalizations. The written and oral reports of students can be analyzed for the same skills. It is often desirable to have pupils evaluated more precisely than by such observation and tests become significant. The teacher can formulate his own tests for each step. The section of this chapter concerning teacher-made tests has items on thinking skills as the basis of discussion and a list of commercially available tests of thinking skills follows.

There is little to be gained in asking whether the teacher should make his own tests or use standardized tests. The only good answer is that he should develop skill in devising tests by compiling and using them, and, at the same time, make himself cognizant of the tests available in his field and become adept in their use.

TESTS OF THINKING SKILLS

In the first chapters, the concept of the existence of thinking skills was introduced. These skills, it was stated, are identifiable and measurable. Over the last three decades some very significant work has been done in this field and several tests are available which purport to measure such skills. Some of them are:

Commercial Tests of Thinking Skills

"Critical Thinking in Social Science"
"Science Reasoning and Understanding"
  135 South Locust Street
  Dubuque, Iowa: Wm. C. Brown Co., 1954

"Iowa Tests of Educational Development"
  Subtests:
      "Correctness and Appropriateness of Expression"
      "Ability to Do Quantitative Thinking"
      "Uses of Sources of Information"
        259 East Erie Street,
        Chicago: Science Research Associates, 1956

"Test of Logical Reasoning"
  Beverly Hills, California: P.O. Box 837, Sheridan Supply Company, 1955
"Watson-Glaser Critical Thinking Appraisal"
  Yonkers, N. Y.: World Book Company, 1942-56.
    (Now Harcourt Brace and World, Inc.
    Tarrytown, New York)

In addition to these tests designed quite specifically to test thinking skills, the teacher might be helped by any one of the several study methods tests which are available. Certain tests of reading also include the evaluation of some of the abilities we have considered to be thinking skills.

The Evaluation of Daily Work

If one accepts the principle that the evaluation of the pupil's work should be continuous, the judgment of his work from day to day is called for. This is not to say that a pupil must hand in a written assignment daily or that the teacher must judge one from every pupil every day. It does mean that frequently a pupil is to submit oral or written work, and that he must be informed as to its quality. This latter point is of the utmost importance. It is extremely frustrating to pupils to hand in work which is not seen again for a week or more. Mistakes are not corrected when work is not judged; unsatisfied curiosity dies; and points which could have aroused lively discussion become stale. Many of the laws of learning are broken.

The teacher is unable, on the other hand, to spend every evening of his life reading papers although more than one teacher has broken down under the strain of trying to do so. This makes it important for each to discover or devise ways he can promote the learning of his charges and, at the same time, retain his own mental health. High school students are capable of reading and judging a great deal of their own and others' work. This is especially true in methods making use of group planning and committees. Committee evaluators and chairmen can do much to benefit their own learning and to help the teacher evaluate the efforts of other pupils. The old-fashioned standby of pupils' exchanging and correcting papers is a sound practice if it is used only occasionally and if some checks are made by the teacher. It is quite permissible to record the marks so derived and to use them for general evaluations. The teacher is to avoid, however, basing important judgments on the word of students.

Many reports and other written work assigned by teachers are too long for careful grading. If each theme or other written task taking pages presents an overburden to the teacher, it might be that paragraph-length exercises would be sufficient for the judging of both content and mechanics. Longer assignments may be demanding unwarranted work on the part of both student and teacher. For the beginning teacher, the use of workbooks and other commercially prepared material can be considered. Such devices are acceptable in our schools and serve a good purpose when properly used. A discussion of workbooks is included in the chapter devoted to instructional materials.

The Evaluation of Projects

The judging of projects affords the teacher an ideal basis for measurement and evaluation of the high school student. Initiative, imagination, persistence, and other qualities are called into play by project work. The assigning of marks for projects offers much difficulty however, unless, as in many home economics and industrial arts classes, each member is assigned a similar task. In connection with the science fair sort of project the assigning of a definite mark to be entered on a report card is often best avoided because of several reasons. Some families can afford more money than others for raw materials and some fathers, or other relatives, are more skilful than others. There is no good reason why a father and son should not work together, but such cooperation makes the evaluation of the boy's work difficult. It is best to limit the significance of the evaluation as far as reported marks are concerned. Such limitation does not curtail the value of the project to the learning of the individual or the progress of the class.

SUBJECTIVE AND OBJECTIVE TESTS

Definition. The terms "subjective" and "objective," when applied to examination, reflect the latitude granted the examiner in awarding marks. In general the subjective test calls for an essay kind of response in which the teacher has great latitude in awarding points. This does not mean that items on subjective examinations might not be answered with short sentences or even single words. This fact emphasizes the subjectivity involved, as one teacher might see the germ of the idea sought in a single word and give credit for it while the next teacher might deem the single word worth nothing. Each item on the objective type of examination calls for one very short definite answer. The answer either appears and the examinee receives credit or it does not appear and he does not receive credit. The objective test was designed for its own purposes rather than to replace the subjective type. Many teachers, however, seized upon it as the only kind to use and the subjective test, or at least the essay type, was neglected. One can conclude only that both types are valuable in the teaching process.

TEACHER MADE TESTS

It is strange that the making of tests received so little attention in the early books or pedagogy. It was assumed, apparently, that one simply has to formulate questions from subject matter which has been taught without much attention to the quality of the questions. After the advent of the commercially prepared test, it seemed for awhile that the teacher would not be called upon to make tests. In reality, the teacher can improve his teaching by preparing carefully both subjective and objective examinations.

Subjective Tests

There have been many reports that teachers throw subjective examinations down a stairway and affix marks according to the step on which the individual papers fall. Such reports are, for the most part, highly exaggerated. There was, however, quite a body of research a generation ago which supported the hypothesis that marking of subjective examinations was very unreliable. In experiments, copies of responses to one examination were marked by several teachers. In some cases the results ranged from the highest possible mark down to utter failure. If these experiments were to be repeated, there is little doubt that similar results would be found today. This is inevitable if the test items are not good and if the marker is not skilful. Even one of these factors makes grading unreliable.

Despite the attacks which have been made upon it, the subjective examination can be extremely valuable in the learning process. It affords the pupil review of broader ideas than those often found on the objective tests and a measure of the student's power of self-expression. This latter function includes many of the skills so important to good scholarship — skills of writing, spelling, punctuation, and so on. As a matter of fact, some of the criticism of the high school concerning graduates' lack of ability to write well seizes upon the neglect of the essay as a salient point. Young people, the critics hold, who answer only by filling spaces with single words at best can hardly be expected to write or spell well. Although overdrawn in some cases, these criticisms cannot be dismissed lightly.

The subjective examination item must be so formulated that a significant fact or generalization is involved in the answer. It must be worked so that ambiguity is not possible. It is much easier to say this than to achieve it, and horrible examples of teachers' mistakes can be found. The item must be worded so that the response is kept within limits of value. For example. "What did Lincoln do?" could be answered by so many correct but not significant responses that almost anything would have to be given credit. On the other hand, the item "What did Lincoln do in regard to the slavery question?" would limit the answer somewhat and would be better. Finally, "What opinions of slavery were expressed by Lincoln prior to the outbreak of the Civil War?" would demand a general understanding of the President's outlook and would reward particular knowledge of his speeches or writing.

Examples of Subjective Test Items To Evaluate Thinking Skills. In addition to testing knowledge of subject matter, subjective questions can be asked to evaluate progress at each step of the thought process outlined earlier. Some examples are submitted.

The identification and delineation of a problem:

1. Why does the ordinary automobile use gasoline instead of much cheaper diesel oil (General science or physics).

2. Identify and explain one difficulty presenting itself in a consideration of better traffic control in your town. (Social studies).
3. Why were the earliest Shakespearian play productions often presented at an inn? (English).

The formation of hypotheses:

1. Why have important wars been fought along the Rhine River between France and Germany and none in the Pyrenees between France and Spain? (Social studies).
2. Why have certain characters from Shakespeare's plays become so famous that their names are used to describe types of people? (i. e., Shylock, Portia, etc.) (English).
3. Why is virtually all long distance transmission of electricity done with AC rather than DC? (Physics).

Evaluation of hypotheses:

1. Why was the production of the Edsel car by the Ford Motor Company discontinued so soon after the car was introduced? (Economics, social studies).
2. Was France more or less free under Napoleon than under King Louis XIV? Why? (Social studies).
3. Kerosene freezes only at very low temperatures and, therefore, would make an efficient antifreeze. Is this true? If so, why are more expensive coolants used? (Physics).

Collecting evidence:

1. Name the physical properties of oxygen. (Chemistry).
2. What products are exported from Japan to the United States? (Social studies).
3. What meter was used by Wordsworth in "The Daffodils"? (English).

Evaluation of evidence:

1. Jonathan Swift, author of *Gulliver's Travels*, wrote stories for children only. Is this statement true or false? Defend your answer. (English).
2. Was the slave question the main cause of the Civil War? Support your answer. (Social studies).
3. Ice floats on water. Water contracts as it gets colder. If these interpretations of evidence are true, then ice forms first on the bottoms of lakes. Does it? Why? (General science, physics).

Drawing conclusions:

1. Does a mountain range or a navigable river make a more peaceable boundary between two countries? (Social studies).
2. Should safety belts be compulsory on all new cars? Why? (Driver education).

3. If you were to build a house in this town, what type of heating system would you install? Why? (Industrial arts).

Evaluating conclusions:

1. Some companies marketed electric automobiles just after 1900. Why did these not succeed? (Social studies, science).
2. The metric system of weights is far simpler than ours using pounds and ounces. Would it be wise to change to this system in the United States? (Mathematics).
3. It would be simpler to do business in Canada if all the people were to speak English. Why should they not do so? (English, social studies).

Correcting and Marking Subjective Examinations. Correcting and marking the essay examination often takes time and skill. The beginning teacher often is bewildered by the variety of responses to a particular question and finds it difficult to reward them all favorably. It is wise to enumerate the good and definite points that can be made in response to a subjective question and then search for these points in the answers. Maximum marks can be assigned to the answer covering all the points. Less credit probably should be given for the answer that covered few points, even though they are covered well. The teacher will have to weigh the unforseen replies and mark them accordingly. It seems that, in general, good knowledge and sound thinking deserve credit even though they produce unpredictable replies.

Ambiguity is the great pitfall for teachers composing examination questions. If items are written well ahead of examination time and then studied by the teacher, some of the ambiguities will be discovered. If the teacher has his items proofed by another teacher, or even by a lay person, some errors will be found and corrected. The hurried test, composed at the last minute, is often a poor one.

Oral Tests. In one social studies situation, the teacher prepares envelopes with two questions in each. An envelope is picked at random from a container by each student, who answers the questions enclosed orally. Each question is designed to afford the pupil an opportunity to treat a topic rather fully, that is, a reasonable answer would require two or three minutes instead of only a few seconds. The student is evaluated on the material he has available and his treatment of it. He has to defend what he says before the class and reply to any who wish to challenge him. This device provides the teacher an opportunity to evaluate each student's knowledge and his ability to draw conclusions from it. Of course, it can be said that this plan favors the glib talker; on the other hand, the ordinary written test favors the good writer.

The technique of having boys and girls prepare and present oral reports can work well or can prove deadly. If a report is the product of the student's studying and thinking about the topic, it is likely to be lively and interesting. If it is aimed at delineating a hypothesis, or some other such goal, the individuality of the reporter becomes involved. Such reports are generally quite valuable. Not much good can be said, though, of the class period consisting of oral reports taken bodily from encyclopedias and read just like so much more textbook material. The evaluation of this latter type is difficult since it comprises either a criticism of oral reading or the authority of the source, rather than a measure of the student's ability to study and digest material.

Daily Participation. "He seems to contribute well in class, but falls down when he writes a test." How often is the failure to get good marks explained in this fashion! There is some doubt that an evaluation of a pupil's work which does not take into account his participation in class discussion, his contributions to the development of the group's thinking, is entirely fair. Yet this situation is often found. The reason is essentially the great difficulty of measuring the diffuse and intangible qualities of daily discussion. The teacher is faced with choosing between having a grade book at hand at all times and assigning marks as the class progresses or committing judgments to memory to be recorded later. The first technique is deplorable. Who can think and speak freely if he is to be measured and marked on the spot? The alternative is preferable. Over a period of months the teacher's appraisal of the pupils' contributions will be valid to some extent — perhaps as valid as any other judgment of the students' work.

The brisk oral quiz, to the degree that the questions are well-formulated and searching, provides a good type of review, a good basis of evaluation, and often speeds up the last few minutes of a class period.

STANDARDIZED TESTS

In the 1890's Alfred Binet was commissioned by the schools of Paris to devise means of identifying the duller of the very young children so that they might receive special attention. After many efforts, he concluded that a series of simple short questions were the best answer to his problem. One item demanded that the child count several coins held in the examiner's hand; others were of a similar nature. Binet's work came to America where it started only as the measurement of intelligence, but the principles upon which it was founded were soon the foundation of a whole movement in objective and standardized testing. Binet's test was an individual one in which one examiner worked with one child, but with the advent of World War I group intelligence tests were formulated and after them tests of achievement, personality, and several other areas.

The achievement tests now cover the curricula from kindergarten through graduate school. A listing of the tests in even one area of the high school curriculum would take several pages, and any comprehensive account of all the tests suitable for secondary schools would comprise a volume in itself. Fortunately a listing has been compiled and is kept up to date by periodic revision. This work by Buros[1] constitutes a very valuable source as it presents the title and a short description of each test, an outline of its purpose, and one or more critiques of it written by authoritative persons.

Definition. A test is standardized when it has been administered to a sufficient number of examinees to determine the distribution of its scores in a typical population. The pattern of the scores has to meet several statistical criteria. The average score has to remain constant through many administrations to similar groups and its dispersion must be consistent. Dozens of administrations to thousands of subjects are often required for the standardization of one test.

The Use of Standardized Tests

The commercially prepared standardized test is very widely used in this country. Some form of the intelligence test is administered to almost every child in our public school systems at one or more times during his school days. The results of such testing often are used in screening groups into advanced, normal, and slow classes. The guidance function of any school is based to some extent on these findings. In practice, the result of one intelligence test in regard to one particular child is rarely used by itself. The results of other evaluations are considered, and, if very important decisions rest on the determination of intelligence quotient, an individual examination is administered by a qualified person.

The intelligence quotient is an index obtained by dividing the mental age of a child by the chronological age and multiplying the result by one hundred. Hence an average child has an I.Q. of 100. Because the very dull children do not reach high school, the average I.Q. of our high school population is somewhat more than 100. The range in a large high school may be from below 70 to above 150.

Achievement Tests

Many achievement tests are published. Batteries often are used at both the elementary and secondary level to determine the pupils' stand-

---

[1]O. K. Buros. *The Fifth Mental Measurements Yearbook.* Highland Park, N. J.: The Gryphon Press, 1959.

ings in several areas of the curriculum. The best of these tests are very well designed and yield scores that can be used as a basis of evaluation for class standing as well as for guidance purposes. Several series of such tests are administered high school juniors and seniors on programs that are nationwide.[2] The results of these batteries are made available to colleges and scholarship organizations in an attempt to direct the students in their choice of college, in their search for financial help, and in their selection of courses. A more detailed discussion of this aspect of testing will be found in Chapter 12, which deals with guidance and scholarship opportunities.

RELIABILITY AND VALIDITY

How good is a test? To be any good at all a test has to perform consistently, for example a test in mathematics must always yield results which place the able student toward the top of the group and the less able lower down. The extent to which a test can be depended on to be consistent is termed reliability. A watch is reliable if it ticks off exactly twenty-four hours each day. It is not reliable if it gains a few minutes one day and loses a few the next. So it is with an examination; the reliable examination performs consistently.

To establish a statistical index of reliability of a test it is necessary to measure one part of a test against another or the whole test against itself. Some tests have alternate forms. In these cases the correlation or the results of one form with those of the alternate yields an index to the degree to which both forms are measuring the same characteristics. In some cases the "split-half" technique is used. In this the odd-numbered items are used as one form of the test and even-numbered as the other or the alternate. The correlation of the results then yields an index. In some cases the first administration of a whole test is correlated with a second and the results are correlated. The statistical treatment involved in these techniques is not difficult and can be found in any textbook dealing with elementary statistics in education.

If a sailor were cast on a desert island and found among his salvaged items a watch in good condition, he might set it at what he thought to be noon and could then know exactly how many hours had passed since that time if the watch were reliable. He would never be quite sure, however, if he were correct in his judgment of noon that first day, so he could never be sure that his reliable watch was telling him the correct time. In other words, the validity of the time of day would be in question, and the watch might or might not be valid. So it

---

[2]See Appendix A

is with a test. A test is valid to the degree that it does what it claims to do. If it does not do what it purports to do, it lacks validity. As an illustration, an intelligence test which depends on reading skills may be more valid as a test of reading ability than as a test of intelligence, which it claims to be.

The validity of a test is determined by measuring its results against those of an accepted and established test in the field. Thus in intelligence testing the earlier tests were correlated with Binet's own work. As some of these tests proved helpful and efficient, newer tests were correlated with them. The reader is justified in asking how the first was validated. The only answer is that the validation was done empirically; the results yielded by the earliest test were in accord with the knowledge the authors had from other sources and were substantiated by further experience with the children who were tested.

The statistical treatment of results to determine validity does not pose a great problem for the teacher. It is far more difficult to obtain results from sufficiently large numbers of examinees to make the findings significant. Those tests which are properly standardized demand answers from thousands of respondents. Such numbers are generally beyond the opportunities of the classroom teacher.

TYPES OF OBJECTIVE TESTS

The teacher can use the technique of the standardized tests which are, typically, also objective. Although he may not go through standardizing procedures nor even do much about determining reliability and validity, he can evaluate aspects of his students' learning which are difficult to measure by other means. There are several types of objective tests.

True-And-False Tests

The true-and-false test usually presents the examinee a series of statements which are to be answered true (T) or false (F), for example, "Electricity is generally brought to our homes by wires made of steel." The obvious weakness of such an item is that a pupil can guess the right response half the time. To counteract this, examiners often use the R-W formula which subtracts the number of wrong from the number of right answers on the ground that the examinee guessed as many right as he did wrong. Statistically this is a device to meet a demand, but it is impossible to persuade all the students in a high school class that one should receive only 60 per cent of a possible total of marks when he had 80 per cent of the items answered correctly. Further-

more, if the number of items in a true-false test is insufficient to eliminate the effect of chance responses to a considerable extent, the results
are not reliable and the use of this type of examination is to be questioned. A rule of thumb might demand a hundred items for reliability.

A modification of this type improves it as a testing device and also as
a teaching device. If, instead of responding with only a T or an F, the
student must respond with a T or a corrected answer, then the guessing
element is lessened and, more important, the student is not permitted
to leave a statement incorrect. To return to our illustration, "Electricity
is generally brought to our homes by wires of *steel.*" In this case the
respondent must know not only that steel is incorrect; to gain credit he
must know that "copper" is correct.

If the teacher reviews the test with the class, as should be done,
then eventually the student has the correct answer to each question.
From a learning point of view, this is important.

The Completion Type of Test

Many of the earliest objective tests were of the completion type.
Some of the items included were crude, as the tester sometimes merely
copied sentences from the book and left out a noun or two to be filled
in by the pupil. Such questions depended almost solely on recall and
offered little opportunity to think. As a matter of fact, students were
sometimes advised to answer such items as quickly as possible without
"stopping to think," because carefully considered responses were less
often correct than quick recall responses. Some modification of the completion type was attempted by teachers using devices such as presenting the initial letter of the required word. Such artificial clues to a correct answer are not sound practice. Completion items are valuable where
recall is to be evaluated, and they are often used in teacher-made tests.
Because of scoring difficulty, they rarely are found on commercially
prepared tests.

The Matching Type of Test

The matching type of test demands that the examinee discern a relationship between two ideas. The test does not go into a description of
the relationship, but asks merely that it is indicated as existing. This
type of item might seem to be a test of thinking of higher calibre than
the true or false or the completion types, but this is not always the case.
No word is demanded of the examinee. He has to choose only one relationship from several presented, and there often are clues present
which help him to do this. He does not have to establish or describe
any hypothesis which would lead to a relationship. Because of these

things, the matching item is also used largely to test the ability to recall. In any completion test, if items in list A are to be matched with items in list B, then list B should have more items than list A. A rule of thumb is to have 50 per cent more items in the list from which the matched responses are to be chosen.

For example:

Following is a list of inventors and one of inventions. Place before the name of each inventor the device for which he is known.

Inventors	Inventions
————— Edison	a. the automobile
————— Cartwright	b. the telephone
————— Newcomen	c. the radio
————— Fulton	d. the spinning jenny
————— Bell	e. the power loom
————— Marconi	f. the steamboat
	g. the electric light
	h. the steam engine
	i. the television

Multiple Response Type of Test

The advent of the automatic scoring machine such as that leased by IBM did much to standardize the type of test produced commercially. In this type the examinee identifies one response of several, generally five, as the right one. Five is a compromise number, of course. If only two responses were offered then, as in the true or false type, guessing would be an immense factor. The guessing factor becomes less and less with the increase in number of possible responses, but printing and scoring costs increase correspondingly. Five responses reduces the guessing factor to a reasonable size and keeps the scoring difficulties within logical boundaries. Because of these considerations, five has emerged as the usual number of responses offered.

The teacher will find advantages in designing his own tests to the five-response standard. He can use commercially prepared answer sheets and, in some school systems, have them scored by machine. The statistical considerations dealing with guessing hold for the teacher-made as well as for the commercial tests. It must be remembered, however, that the latter examinations are prepared with professional services and standardized on more cases than the teacher can afford, and the guessing in them is decreased to a degree smaller than the ordinary teacher can achieve.

The preparation of multiple choice test items should include more than simply submitting five answers. The following considerations should be borne in mind: Are the wrong responses simply misplaced words or are they foils to catch the unwary? Should they be so close to the right response that only the most particular student will note the difference? Is the item to test memory by using words suitable for recall only, or will the foils (the incorrect answers) be logically incorrect so that a test of thinking is involved? If such is the case, is the item valid, that is, is it testing a knowledge of chemistry, for example, or one of thinking? Either function of the item may be defensible, but the teacher must know just which he is utilizing.

Some examiners use only three or four responses in some questions and combinations of these as the other responses. As illustration:

The telescope was discovered and used

a. in the seventeenth century
b. by Galileo
c. by Copernicus
d. ab
e. abc

In this item a, b, or c is correct, but more information can be conveyed by using d (ab) if both a and b are correct and even more by using e (abc) if all the first three are correct. Of course, such items must be preceded by directions indicating that the best possible answer is the only one for which credit can be awarded. Another modification includes three responses followed by (d), all of these and (e), none of these. For example:

Explorers to the New World were

a. Columbus
b. Cartier
c. Hudson
d. all of these
e. none of these

The generalized answers attract many responses and if the teacher often identifies them as correct, the pupils will choose them as a matter of course rather than after adequate thought.

Other Types

Beyond the types of items dealt with, there are several others which can be found on a very small scale. The teacher has every right to experiment with these. Often an unusual type of test will suit a particular evaluation demand and will prove very valuable. The possibilities of machine scoring tests should certainly be explored by every teacher not familiar with the technique. With increased automation in teaching, there is little doubt that such scoring will become more common. One must also keep his mind open to more advanced testing procedures on the part of nationwide examining groups. With all of this, it must not be forgotten that a test should be a teaching device, and opportunity should be found, or made, for a review over every examination administered. No pupil should be left with incorrect conclusions in his thinking. For the sake of scholarship alone, if not for more intrinsic reasons, the essay type of examination is not to be neglected. As a good craftsman can use many tools to advantage in his work, so the good teacher can use skilfully many testing techniques.

REPORT CARDS

A wise man has said that you do not increase a child's growth by measuring him. In spite of this, schools have been sending home report cards with marks on them for many generations.

Absolute Marks

From earliest times in our educational history until very recently, the marks on these report cards were absolute. The report indicated a mark of 95, or 82, or 68, or some other such number. The number did not always indicate the percentage of answers correct, although sometimes it claimed to. The passing marks in some systems was 50, in some it was 75 and other systems had other passing marks. Each was also a failing point because, if one did not reach it, he failed the examination and often the course. As with so many measuring devices in education, the passing or failing point was arbitrary and, away from its own system, was probably meaningless. The school with its passing point at 75 was not necessarily tougher, nor yet easier, than that with the indication 50. Examinations were almost always subjective and the marking depended on the system rather than on what was written by the examinee.

The absolute mark is not currently popular in this country, but it is not unknown. Some schools, particularly private ones, still use it. In foreign countries, it continues to be the acceptable procedure.

The Letter Mark

The letter mark (e. g., ABCDE) was designed to avoid the pretense of marking pupils' work more closely than was possible. If 50 is a passing mark and 49 is a failing one, the teacher has claimed, if he has awarded a student a mark of 49, that he has been able to measure the student's achievement to the nearest one per cent and that he has failed him on this narrow margin. Experimentation showed that the marking was not reliable enough to permit teachers to claim such accuracy. By dividing the total number of a class into five discrete groups rather than into many more, often 100, it was felt that the grouping would be more accurately done and hence reporting would be fairer to the student.

The five-step marking system was a generalization of systems having the number of steps ranging from two up to seven and even more in some schools. Where only two steps are used they are often "satisfactory" and "unsatisfactory" and this procedure is sometimes found in the elementary schools. There are also three step systems. In these cases the steps are often as above the "improvement" as a middle step. The five-step systems do not always use ABCDE. Many use F as the fifth mark, as it emphasizes failure. One large school organization uses Excellent, Very Good, Good, Poor, and Failure with the initial letters recorded on the card. Teachers are advised to make the F backward so that the pupil could not easily transform it into an E! The five-step system is common in the American high school today. The ABCDE (or F) range has been somewhat violated by the addition of + and − so that in reality a fifteen-step device is being used. A boy was once heard to exclaim, after receiving his report card, "How on earth does she figure that I am worth an E+?" Many schools drop the suffixes for recording purposes.

Marks and Class Standing

The absolute mark was sometimes determined by the competition involved, but it did not have to be and often was not. If the whole class scored above 90, the teacher would accept the results as they were. He concluded, perhaps, that he had a good class or that he was an excellent teacher. In the letter system, however, the supposition is that the class will spread itself out to some degree so that the teacher can discover gradations which justify giving one pupil a high mark and another a low one. In this procedure it is assumed that the class is heterogeneous in ability, that the differences follow the laws of chance to a degree, and that the marks should be distributed so that a definite percentage will fall into each of the five categories. Of course, classes differ greatly in heterogeneity — some do spread out, but some clump together — and the ordinary class of about thirty members is not large enough for laws of chance to work. All marking systems assume, by definition, that the teacher can evaluate the pupils' ability well. Practically, this is not the case.

Of recent years colleges have made much of the class rank of graduating high school seniors. It is reasoned that class rank consideration avoids some of the pitfalls of accepting the marks of many teachers from many school systems. It must be remembered that the competition involved is within each local school. It is obvious that in some schools this is strenuous and in others it is not. By and large, however, class rank, especially in a large graduating class, is indicative of the success of the student in high school, and this is the best predictive factor yet discovered for success in college.

Individual Progress versus Group Competition

Of the many ideas stemming from the child study movement, that of reporting a pupil's achievement in light of his own growth rather than according to group standards has had its share of support from educators. When a class is marked on this basis, the grade indicates how well the student is doing as compared to what he has done and what the teacher feels he can do. The teacher's "feeling" should be based on some objective criteria such as standardized tests. It has been argued that this is the only fair and logical way to measure a child. Competition, though important in our society, is a forced business in school with little choice afforded the pupil. It is true that he will meet competition in his vocational life when he grows up, but it must be pointed out that college graduates in medicine compete with others of similar ability and by choice. Plumbers compete for business with other plumbers, and only a college professor can replace a college professor. Yet in school all pupils are placed together and some face overwhelming odds. When this system forces a young person into an academic situation and then brands him a failure, it has done something it was not designed to do. The very branding of a boy or girl is counter to the aims of education and defeats its purpose. The school is at conflict with itself when it demands that all children attend, but cannot take into consideration all their ranges of ability.

For the most part, the secondary school has not subscribed to the idea of reporting marks based on individual progress, but has clung to marking by standards set by the group or by absolute standards set by the teacher or some agent of the school system. In the past few years, reactionary sentiment has made the foregoing statement truer than it has been at times in the past. Once again, competition becomes the basis of argument. Colleges and employers, it is held, expect to be able to judge marks by accepted standards. If a boy has A marks in mathematics and sends the college registrar his transcript, the college personnel feel free to place him in courses of mathematics. If the A's mean

that a dull student had been making steady but laboriously slow progress, then the college has little on which to build. In a parallel case,
if a local firm employs a girl with A's in typing, they expect an employee
with the ability to type with speed and accuracy. If the A's mean that
a poorly-coordinated girl advanced a few words per minute each year
with mighty effort, the employer feels that he must distrust marks. He
is more confused if he is told that the C pupil may possibly be a better
typist than the A pupil.

Current practice favors reporting a pupil's progress according to
his own growth and ability in the elementary school and by group
standards in the secondary school. This discrepancy of outlook often
offers problems of articulation in the seventh, eighth, and ninth grades,
and no simple solution is yet in sight. Since the procedure to be used
is often a matter of school policy, the beginning teacher is to be aware
to the advantages and disadvantages of each.

Parents and Report Cards

"Your son could do better if he studied more." This statement is made
by hundreds of teachers at thousands of PTA meetings and teacher-par-
ent conferences. It is a device used to soften a blow and often to turn
away wrath. Is it a wise thing to say? Obviously it is often true, as most
of us would do better if we were to work harder. There is no record
of parents who reply, "Yes, and you could teach him better if you
worked more at it." It is certain some think it even if they are too
polite to voice the words. Nor do parents often say, "He is in your hands
and it is your duty to inspire him." But they might so answer with a
great deal of reason. Perhaps we should seek other ways of dealing with
unpleasant truth.

It is certain that parents should be warned of impending failure
while time remains to recover lost ground if this is possible. Parents
can be invited to the school for conferences dealing with their children's
poor marks. A deeper and more realistic treatment of the problem lies
in the proper guidance of students into areas and courses in which there
is little discrepancy between the demands of the school and the abilities
of the pupil. This matter is discussed at greater length in Chapter 12,
which deals with guidance.

Public Relations. "Well, you know, with that report card, I haven't
been cheating." Thus runs a caption under a cartoon in which a teen-age
boy has just shown his father his report card. This cartoon is one of
hundreds devoted to the topic. As with most nonsense, there is a truth
behind this joke. Fathers and mothers are intensely interested in the
growth and advancement of their offspring, and the worth of the school

is often judged by the report card. If reports are poor, the conclusion is that the teachers are not efficient. If marks are high, the school is "soft" and is making it difficult for the pupil to do college work in the future. Recently a chemistry teacher in a small town was adversely criticized because a boy, having gone from the local high school to college, had failed in chemistry. The teacher's defense, that the student had avoided the subject in high school and had never enrolled in the course, was not listened to by those wishing to attack the school.

Many school systems have devoted long hours to the question of the type of report card to be sent home. Their answers range from pupils' getting a separate card from each teacher, and thus presenting six or eight cards to the parents, to none at all. In the latter cases, a letter is written by the teacher about each child and mailed to the parent. There is little evidence to show that any one type will lessen parental disturbance. One fact has become clear: the report card must be simple and conventional unless the community has been prepared for radical change.

THE RELATIONSHIP OF EVALUATION TO REFLECTIVE THINKING

The techniques of evaluation very often yield measurements of knowledge of facts. In regard to the reflective thinking process, this means the judgment of the amount of evidence collected and remembered. The objective type of test has been severely criticized on this point, as too often it merely checks the knowledge of single facts which may or may not be contributing to the thought process of the learner. The essay type of question is credited with demanding more thought of the student. Neither of these generalizations has to be accepted. Objective examinations can be devised to test specific skills in thinking. On the other hand, essay questions can result in answers which are nothing more than the parroting of the authority of the teacher or the textbook.

When teaching is done toward reflective thinking, the process should produce answers on conventional examinations as good as those resulting from the teaching for which the test has been designed. As a matter of fact, because the learner who is taught to think reflectively has his knowledge organized into large patterns and can proceed deductively from generalizations to specific points, he can be expected to do work of a higher quality than he otherwise would.

SUMMARY

The evaluation of the student's ability and the appraisal of his work is one of the teacher's most exacting tasks. Much attention has been paid to measurement of this type since the turn of the century. Many tests of intelligence and knowledge are available from commercial firms. These tests serve very important purposes but the teacher still must prepare at least some of the examinations he uses. These may be of the subjective or objective type.

Reporting the student's progress to parents through report cards is traditional and there seems no move to abolish the practice. Just how the report is to be marked is debatable but in gnereal the high school uses a five step system (ABCDE or F). In recent years nation-wide testing services are used for college placement and the awarding of scholarships.

These are tests designed to measure the thinking skills but the student who has developed these skills may be expected to do well on conventional examinations when he has prepared well for them.

SUGGESTED ACTIVITIES

1. List the thinking skills as identified earlier in the book and devise a question or two for the evaluation of each from your own teaching field.
2. Devise a check list for the evaluation of projects submitted to a science fair. Indicate the qualities you would look for and the weight to be assigned to each.
3. From a unit in your field designed for Chapter 4, compile an evaluation device for one or more major generalizations. Use at least two types of questions.
4. From Buros, or another source, compile a list of standardized tests in your field and analyze at least one of them.
5. From the foregoing list rate the tests as to reliability and validity, using as your basis the reports in Buros.
6. Identify several types of report cards. Have mimeographed samples of each made available and determine the advantages and disadvantages of each.
7. In a role playing situation, have an irate parent, angered by a report card, face the principal and the teacher involved.
8. Write a letter to a hypothetical parent saying that his child is failing in two subjects. Have several of these letters read in class and discussed.
9. Analyze one of the several tests of thinking and identify the several skills it attempts to evaluate.

QUESTIONS FOR SELF EVALUATION

1. Define both measurement and evaluation and show how one is not synonymous with the other.
2. To what extent does knowledge of progress facilitate learning, if it does? Indicate a situation in which there is no knowledge of progress and identify the outcome.
3. Can you see a relationship between types of evaluation used in high schools and disciplinary problems in these schools? If so, describe it.

4. How much of a student's credit in a course can be properly based on his daily work as compared to that given for tests and examinations?
5. A boy has assembled a radio kit and enters it as a project for a science fair. In what ways can this be considered as deserving credit in a general science class? In an industrial arts class?
6. In your own experience, was the subjective or objective type of examination more popular among the students? Why?
7. In the essay type of examination, is the teacher of a social studies class or a science class justified in awarding or withholding credit because of the mechanics of English involved? Defend your answer.
8. On what points can one judge an oral report? Should ability in speaking before the class enter into the judgments made on the report?
9. What are two or three of the better known standardized tests in your field? Describe at least one of them in some detail.
10. What type of item on objectve tests do you think is most discriminating? What are the disadvantages of this type?
11. What attack can you make on the letter-mark (ABCDE) system? What defense can you make for it?
12. What type of report card was issued at the high school you attended? Was this efficient? If you could replace it, what would you use? Why?

BIBLIOGRAPHY

1. BURTON, WILLIAM H., *The Guidance of Learning Activities*, New York: Appleton-Century-Crofts Inc., 1952.
2. BARON, DENIS, AND BERNARD, HAROLD W., *Evaluation Techniques for Classroom Teachers*, New York: McGraw-Hill Textbook Company Inc.,
3. DOWNIE, N. M., *Fundamentals of Measurement*, New York: Oxford University Press, 1958.
4. GREENE, HARRY A., JORGENSEN, ALBERT N., AND GERBERICH, J. RAYMOND, *Measurement and Evaluation in the Secondary School*, New York: Longmans, Green and Company, 1954.
5. KLAUSMEIER, HERBERT J., *Teaching in the Secondary School*, New York: Harper and Brothers, 1958, Chapter 9.
6. LINDQUIST, E. F., *Educational Measurement*, Washington, D. C.: American Council on Education, 1951.
7. ROSS, C. C., AND STANLEY, JULIAN C., *Measurement in Today's Schools*. Englewood Cliffs, N. J.: Prentice Hall Incorporated, 1954.
8. ROTHNEY, JOHN M. W., DANIELSON PAUL J., AND HEIMANN, ROBERT A., *Measurement for Guidance*, New York: Harper and Brothers, 1959.
9. WATKINS, RALPH K., *Techniques of Secondary School Teaching*. New York: Ronald Press, 1958, Chapter 6.
10. WIGGINS, SAM P., *Successful High School Teaching*. Boston: Houghton Mifflin Company, 1958, Chapter 13.

CHAPTER 12

The Guidance of Adolescents In the Classroom

OVERVIEW

A classic tribute to a teacher has been quoted many times. It was the dedication of a book to a teacher who "taught me Latin and more than Latin." We are concerned with the "more than Latin" aspect of the teacher's work in this chapter.

A teacher has obligations to two contracts. One is a legal document which specifies the duties to be met and the salary to be paid. In regard to this contract, every teacher has the right to look out for himself and to seek the highest return posssible for his services. The other contract has no document because it cannot be written; in many ways it is more binding than the first. The child invests in the teacher a very precious part of his formative years and the teacher must return the very best value to him for this investment. In meeting the second contract, the teacher tries to impart to the child a sense of values. This is not done through sermons, of course, but through the great lessons of mathematics, history, and other studies. In all such work, the teacher guides the student in making extremely important decisions. This guidance is sometimes direct but more often it is indirect and does not come under the formal guidance program. Great decisions are made in the classroom, in the shop, in the laboratory, and on the gymnasium floor.

Some of this significant work with boys and girls deals with intangibles but some can be reduced to very practical considerations. In this chapter we deal with some of the tangibles and also will reach out for some of the intangibles.

MENTAL HEALTH IN THE LEARNING PROCESS

"He was my teacher!" This simple sentence is often spoken with affection and pride, to express a relationship that is easily recognized but difficult to convey. The student has sensed an awareness, on the part of the teacher, to his own personality. Traditionally, it is part of the picture of the great teacher that he can remember the names and characteristics of boys and girls whom he taught years ago. We may not all be Mr. Chips but there is a principle involved that is important. The effective teacher recognizes each student as a person in his own right and affords the young person every opportunity to express himself as an individual. On the other side of the coin, he avoids imposing on the student any experience which will tend to lessen or destroy the dignity of the person. Demeaning punishment, sarcasm, and ridicule are some practices which destroy personality.

Motivation

Many a teacher has been heard to say, "I can't motivate my students." Of course he is right because one cannot motivate another; one motivates himself. Motivation is a catalyst that brings into play the energies of an individual so that he can acquire a desired result. The learner must feel the urge within himself, he must desire the learning, before his learning is properly achieved. In practice, this means that the student must not only understand the aims of his efforts, he must also have accepted them as worthy of his endeavor. If the aims are clear only in the mind of the teacher or some other authority, or if they are imposed arbitrarily on the learner, the motivation is lacking. This is too often the situation in the high school, so extrinsic agents such as detention, threats of failure, and deprivation of privileges are called into play.

Motivation Through Pressure From Peers. Motivation through pressure from peers is ever present in our high schools, is exploited extensively by teachers, and is easily recognized. Research workers concluded a generation ago that personal rivalry is a strong incentive and that group rivalry, putting one class against another or one section of a group against another, is almost as strong. One must bear in mind, however, that there are undesirable effects from competition. Accuracy is quite likely to suffer. More important, overstimulation of young people is entirely possible and the disappointment experienced by the losers can do much harm. Nothing much has been said about the effect of conceit on the winners, but it is an area in which some questions could be asked.

For some time the pressure of competition was lessened on the high school students as far as marks were concerned. In the last five years, the reverse has been true. Because of intensification of rivalry for world power involving our country, emphasis has been put on scholastic achievement. In science, mathematics and foreign language this has

Carl Purcell, NEA

The Teacher Guides the Student Through the Learning Process

been particularly true. There are several reasons why there has been pressure on boys and girls to master science and mathematics. The great amount being written about the college entrance situation has added its weight to the pressure. Nationwide systems of examination for scholarships also is contributing. All these work together to produce a situation in which the status in the group is gained through scholastic achievement. Although many teachers have thought of this as something to be wished for but unattainable, they now have to pause for an evaluation of the situation. One school is illustrative. The emblem of this school is the eagle and traditionally the boys who played on athletic teams were awarded gold E's. The administration had a different type of letter designed for those who attained scholastic excellence. In addition a comfortable lounge was provided in which the students with a B average or better could spend their study hall periods. When asked how all this worked out, the principal said ruefully, "Now to the athletic snobs, we have added the bright snobs."

It must be remembered that competition in the public school is a forced situation. The students have to compete with others in spite of disparity of talent. This is true of athletic competition as well as scholastic. While we cannot decry efforts of boys and girls to learn, we must see the mark (ABCDE) as an extrinsic factor of motivation and keep it secondary to the intrinsic factors.

Cooperation with peers is a factor in motivation although it has been used less by teachers than competition. One might point cynically that cooperation is often involved in cheating but this is not what we are looking for. In a teacher-pupil planned unit there is unlimited opportunity for boys and girls to work together in learning experiences in which they stimulate, test, and solidify each other's ideas. Unfortunately, with the stubborn holding to the marking system the schools have neglected this avenue toward learning in the secondary school.

Motivation Through Pressure From Teachers. In the typical high school, almost every response of the teacher to the student is either reward or punishment. If he says about a task, "That is good," the pupil is rewarded. If he knows that the response is to be interpreted in a grade book, the reward is tangible. If the teacher says, "No you are wrong," then the student is punished. Proceeding to things on a larger scale, the examination results are rewards if they are as high as the student expects them to be or punishment if they are not. Since many young people exhibit a high discrepancy between their aspirations and their ability, examination results are punishment more often than they are reward. In many schools punishment is the rule under which the students exist. This does not say that the youngsters are beaten unmercifully; it means rather that the scolding is heard much more often than praise, that low marks are held as a threat, and various deprivations are used in admonition. In this pattern, the teacher is a figure to be feared rather than trusted, and avoided rather than sought out. The respect accorded such a teacher often is one based on fear rather than admiration or affection. In a cooperative situation in which teacher and student feel united in the search for knowledge, the respect of the student for the teacher is more often based on admiration and trust.

The Gifted Student

Only a decade ago one could point to the gifted boy or girls as the misfit in our high school. Present emphasis in curriculum and method have changed the situation radically. A teacher often struggled against odds to find time to recognize the gifted, to give him some challenge, and to find help for him to further his education if his parents could not afford college fees. Now the guidance of the gifted may include protecting him from exploitations. The gifted student in science or mathematics may be urged to specialize highly in these fields on the high school level at the expense of studies which would benefit him greatly as a human being. These very bright youngsters are taken from high school classes, in some instances, and permitted to go each day to a nearby university for college courses. Many are being accelerated through summer schools so they can get to college a year earlier and some are even being snatched from the school by the university at the end of the eleventh year! One must ask the reason for pushing young people through school and college at an accelerated pace. They do not learn better at younger ages. If a boy can do calculus at the age of seventeen, he will be able to do the same work at the age of eighteen or nineteen. The nation probably will not perish waiting for his contribution. For the sake of the boy, rather than accelerating his progress it might be much better to allow him to mature at a steady pace and spend some of his time in general education areas preparing for the long and complicated adulthood waiting for him.

The teacher has many responsibilities to the gifted. He has the obligation to find the gifted among the many boys and girls who come to him. He must detect the spark of interest in its early stage and feed it with interesting and challenging learning material. He must afford the younger person a vista of the possibilities within the reach of his talents. He will want to assure the student that he can take advantage of the opportunities available in his field of effort. This may well mean telling him of colleges and universities and the scholarships they offer.

The Slow Student

There is the story of the man who, being too light for heavy work and too heavy for light work, never got any work. The slow student is often in this man's predicament. Too bright to be classed as a special problem who could be assigned to a class designed for those who do not learn easily and too slow to keep up with the group in an ordinary class, he sits in the back row of the typical high school class and does little if anything at all. In some situations he is permitted to sleep. If there is sin in teaching, it lies in the treatment of such boys and girls.

What can the teacher do? The ordinary high school offering often is beyond the ability of the slow learner. Assigning him to industrial arts courses, unless he has ability, is no good answer. Forming homogeneous classes and teaching groups of low ability together at a suitable level is practicable only in very large systems where such practice affords economically-large groups homogeneous enough to function. In the common-assignment and common-recitation method of teaching, there is no place into which the very slow learner can fit. In the unit approach in which teachers and students cooperate in planning experiences, assignments are flexible — if they can be called assignments — and the slow pupil can take upon himself certain tasks which contribute to the group as a whole, which include him as a member of the group, and yet are within his capabilities. It is inevitable that the slow learner's inferences and conclusions will not measure up to those of the more able. It must be added, however, that not all the boys and girls with low achievement are slow learners. Often a friendly and cooperative approach with freedom of individual choice will challenge the able student with low achievement to great effort and very happy results.

The teacher may be able to do little with the truly slow learner in the ordinary classroom as far as intellectual growth is concerned. This does not say that the older person is not able to help the younger. He can adapt work to the student's abilities so that some progress is made with each effort; he can encourage the youngster to accept roles of leadership — or followership — if this seems wise. In short, he can maintain a respect for the individual in the pupil's own thinking and instill it into his classmates. By carefully guarding such principles in the treatment of the slow learner, the high school teacher can aid the growth of a calm, well-adjusted citizen with a respectable concept of his own worth rather than the development of a disturbed delinquent.

The Aggressive Child

One day the writer visited a school and observed a class in instrumental music. The band had verve and precision worthy of professionals. He asked the teacher how this was achieved. "I have a system," the teacher replied. "I visit the elementary schools which send their pupils to me in the seventh grade. I ask the teachers to identify the meanest and most aggressive boys and girls they have. When these kids come to junior high I get them as band students and give them trumpets and trombones. They don't all continue, of course, but from them I get enough to put real spirit in my band." If the musicians do not support this practice, there is little doubt that the mental hygienists do. The aggression within a child is of necessity a pent-up pressure that vents itself in some way or another. Often the way is undesirable. Much of the routine of the classroom and the repetitive and sometimes meaningless teaching done increases the frustration of these young people who come to school already frustrated for reasons of their own.

The function of method in the school is to alleviate rather than to increase the trouble.

The band teacher had one answer which was successful in his particular case. Other teachers have developed other successful methods. They have understood that aggression is an aspect of the teen-agers' struggle for independence which builds up to harmful proportions when young people are thwarted too much in responding to their own drives. Very often parents and police officers are the thwarting agencies in the youngsters' minds. If the school is added to these agencies, then it is quite likely that it will contribute to frustration. On the other hand, if the school can offer the disturbed person an opportunity to express himself and win approval too, the student will feel less hostility toward the school and his frustration will be abated.

What has been said means that freedom for learning within the school is of especial significance in the case of the disturbed boy or girl. This freedom has been discussed in Chapter 4 and from that discussion we can draw several factors in the methods of teaching which help to alleviate aggression. The identification of the student's needs, the opportunity for him to work with his fellows, and his association of himself with problems to be investigated are extremely important considerations. Above all, however, is the acceptance of the teacher as a leader and a guide rather than an authoritative ruler. In many cases, the aggressive child has accepted the teacher without hostility and this has provided a bridge over which the youngster has crossed to a responsible role in society.

The Quiet Child

Because silence and conformity have so long been characteristic of the "good" boy and girl in school, the youngster whose trouble is evidenced by such behavior is very often neglected. Sometimes this type of pupil achieves well enough to rank high in class and no one suspects any trouble. Sometimes he ranks low but little is done because there is no nuisance involved and the teacher, often too busy for individual remedial work, simply does not look below the surface. Yet the anxious person, the victim of feelings of inferiority, often is known only as the quiet one who is not a troublemaker. Of course there are many quiet children who are quite happy and well adjusted but the teacher must realize that some such apparently healthy youngsters are deeply disturbed and need help.

The identification of the quiet and troubled student is not always easy. Discrepancy between ability and achievement is sometimes a clue. The brilliant student with a mediocre achievement record need be studied. On the other hand, the child of mediocre ability who ranks high in his class because of a self-enforced overachievement is fearful of something and needs understandnig and consideration. In each case it is important for the sake of the individual and the welfare of society that the fear involved be uncovered and, if possible, dissolved. This is hardly possible in a highly authoritative school situation but in a free and integrative situation skilfully managed fears can be lessened and strength built up.

HELPING THE STUDENT TO STUDY

The Russell Sage Foundation[1] has conducted a study to determine what outcomes indicated by changes in pupils' behavior should result from general education in the high school. Four pages of the work are devoted to the improvement of the students' study habits, study skills, and other work habits. Many of the behavioral goals have been identified in this work. It is believed that the method of teaching illustrated by various examples which put an emphasis on unit organization and teacher-pupil planning results in more desirable behavioral outcomes than much of the conventional teaching.

A great service is done by those who have listed objectively the aforementioned goals, but one must ask how he can help a youngster to be skilful in securing information, organizing, evaluating and reporting results of study and research. The answer can be only in recommendations: instruct the learner in the essential techniques, which are relatively simple, and then afford him practice in meaningful use of these tools. Success in study involves knowledge of progress and its constant evaluation. It also demands learner motivation which comes from identification with the problem. Of course the teacher himself must be skilful enough in the use of techniques to afford the learner a good pattern.

How does one guide a pupil so that he becomes, or remains, intellectually curious and industrious? One can do this only by allowing the learner the initiative in seeking problems and the honest opportunity of pursuing a solution through his own capabilities. This is a far cry from imposing on him the dictates and conclusions of authority. To achieve this end, one must conduct a classroom in which the students feel free enough from demands of the teacher to follow their own inferences, conclusions, or even hunches.

---

[1]Will French, *Behavioral Goals in General Education in High School*, New York: Russell Sage Foundation, 1957.

We have emphasized independence of thought throughout. One can learn independently only if he practices doing so. In the classroom, this means placing faith in the learner after he has mastered techniques of independent study, and permitting him to work by himself for some proportion of the time. Some proponents of the team teaching technique place this at 40 per cent of the total school time.[2] This is certainly much more time than the typical high school pupil spends in individual study, but the well-motivated student can use this time efficiently.

HELPING STUDENTS TO SELECT PATHS TO VOCATIONS

A child of thirteen can seldom form a definite picture of his vocation. If he has an idea of what he wants to be, it is only tentative and very often not even realistic. The graduate of eighteen years of age often has not only decided on his vocation, but has taken steps toward it. Thus in the secondary school years, vocational choice is very important. In this area the classroom teacher has some obligation even though a guidance service is maintained by the school.

Exploration

The junior high school years are exploratory as are, to some extent, the senior high years. To serve this function, the teacher has every right to spend time on various vocational areas as they touch on the subject matter he is teaching. It is obvious that the industrial arts teacher will have many opportunities to disseminate vocational information and even to go into some detail on certain callings closely related to his work. As an illustration, in a unit on wiring a house for electricity, he can justifiably conduct a discussion on the opportunities for boys wishing to be electricians. The teachers of vocational agriculture and vocational home economics, of course, may expect a significant percentage of their students to go into their respective fields. The teacher of general home economics, on the other hand, dircts much of her work to preparing girls for home-making and they are engaged in general rather than vocational education.

The English teacher, the social studies teacher, and all other teachers have similar great opportunities. Very often the textbook assignment method of teaching falls down in this respect. Textbooks are often written to appeal to readers in every corner of the country, and are too general to deal with local vocational needs. The unit method, which is more at liberty to go beyond subject matter limits and to involve

---

[2]J. Lloyd Trump, *Images of the Future*, Washington, D. C., National Association of Secondary School Principals, NEA, 1959, p. 10.

local phenomena, can sometimes introduce many vocational choices to the students. The illustrative unit of Chapter 5 might involve contractors, realtors, lumber merchants, masonry experts, plumbers, electricians, and any of another half dozen occupations. It can be noted that their lines of of work ordinarily do not demand college preparation. It is of the utmost importance to our young people, half of whom do not go to college, to know that there are many vocational choices open to them and to understand that the people in various businesses and trades are proud of their skills, enjoy their work, and are extremely valuable citizens. It may well be that some schools and some teachers are going too far in encouraging boys and girls to attend college because of vocational goals.

The work of the teacher is important in the vocational choices of those boys and girls who do go to college. Although many college students do not know what choice to make and many change directions in their college years, it is an advantage if the entering freshman knows where he wants to go and what courses he needs to get there. Because of this, discussions in the high school of vocational choices and the dissemination of information are highly important. In our unit, sanitation might well be introduced. This might involve a visit to a state health department laboratory or a talk by a member of the department of health. This might lead to students' obtaining information about the numerous jobs and positions in the general field of medicine. In addition to the great need for medical doctors is that for hundreds of workers in the less publicized occupational areas of the world of medicine.

One could draw a similar parallel for educators and musicians in our churches, for secretaries and researchers in the legal field, and for laboratory technicians to assist our scientists. Whereas relatively few of our boys and girls can do seven or eight years of college work because of intellectual or financial obstacles, there are many who could manage a four year degree and have happy careers in these lesser positions.

"He worked well for me. I was able to reach him and perhaps I even inspired him." Almost every teacher of several years' experience can say this of at least one boy or girl. It is one of the true joys of teaching to discover ability which others have missed. It is not enough, however, to discover. One must have his treasure assayed, as it were. Today there are several testing programs operating on a national basis which not only determine, to a degree, how promising each student may be, but also provide for him a good deal of help in choosing a college to attend. In cases of need these scholarship examination agencies often make financial assistance possible. Detailed descriptions of the agencies are found in Appendix A.

HELPING THE STUDENT TO ACHIEVE A SENSE OF VALUE

We have discussed the needs of young people in our society in Chapter 3. It was pointed out that although most of our people have high ideals and live by them, there are members who exploit youth by presenting to them very warped and undesirable ideas. Many of our young people are strong enough to withstand the impact of the unsavory film, the pornographic magazine, or the spectacular newspaper. Others, however, are more impressionable or have a less secure foundation for their lives.

The basis for security is found in one's faith, which is a matter of religious convictions. Within this body lies faith in one's own abilities. It is here the public school teacher finds his opportunity to help the young people in his care. The characteristics which he may hope to develop are initiative, self-reliance, persistence, and intellectual honesty.

The method of teaching is very instrumental in the growth of these virtues. Unfortunately the sterile classroom isolated from the problems of the world and in which authority is accepted without question does little to advance this growth. This does not mean that the boys and girls do not grow at all because other agencies such as the home and the church are contributing all the time. It does mean that the young people are denied some opportunity to develop, especially in the areas where the school could be most effective.

If the methods of teaching afford the student the chance to attack problems which he identifies as problems and to which he devotes some thought and effort and also the chance to reach his own conclusions, then we can expect growth in the characteristics being considered. In other words, the teacher must give the learner the right to participate in the learning process so that he has practice in being persistent, intellectually honest and so on.

Beyond this consideration, we have the everyday person-to-person relationships of the classroom which contribute much to the personal development of young people. The closer the teacher gets to the boy or girl, the more effective these relationships become. The cooperation and mutual respect of the unit method of teaching are effective in the furthering of these objectives.

MORALE IN THE CLASSROOM

The morale of a classroom is an easy thing to determine and a hard one to define. It is the tone of a class. Some classes are dull and lifeless, some are bright and cheerful. Some are quiet and studious and some are quiet and sullen. By some technique or another, almost any group of boys and girls can be kept reasonably quiet. The fear technique is the simplest and most widely used. The fear of simple corporal punishment may have been eliminated from most of our schoolrooms but other fears are called on by teachers who themselves are afraid. Some of these are fear of failure in school work, fear of loss of privilege, fear of loss of status through ridicule and sarcasm. Many critics of the school would have these fears intensified and some even call for the return of corporal punishment. If the teacher believes that a child can be creative, if he hopes to lead the learner into independent thinking, he must know that fears such as those identified can only hinder him in his efforts.

A Quiet and Orderly Classroom

Do we work toward a quiet and orderly classroom or do we support an independence which leads to every pupil's doing what he likes and making any commotion he wants to? The answer is, of course, that control is essential and that orderliness is necessary to any concerted effort. The order is achieved when each pupil understands that he is a contributing member of the group. If he does not pull his weight, other members will not accept him. This situation does not come about easily. The teacher must first gain the confidence of the group so that they believe he can help them. He must impart to his class some of the skills of reading, discussion, and research in order to fit them for what is ahead. Above all, he must plan wisely and carefully so that interesting experiences will be provided for the class in a sequence which assures that the curiosity of the learner will be satisfied and further curiosity aroused.

The boys and girls any high school teacher meets in the classroom have already been trained and indoctrinated by many other teachers. Largely because of this, undesirable behavior is almost bound to occur in the early part of the school year. If a simple request that such behavior be discontinued proves insufficient, it is best to ask the student involved to remain for a conference after the class period if possible, or after school. What is said in the conference depends on how much the teacher knows about the learner because this conference is a guidance device in the best meaning of the word. Because of this, it is important that the teacher have access to the past records of the student and an opportunity to study them before the interview. It is well to remember that the high school student who causes trouble in class has probably been scolded and punished by experts for years. A logical explanation of his situation based on factual material about himself is very likely to strike home. Because he is all braced for scoldings and threats, he often is very surprised by such a new approach and frequently glad to pursue it.

DISCIPLINE

Sooner or later every teacher has to come to grips with the problem of control over children in the classroom. The personality of one teacher may be such that boys and girls are willing to follow his guidance without question. The personality of another may be much different. In this consideration, the beginning teacher is often at a disadvantage because of his youth and lack of experience. There are some hints and helps the more experienced can pass on to the less.

The First Day

The first day is important. The impressions gained by the students stay with them for a long while and influence their behavior profoundly. Most experienced teachers, and some authorities, advocate a "tough" attitude for this period of time. One can always relax and be friendly after a few weeks. There are several points regarding this "tough" attitude that have to be questioned. Are the boys and girls much impressed? Have they not seen other teachers putting on the same act? More penetrating is the question of what boys and girls are like in their relationships to other people. If they are like most other humans, they tend to react to toughness with hostility and resentment. If these attitudes are included in the impressions of the first day, they may hinder the formation of a good teacher-pupil relationship. We advocate a business-like, firm attitude the first day because we feel that with this start the teacher does not have to change his nature somewhere along the way but can remain business-like and firm throughout his relationship with the group. True kindness and consideration are never out of place.

How to Face the Class. In the first few days, at least, the teacher will be before the class a good part of the time. It is unwise to spend all of this time seated behind a desk. As a matter of fact, the young teacher has the strength and energy to stand when he is speaking with the group and will find it better to do so. Teaching involves communication and eye-to-eye contact between teacher and learner helps in this process. In the typical classroom situation, the teacher seated behind a desk can attain this contact with only the first two or three rows of pupils. The several rows behind these are often left out of the lesson. The experienced teacher studies his whole class all the time. He does not limit his attention to the student responding or the one working at the chalkboard; he glances at the boy in the back corner, the girl sitting by the window, and all the others in his class.

Obviously the person seated behind a desk does not move around very much. The effect of the human personality is somewhat like light in that it diminishes in intensity as it is projected farther from the source. If the teacher moves about a little he actually pulls in more attention from various sections of the group. Moving about can be easily overdone; casual movement and nervous pacing are two entirely different things. If one uses the chalkboard occasionally during a lesson, draws attention to a map or chart, demonstrates with apparatus, or in other ways moves naturally about the front of the room, he will probably introduce enough motion to the lesson.

Variation of Activity

The attention span of the high school student is only a very few minutes. An attempt to keep him interested through one type of activity for an hour is almost a hopeless task. After a class is organized so that the demands of the work bring about a good deal of movement and change of pace, there is little problem. In the first days of the school year, however, there is a tendency for the teacher to spend a great deal of time merely talking to the class. This must be avoided. The wise teacher has several class writing assignments ready before school opens. When the group shows signs of restlessness, he assigns them written work. The old adage that "the devil finds work for idle hands" is still true. The busy class is rarely a misbehaving class. In many schools it is a practice to have some part of the class period spent in supervised study. This seems to be a very wise use of time in school. The Trump plan, mentioned before, calls for the student to spend 40 per cent of his time in individual study. The conventional classroom does not always permit individual study but it does offer the opportunity for study in a supervised situation. In general it is considered good practice to have fifteen or twenty minutes of a 50-minute period devoted to this activity.

Seeking Administrative Help

The beginning teacher often is told by friends not to send any one to the principal because this act will mark him a weak teacher. This frequently is very bad advice. Let us consider a young person, new in school, who has a class which includes a troublemaker who has been in the principal's office at least once a week for several years. If such a student is not sent to the office in the first few days the principal wonders what is going on. If the new teacher can handle the trouble better than anyone else has been able to, so well and good. If, however, the new teacher is merely hiding his trouble behind a closed door, the principal knows that sooner or later it will break out and, in the meantime, the better pupils are losing out if the troublemaker is not yet reformed. If the miscreant is sent to the office then the principal knows that the new teacher knows trouble when he sees it, to say the least. It is not a disgrace to get a student out of the way of others if he is willfully hindering their progress through undesirable behavior.

The "Bag of Tricks" Procedure

The new teacher is often tempted to confide his trouble to an older and more experienced person. This may be a very good idea and in other situations it may not. If the inexperienced is told of a little technique to take care of the present problem and next week is told of another little technique for another problem, he soon has a series of little techniques to deal with various problems as they arise. The use of such devices not based on an understanding of adolescent behavior and not part of an organized body of knowledge about their behavior, we call the "bag of tricks" procedure. The sad part about it is that many teachers have taught for years using such a hodge-podge technique and some of them have established good reputations being one jump ahead of the students all the time. Making boys and girls write out sentences hundreds of times, having them stay after school to do more algebra problems, forcing them to memorize verses, and so on are illustrations of tricks. Of course there is a double crime committed against education in these devices. They make algebra, writing, and poetry a sort of punishment with all the undesirable associations which accompany it. Against the "bag of tricks" theory is logical treatment of the behavior of adolescents based on a knowledge of what reward or punishment will bring out desirable behavior and which will bring about undesirable.

Opportunity for Expressive Behavior

Man is a creative being with a strong urge to create. There is no stage in life when this urge is stronger than in adolescence. When one contemplates how dull and uninteresting a high school class can be when the teacher attempts to teach it using only one technique and that a questionable one, he can understand some of the restlessness and lack of attention characteristic of the poorly taught high school group. The inexperienced teacher cannot promise more than he can deliver but if he can show the students in his class that his teaching is to be provocative and stimulating, he has his battle half won. If he can

Indiana University School
Courtesy of William Garrison

The Idea of Following in the Footsteps of the Pioneers Becomes
a Cold Reality

organize his group so that they become independent thinkers to some degree, he is on his way to becoming an effective teacher.

One cannot present a formula for imaginative teaching but it can be illustrated by a diversity of ideas. For example, one young biology teacher starts his unit on reptiles by pulling an eighteen-inch long snake from under his shirt. This provides a sharp dramatic introduction. Some projects are far more ambitious. In one case, the study of the journeys of William Rogers Clark led to quite an adventure. The students of William P. Garrison,[3] of the Indiana University High School, came to the conclusion that reading about such adventure was not enough — why not retrace a journey under somewhat similar conditions? Preparations were not simple and obstacles presented themselves, but in the

---

[3]William Garrison, "A Personal Account of Clark's Trail," *Outdoor Illinois*, (Benton, Illinois), 2:2, April, 1963, p. 6-10.

winter of 1963 Mr. Garrison and his students traveled afoot from old Fort Kaskaskia, Illinois, to Vincennes, Indiana, much as their predecessors had years before. On the trip, sore feet, cold, and fatigue doubtless made more impression on the boys and girls than American history, but we can be sure that this is one group who will never forget this chapter in the building of the United States of America.

Punishment

The teacher who is the subject of our illustration of the teaching of English believes no punishment at all is needed in teaching high school students. He teaches very successfully. Many teachers will not go as far as he does in their scorn of punishment. The new teacher may find himself in a situation where punishment is the only answer. If so, he must be certain that some principles are followed:

1. The boy (or girl) knows why he is being punished.
2. The punishment is reasonable and not vengeful.
3. The punishment is adminstered soon after the cause.
4. Only the guilty is being punished. Nothing is worse than hurting a group because of the behavior of some individual.
5. The punishment clears the slate.
6. The punishment is within the law of the state.

Any punishment not the logical outcome of behavior must be looked upon as an emergency device not good in itself but apparently necessary at the time. A doctor might cut a hole in a person's throat (tracheotomy) to make it possible for him to breathe in an emergency. In doing this the doctor knows that he really has compounded his trouble because he now has the throat wound to deal with as well as the original problem. Nonetheless it is better to perform the operation than to have the patient choke to death. So punishment is almost always undesirable and harmful in itself. The good school and the good class are marked by the lack of threat of punishment as well as punishment itself.

Self-discipline

Self-discipline means that the individual finds in himself the ways of determining which paths he wants to follow and the strength with which to do it. When the teacher uses the term to mean that the students are obedient enough to do what he expects without any trouble, then he is not using the term correctly and perhaps is not wholly honest with his boys and girls. True self-discipline must stem from an independence of thought. The individual must see his ways of acting and reacting as they affect him and society. He must study each path from the evidence available. He has to reach his conclusions concerning the desirable and undesirable paths and then must have the freedom to follow them. In short, he must be free. It is true that there are degrees in this freedom but as the youngster matures his good judgment, which is the result of thinking, matures along with him so that the freedom granted him can be increasingly great. As has been pointed out several times previously, anything that is the result of thinking depends on the skills involved in it. These skills are developed through instruction which includes opportunity to practice. The boys and girls described in our illustration of the teaching of science had perfected self-discipline to a high degree. They could not have done so had they not been able to think independently.

SUMMARY

The guidance of adolescents in the classroom includes the mental health involved in the school situations. While he can do a great deal of harm if he is inefficient, the teacher has much opportunity to contribute to the welfare of the boys and girls in his care. To take advantage of this opportunity an understanding of the motivation of the young person is called for. Wise guidance of the gifted aggressive student, the quiet child, and the slow learner is based on a knowledge of such boys and girls and an appreciation of their potential ability.

The classroom teacher of necessity functions to some extent as a vocational counsellor. Imaginative teaching provides a dissemination of vocational knowledge and some opportunity for exploration. The teacher also influences every student in his search for values on which he builds his life.

To some degree the morale of the classroom is an expression of the ability and attitude of the teacher. It is closely tied in with disciplinary control of boys and girls. Such control is directly a function of method and punishment as well as reward; all are very directly involved.

The aim of the school in this aspect of function is the development of a strong self-disciplined personality who has faith in his own creative power.

SUGGESTED ACTIVITIES

1. Determine what scholarships, if any, are available to the students in one particular high school. (Omit the scholarships that are open to students in all high schools.)
2. Learn about the scholarship opportunities provided by the state in which you plan to teach.

3. In a role playing situation, set up the class to exemplify a repressed and quiet classroom, a repressed but noisy room, a free and noisy room, a free and quiet room.
4. Visit a high school class and try to identify a pupil who has a personality problem. Seek a conference with the teacher to discuss the help being given him.
5. Secure the handbooks of several high schools and from them determine policies concerning disciplinary control.
6. Observe several styles of teaching and report how proper control was achieved in each case.
7. View if possible the film *No Bells Ring* and discuss the control of students implicit in the technique portrayed.
8. Seek a conference with a high school principal to get his views on the practice of sending problem pupils to his office.
9. Analyze the vocational areas of the high school which you attended and determine, if possible, the degree to which the school met the demands of its locality.

QUESTIONS FOR SELF EVALUATION

1. Define "discipline" in your own words and outline its main purpose.
2. Recall a situation from your school days in which a teacher used ridicule in an attempt to change a pupil's behavior. Can you suggest a better way to accomplish the same purpose?
3. To what extent can competition be used in the high school classroom with respect to mental health?
4. Explain what is meant by the statement that marks are often used for extrinsic motivation. Is the practice justifiable in your opinion?
5. Outline a technique by which one might identify the quiet but disturbed pupil in a high school class.
6. What responsibility does the classroom teacher have to the dissemination of vocational information in the junior high school?
7. To what extent should the teacher seek the help of administration to control his class?
8. How do you define classroom morale? Describe that which you think best.
9. Outline plans for your first class period in your teaching field.
10. What do you understand by the "bag of tricks" technique. Can you identify several tricks used by your teachers in the past?

BIBLIOGRAPHY

1. CROW, LESTER D., RITCHIE, HARRY E., AND CROW, ALICE, *Education in the Secondary School*, New York: American Book Company, 1961. Chapter 16.
2. DE HAAN, ROBERT F., AND KOUGH, JACK, *Helping Students With Special Needs*, New York: Science Research Associates, 1957.
3. FRENCH, WILL, *Behavioral Goals of General Education in High School*, New York: Russell Sage Foundation, 1957.

4. KLAUSMEIER, HERBERT, *Teaching in the Secondary School*, New York: Harper and Brothers, 1958. Chapter 14.
5. NATIONAL SOCIETY FOR THE STUDY OF EDUCATION, *Adapting the Secondary School Program to the Needs of Youth*, 52nd Yearbook, Part 1, Chicago: University of Chicago Press, 1953.
6. ROTHNEY, JOHN W. M., *The High School Student*, New York: The Dryden Press, 1953.
7. SCHAIN, ROBERT L., *Discipline: How to Establish and Retain It*, Valley Stream, N. Y.: Teachers Practical Press, Inc., 1961.
8. WIGGINS, SAM P., *Successful High School Teaching*, Boston: Houghton Mifflin Company, 1958.

CHAPTER 13

The Professional Life of the Teacher

OVERVIEW

The professional life of the teacher involves human relationships and the quality of these determine not only the happiness of the teacher himself but also of the people with whom he works. Some of these are his students and their parents, some his administrators and some his fellow workers.

This chapter considers these relationships and attempts to give direction to the teacher as he faces the problems involved in getting along with others. Occasionally happy relationships break down and the power of the law is called upon. Although the typical teacher is never involved in a lawsuit in connection with his work, some principles concerning the legal aspect of teaching are presented.

THE TEACHER'S WORK WITH STUDENTS

A teacher spends about a thousand hours per year in the classroom. So do his students. Because of this it is important to the mental health of all that a climate be established in which work progresses evenly, each party respects the other, and each is happy with a sense of achievement. Because teachers and students are human, the perfect classroom with the perfect learning situation is an ideal to be wished for rather than a reality within grasp, but there are principles of teaching and classroom management that can guide the teacher to a rewarding and satisfying relationship with students.

Honesty

It probably is true that one can fool some of the people all of the time and all of the people some of the time, but one cannot fool a high school class for very long. If one is allied with them in a search for truth day after day he cannot stray from the truth at all. In the academic world one speaks of intellectual honesty — the recognition of truth and obedience to it at any price. High school students are quick to recognize this honesty in a teacher and are just as sharp in detecting the lack of it. In a conventional classroom taught through textbook, the boys and girls see truth as established by authorities out of their sphere, but when learning is teacher-pupil planned and conducted by a group process, truth is established in the classroom and every source, including the teacher, is closely questioned.

The Teacher as a Leader

A very effective teacher of English who has many years' experience has stoutly held that the teacher has no right to punish and is not to act like a policeman. He also believes that competition, such as in essay contests, is not in accord with the best interests of boys and girls. The high school graduates from this man's classes do well in college work, generally like to read, and, in spite of his discouraging advice on the matter, have won many contests in both prose and poetry writing. It goes without saying that he is a very well-liked teacher and is highly regarded by his administration. What characteristics and attitudes are found in such a successful and happy teacher?

He is enthusiastic. He loves English and knows it thoroughly. His students are secure in that they accept his judgment and his corrections of their work. His enjoyment of the classics is so genuine that boys and girls are infected with it. His use of the language is skilful and beautiful, and he can direct their growth in this skill through the writing of class newspapers, little books of verse, and other such creative activities. In his room the students proofread, correct, and edit in small group periods so that only fairly well finished material has to be read by him. His own zest for his subject is not dimmed by long meaningless drill in grammar nor in midnight sessions of paper grading. Neither he nor his pupils are bored by dull literature periods. Everything in his room is bright, lively, and means something.

He likes children, not in a mawkish, sentimental meaning of the word. He likes them because he is aware of the aspirations of each of them and knows what potential each has. When he says that he does not believe in punishment, he includes in the term sarcasm, ridicule, and other such weapons used by some teachers. The worth of the individual in his class is always upheld, never destroyed. This is the sort of man boys and girls will follow in a group learning situation which we have tried to illustrate in other parts of this book.

He is discreet. This man knows enough about teaching to realize that the teacher must not only avoid doing evil, he must also avoid the appearance of evil. There are some laws in our society which the teacher must follow. Both a written and an unwritten code demand his strict obedience. Sexual misbehavior in the classroom is the cardinal sin and even suspicion of it is enough to force suspension of the teacher on the spot. This is a fact that almost everyone knows, yet every year teachers get into deep trouble on this count. Instances of homosexuality are, unfortunately, on the records of too many schools. Heterosexual acts between teacher and student are not unheard of. Less serious charges, such as undue familiarity, have cost teachers both the respect of the community and their employment. "Hands off!" is a good slogan for every teacher to keep in mind. To the fanciful and imaginative adolescent, even the slightest friendly gesture involving contact may be interpreted as much more meaningful than the teacher ever intended it to be. The wise teacher does not spend lengthy periods of time alone with individual pupils in the classroom or laboratory. If one student is to be detained after school, it is wise to have it done when some other person is to be in the room also.

Our friend used as an illustration does not prescribe and administer drugs to students. If a pupil has a headache, he is sent to the school nurse, sent home, or left to suffer. The teacher has no right to say to him, "Here is an aspirin; take it and you will feel better." In emergency cases, the teacher must act and do what he can, but he must make it clear to the student and his parent that his ministrations are first aid only and that professional attention is called for.

He is friendly in a sincere way. He does not seek popularity, although in many senses of the word, he is popular. The particular man we have in mind has the quiet dignity of self-assurance without trace of the pomposity of conceit.

THE TEACHER'S WORK WITH THE ADMINISTRATOR

When an administrator employs a teacher and gives him an important part of the functioning of the school, he is involving himself in some risk. The morale of the school, the welfare of the students, and his own reputation are at stake to some degree. The less experienced the teacher, the greater the possibility of trouble. When he signs a contract, the teacher obligates himself to support the administration in his dealings with the students and in the community. Every teacher has the right to disagree with his principal or superintendent on points of theory and even on points of operation, but it is his duty to talk these things out with the men involved rather than to discuss them with people outside the administrative offices. As in the army, there is always some-one who has a gripe. It is important to see such complaints in their true light and to remember that it is often wisest to keep one's eyes and ears open and mouth closed. When one is asked direct questions, an appeal to reason rather than prejudice is frequently effective.

The teacher's responsibility to the administrator includes the accounting of his work as set down in the several records to be filed in the office. Attendance records are of the utmost importance, since school financial support depends on them. A teacher new to a school system should not hesitate to seek direction in this area if he is uncertain as to proper procedures. It is best to go directly to the school office rather than to get help from a colleague who might be doing things improperly. The recording of marks is also the responsibility of the teacher and the detail in this work must be faultless. With graduation pending, promptness with final grades becomes exceedingly important.

Responsibilities

The legal responsibility of the school lies essentially in the school board who are empowered by the tax paying voters to operate the system. They delegate their powers in part to the superintendent who turns over certain duties to school principals. These men entrust much of their duty to the classroom teacher. As the teacher goes about his work making decisions concerning classroom management, he must keep the hierarchy under which he operates in mind. This means he must make no threats whose consequences would be against good school practice; he must condone no behavior which the principal deems undesirable; when driven to a decision by the exigencies of the moment, he makes them of a pro tem nature. As an example, a teacher may send a boy from a classroom to the principal's office and tell him not to return to that particular class until some decision has been made by the principal. The teacher cannot say to the boy, "Get out of this school and never come back." As further illustration, the teacher is permitted, in most cases, to have people from the community come into a class situation, but to invite a speaker into the school without the knowledge and permission of the administration is going beyond his powers.

Emergencies. With due regard to the foregoing paragraph, it is to be admitted that there are emergencies in which the teacher is the sole school authority on hand. In these cases he has the right, in fact the obligation, to act in the best interests of the school and in accordance with its policy if this covers the situation. In the judgment of the teacher's actions on such an occasion, the term "reasonable" is generally used as the criterion of proper or improper action.

Extracontractual Work

The fact that teachers often have to eke out their income with work other than teaching is not new in educational history. During World War II working a shift in a munitions factory after school or similar employment was such a common practice that the term "moonlighting" became a part of our language. Under the duress of war, such employment was looked upon as an indication of loyalty, but in more normal times it is generally considered that teachers' contracts with the school board to give of their full time and energy for their school work are binding. Certainly it is only ethical to tell the administrator of any intention to seek steady employment beyond the limits of one's contract. Of course, the right to engage in other types of work during the summer is not questioned because as yet in most systems the teachers, rather than having an extaordinarily long vacation with pay, are unemployed during these months and without pay.

There are many student teachers doing their internship in the public schools. Each is with a teacher under some form of contract with a college or university. In some cases the supervising teachers are paid for their work with a student teacher and in some places they are not. In either situation, it is quite professional to cooperate with a college educating teachers. The contractual arrangements, of course, are made through the administration and the proper university or college officials. The teacher does not have the right to promise to take a student teacher without the knowledge and consent of his superintendent.

THE TEACHER'S WORK WITH PARENTS

The Parent Teachers Association

"St. Peter is calling but I can't stay
"I've got to go back to the PTA."

Thus ran a parody on a popular tune a few years ago which exaggerates only slightly the attitude which some teachers have to the PTA. In most cases the PTA is a very valuable institution which brings together those most interested in the children of a school. Where the organization sees itself as an agency dedicated to this task and to that of educating both parents and teachers to understand children more fully than they do, a great deal of good comes from their work. Where the PTA look upon themselves as a coffee club or a fund-raising organization, the teachers have every right to work toward a redirection of effort.

On the individual level, the PTA offers a good opportunity for the parents to meet the teacher and the teacher to meet the pupil. There is reason to doubt that any further purpose is served at the PTA meeting itself. The practice of the teacher standing with mark book in hand explaining to parents as they stream before him the standing of the pupils is to be deplored. Introductions and local amenities belong in the public meeting, but the discussion of the student's work is done properly only in the privacy of an office or in the classroom when pupils are not present.

The Home Visit and the Office (School) Visit

Some years ago it was considered good practice for the teacher to visit the homes of the students. In the early days of our country, it was traditional that the family invite the teachers to dinner. As the invitations fell off, teachers took upon themselves to visit the home of a boy or girl who was failing either in his deportment or his studies or both. With such an ominous purpose, the teacher's visit became an ordeal to be dreaded — rather a visitation than a visit. Today the teacher visit not only is frowned on by many administrators but is considered unprofessional by many authorities.

It seems wiser to have the parent come to the teacher than the teacher visit the parent. In the school situation privacy can be assured. Only one who has been through the experience can tell of all the distractions to which home visits are prone. In the school the student may be present or not according to the teacher's wish. This is also true of other personnel in the school. Frequently the presence of the guidance officer or the principal is desired. In the school, there is no obligation on either side — it is merely a professional arrangement. In the home, the teacher is often invited to stay for a meal, and then he must be either apparently ungrateful and decline or he must accept and, very likely, put the relationship on a basis that may prove troublesome.

The foregoing paragraphs do not imply that teachers should not be friendly with parents. As friends it is quite proper for them to play bridge, bowl, or go fishing, but the discussion of the student's troubles is a professional matter dealt with best in a professional atmosphere.

RELATIONSHIPS WITH OTHER TEACHERS

By far the great majority of teachers are kind and understanding people who are glad to welcome the newcomer into the profession. It is only right for the inexperienced teacher to accept help from the old hand when it is needed. Dangers must be pointed out, however. If the younger person in trouble accepts the advice of the more experienced and patches up his difficulties by some device borrowed from the older teacher and then makes a practice of running to his friend every time he has a hard day, it may work out that he is missing the root of his trouble entirely. In this case, instead of building up a strong system of teaching, he is merely assembling a bag of tricks. Unfortunately many teachers have managed to cling to their positions for years because of such a bag of tricks which serves to keep boys and girls quiet enough to get by. Such policemanship is often a far cry from effective teaching. Furthermore, in the aforementioned practice, the new teacher may be covering up a poor situation in a school, and a down-to-earth professional talk with the principal might be a far better answer.

There is really only one word to say about gossiping with other teachers. The word is: "Don't."

RELATIONSHIPS WITH NONTEACHING EMPLOYEES

The superintendent of a well-run school system can be away from his office for a day or two without dire results, but the secretaries and the janitors have to be on the job every day. These people keep the machinery of the building running and do much to maintain the organization of the persons within it. They often go beyond the call of duty to help children and to make life pleasanter for the teachers. Teachers will find that a kind and friendly attitude toward these coworkers will pay great dividends. There is not a great deal in research and literature on this point, but the reader will enjoy one man's expression of his attitude toward the school janitor.[1]

PROFESSIONAL ASSOCIATIONS

The National Education Association

The lot of the school teacher in the United States has improved greatly in the past two or three decades. Not only has salary increased, but the salary schedule has become firmly established and assures the teacher increases in salary as his years of experience accumulate. Retirement programs are in force in all states. Some of these programs are combined with Social Security; some are entirely independent of the federal government; but each provides the retired teacher a stipend on which he can live. Most school systems have some form of sick leave. Other benefits such as group insurance are available to teachers in increasing numbers. All these benefits did not come by accident or by the action of solicitous school boards. Most of them came through the vision and

---

[1]William H. Patterson, *Letters from a Hard-Boiled Teacher to His Half-Baked Son*, Washington, D. C.: The Daylion Company, 1939.

work of men and women in the profession who struggled mightily to bring them about. The newcomer has the advantage of these things and is not forced to pay for them. If teachers are to maintain their professional growth and material gains, it can be only through the efforts of all members of the profession. The greatest vehicle for the improvement of conditions and the maintenance of working standards is the National Educational Association. This organization has now enrolled almost a million professional people. Within the parent organization are several lesser organizations such as the Classroom Teachers Association and the Association for Supervision and Curriculum Development. The individual teacher has to consider what his contribution to the profession, as reflected by membership in this organization, should be.

The State Education Association

Each state has an association of teachers who strive to achieve at the lower level what the NEA does at the higher. Most of these associations work for desired legislation and try to promote a good understanding of the profession in their area. Many of them support professional periodicals and a research office.

The Local Education Association

Under the state association are the many local education associations. In these groups teachers form a liaison agency with the school boards, help in in-service education and, in general, strive to promote the good of the profession.

In many areas, membership is available in all three of the foregoing associations by the payment of one sum of money termed "unified fees."

The American Federation of Teachers

The American Federation of Teachers is a union. A local of this federation is organized and operated much like the local of any other union. The AFT has as its purpose the improvement of the working conditions of the teacher. In New York City the local group has been conceded the right of collective bargaining for the teachers of that metropolis. One case is too little for generalization, but the New York situation involves many teachers, and the decision must be regarded as an important one.

THE MENTAL HEALTH OF THE TEACHER

The teacher is under a good deal of stress and strain. For four or six hours per day he is with young people notoriously full of energy.

The ineffective teacher wears himself out trying to fight against this youthful vigor. The effective teacher often becomes fatigued trying to use every ounce of it to good advantage. This sometimes means that the teacher feels he has to take much time every evening to prepare for lessons of the following day after several hours of correction. If his constitution can stand nine months of this a year, and many constitutions cannot, his disposition will not, and he will find himself becoming increasingly impatient and harsh. The techniques outlined earlier by which the students themselves become involved in the planning and carry much of the momentum will free the teacher's hours away from school for reading and other constructive activities.

The Adult World

Teaching can be a lonely occupation, since the working hours are spent with persons younger and less mature than one's self. Because of this the teacher should plan his leisure time to include contact with adults. If one works in a church, it is wiser to be with adults in the choir than with school-age children in the Sunday School. If he likes to bowl, he should do so with an adult team, or group, and not with the high school boys and girls. It is often wiser to promise to help some less-prepared person be scoutmaster than to take over a troop by ones' self.

Many teachers indicate that, although they read a great deal when they were youngsters, they no longer find time to do so. This is tragic, because only by continuous reading and thinking can a teacher bring to a class the thoughtful and stimulating leadership it deserves. Time must be found for reading beyond the subject matter area met every day, reading beyond the high school level, reading which will promote the literary maturity of the reader. This is impossible every evening; there are lessons to prepare and papers to be marked. The only answer is found in the organization of work and time which permits some of the marking and much of the planning to be done during the school day. Teacher's aids may be pointed out by some as a good answer, but, to this date, there are too few of them to be considered a general resource.

Enthusiasm

One great teacher declared that if he had to teach without enthusiasm or not teach at all, he would not teach. Fortunately, most people teaching feel there are very satisfying rewards in the work itself. If one does not, he must evaluate himself and his position. It may well be that a move within the profession is the answer. It may be that further preparation in the field, bringing more assurance, will help. Only seldom does one who has prepared to become a teacher and devoted time to the profession feel that he is unhappy with the work, although many have left the profession in order to better themselves financially.

There is no greater work than to teach boys and girls. The teacher stimulates creativity, fosters intelligence, and builds character. All this is done in a climate of friendly personal interaction. Surely there can be no greater effort more worthy of one's faith, nor can there be a more congenial profession than one dedicated to this great task.

TEACHERS AND THE LAW

The telephone in a principal's office rang at about 9:30 one morning. A police officer, who knew the principal well, asked if a certain boy named Eddie were in school. "Yes," was the answer, "I saw him go by the office about an hour ago." "You had better make certain because we have a traffic victim here whom we think is Eddie."

Unfortunately the boy who was supposed to be in school had been killed in a traffic accident near the edge of the small town. There had been a play at the school the evening before and the proceeds of it had been placed in the school safe. A teacher had taken this money from the safe in the morning and had asked Eddie to deliver it to the bank. He had agreed to do so and started out with the family car which he had driven to school. Thinking that he had insufficient gasoline to do the errand, he decided to run out to his parents' farm to fill up from the gasoline pump which they owned. On the way back into town, he collided with another motorist and was killed. What was the teacher's responsibility in this case?

The case never came to court, so no decisions were drawn. It may be worthwhile, though, to study some aspects. The school had a measure of responsibility since the boy was entrusted to their charge for the hours of the day devoted to schoolwork. The school, on the other hand, is a state institution, or an arm of the government, and the state had impunity against suit at the time. This impunity was not always used, so the school board may have been sued. In any case, the teacher is a state employee, not a state officer, and does not share impunity. This means that he may have been sued. Had this happened, it might have been held that he took full responsibility for the boy's safety once he broke the routine practice of the school. Against this any defense would have been difficult. It also might have been held that he had delegated authority which he had from the principal to the boy, who was then acting as the agent of the school, and hence the school itself was liable.

Until very recently, the state has been immune to legal suit, although many states have abrogated this immunity from time to time. A most important decision by the Illinois Supreme Court was rendered in 1959. In a case concerning a school bus accident, they concluded:

.... we accordingly hold that school districts are liable in tort[2] for the negligence of their agents and employees, and all prior decisions to the contrary are overruled.[3]

This decision is effective in Illinois only, and no one can say what the finding in a court of another state would be. To the teacher, however, his path is clear. He must conduct himself at all times on the assumption that neither he nor his employer has immunity against suit. Even the compromise that a school can be sued to the limits of its insurance liability is no longer valid, if it ever were.

Discipline

No court or authority has yet presented a clear-cut decision on the liability of the teacher if a child is injured as a result of punishment. Many cases have been heard and some generalizations can be made. If the injury is the result of unusual and brutal punishment, the teacher's defense would be difficult. No one can define "unusual and brutal" for a court, so it is impossible for us to draw a clear line. In some states a paddle may be used on the pupil's seat, but, in a state where corporal punishment is limited to the use of a strap on the palm, the paddle punishment may be considered "unusual and brutal."

The teacher must not act in anger or from "malice." Again we cannot say what a court will judge "malice" to be. It is certain that teachers, human as they are, may be emotionally disturbed when administering corporal punishment. It is extremely wise of a teacher to confer with the principal before any punishment of this nature and to have him or another adult present as a witness while it is being administered.

It is strongly advised that a woman never punish a boy corporally nor a man a girl. The sex factor is quite likely to be exaggerated in the mind of the pupil and, perhaps, in the minds of the parents and other adults.

A study of reported cases indicates that legal actions are more likely to come from impulsive acts on the part of the teacher than on punishment done after contemplation. As an example, a woman teacher was reported to have hit a girl on the back with a book immediately after the girl, working at the board, had made an error in arithmetic. The

---

[2]A tort is a legal wrong which may be the basis for civil action in court.
[3]Molita vs. Kaneland Community Unit School District. Docket N35249, March, 1959. Illinois Supreme Court.

girl soon afterwards had to have a kidney and the spleen removed. The teacher was sued by the parents.

The wise teacher never hits a student on impulse and uses corporal punishment as a very last resort and then only with the approval of his administration. He also knows the laws of his state which govern corporal punishment.

Medical Attention

Unless he is a physician, the teacher has no rights as a medical person. He has no privilege to prescribe or administer drugs or even to give advice. He has the right to administer first aid, but it must be only first aid. This is defined as help until a doctor can give attention to the patient. In minor cases, the student should be advised to show the injury or explain the condition to his parents. In major cases, the student should be placed in the hands of a doctor or nurse as soon as possible or taken home to his parents. (It should be borne in mind that it often is harmful to move an injured person.) The physical education teacher, the coach, and the industrial arts teacher especially must be aware of their responsibilities and limitations in this area.

Slander and Libel

Slander is defamation of character by the spoken word; libel is the same through published material. If a teacher says defamatory things about a pupil in the presence of witnesses, he leaves himself open to trouble. Even comments on report cards which go beyond the limitations of the teacher's evaluation can be used as basis for prosecution. Remarks about public figures, such as local politicians, of a defamatory nature, must be avoided. If a teacher (let us consider one who is also a principal) in line of duty reports that another teacher is incompetent or lazy, he is not committing slander, but if he makes similar statements unofficially, he may be found guilty.

There is insurance against slander liability as well as other liabilities which may involve the teacher. Very few teachers carried this insurance until recently, but at the present it is included in the membership fee of some state education associations. In actuality, suits for slander are infrequent, but the slight amount of money it costs each teacher in a group insurance plan is most certainly well invested.

Immorality

There is no doubt that a teacher may be dismissed from any contract if immorality charges are proved against him. Beyond this, and perhaps more to be stressed, is the fact that appearances of immorality or records of immorality prior to contract can also lead to dismissal. School boards, with justification, must frequently hold that the teacher they employ must be an example of morality and decency to the young people in their charge. The definition of the terms is very often in the hands of the board and not of the teacher.

WHAT THE TEACHER DOES

For many years numerous efforts have been made to define the good teacher. Many of these attempts culminated in long lists of the attributes. Fairness, enthusiasm, and other such characteristics held high rank in these lists, which did not accomplish much, and one was not much better than another. Of recent years a new attack on the problem, which tries to determine what the teacher does, has been utilized. If the behavior of the effective teacher and that of the ineffective teacher can be determined, then certain behavior can be established as the mark of the effective teacher. Of course this statement begs the question, as it is essential to say which teacher is effective and which teacher is not. In most researches, the opinion of the administration and that of trained observers is used as a base for judgments.

One authority[4] feels that most definitions of teaching are biased inasmuch as their supporters start with a certain theoretical basis and move from there. Because of this, any definition comes from certain postulations which in themselves cause the authority to be prejudiced. He would have us see teaching as a system of actions directed toward the pupil. This definition draws a sharp line betwen teaching and learning. Many would say that if there is no learning, there is no teaching, but in this consideration a man could be teaching before a television camera which, due to technical difficulties, was not functioning. Nobody would be learning in this case unless one judged that the teacher was learning to teach better through practice. The teacher, however, is teaching.

Following Tolman's model, Smith sets up a pedagogical model to outline a teacher's actions when he teaches. There are variables on the teacher's part which produce learner variables. In between are the intervening variables which are extremely difficult to measure or even to identify precisely. The model is as follows:

---

[4]B. O. Smith, "A Concept of Teaching." *Teachers College Record,* 61: 229-41, February, 1960.

A Pedagogical Model

I	II	III
Independent variables (Teacher) ⟶	Intervening variables (Pupils) ⟶	Dependent variables (Pupils)
1. Linguistic behavior 2. Performative behavior 3. Expressive behavior	These variables consist of explanatory entities and processes such as memories, beliefs, needs, inferences and associative mechanisms.	1. Linguistic behavior 2. Performative behavior 3. Expressive behavior

This model demands some thoughtful study. Many of us have dwelt almost entirely on the intervening variable with some sort of assumption that teachers know how to act and that the pupils often know how to learn, but do not follow through. Let us backtrack for a little and consider teacher behavior.

Linguistic Behavior

Most teachers not only talk too much; they also say many wrong things. Perhaps the most common phrase that is to be considered undesirable is "I want you to. . . ." At the early elementary level this is not good; at the high school level it is to be deplored. The typical high school boy is not greatly concerned as to what the teacher wants except as it is smart to follow directions and avoid trouble. As a matter of fact, some high school pupils feel quite a resentment when told that the teacher wants this and the teacher wants that. Instead of "I want you to do page 117 in algebra tomorrow," the teacher might say, "You can fix this idea more firmly in your mind if you will do some of the illustrative problems on page 117." Teachers slip easily into speech mannerisms. "O.K." is acceptable as a term of approval once in awhile, but there are instructors who throw it into the conversation as a question as well as a term of approval and sometimes just throw it in with little purpose at all — it becomes only a mannerism. In a larger area, sarcasm and ridicule fall into the category of linguistic behavior as do scolding, nagging, and shouting. These behaviors, all objectionable, influence the thinking and feelings of the pupils, as intervening variables are affected, and undesirable behavior results.

On the brighter side of the coin, correct use of English and good speech habits also have their influence. As the teacher guides the students in the planning and pursuit of their own work, he will find that it is not necessary for him to talk a great deal. As students identify themselves with him in the pursuit of a certain segment of knowledge, they will listen to him with interest. As the teacher's linguistic behavior takes up less of the time available, the students can have more opportunity to voice themselves.

Performative Behavior

The effective teacher does not look upon himself as a performer in the meaning of an actor, although there is a good deal of the actor in many teachers. The performative behavior of a teacher is defined as the many acts which he performs in the pursuit of his duties. The science teacher often presents a demonstration in which he manipulates equipment and materials. In this case he is performing. The teacher writing on the blackboard is performing. Here again, the teacher is likely to be doing too much and the students too little. If the teacher is to present a demonstration it is his duty to perform it as well as he can, even if it means rehearsing several times before the class meets. Before he does the demonstration, though, it is highly important that he ask himself if he should do it. It may be that a student could do it as well and in addition have the learning experience.

Expressive Behavior

Some teachers have strong bonds of respect and affection with students and some do not. It may be that these bonds are formed in part by the expressive behavior of the teacher. The tone of voice is often expressive behavior; the touch of courtesy and the friendly smile bear their messages, as do the frown and the growl. Every teacher knows what is desirable, and every one also realizes that the effect on the students, whether for good or bad, is inevitable.

Reward for learning is often a great incentive for further progress; conversely, punishment often hinders learning. The most numerous rewards given by the teacher, as well as the most numerous punishments, are those conveyed through his expressive behavior. The climate of the classroom is established to a great extent through the expressive behavior of the teacher. The firm and friendly climate is conducive to learning, while the harsh and autocratic is not. Classroom climate is rarely a matter of black and white — there are many shades of gray — but, in general, the bright and lively class achieves more than does the dull and monotonous one.

The Intervening Variables

It has been stated that the intervening variables are extremely difficult to measure or even to identify precisely. The educational psychologists have spent time considering them and have produced different theories to explain their operation. On one extreme are the behaviorists who say that behavior itself is learning and that this is the only view which can be logically defended. On the other hand, the field psychologies, of which Gestaltism has been discussed, hold that the learner becomes aware of the factors in a problem situation and integrates them through his own insight so that he can attempt a solution. We must limit our discussion of this very wide and complicated field here and seek only the way in which the behavior of the teacher influences these varaibles. One can think of the student's nervous system, including his brain, being ever receptive to impressions. The learner is seeking new material to modify or add to what he has gained. In this search the teacher is, or should be, a never failing source; the facts, hints, examples, approvals, and interpretations offered by him are a continuous source of grist for the student's learning apparatus. Within this apparatus, ideas are formed, strengthened, or awakened, adopted or discarded, according to the impression the student receives from the teacher. Such impressions can come only through the teacher's behavior. It is in this area that teachers create and inspire interests, foster attitudes and appreciations, stimulate aspirations and ambitions.

Dependent Variables

Often with pride, sometimes with anguish, the teacher sees the class as a reflection of himself. Learning is often imitative, and the teacher can see some of his own performance in the behavior of his students. He often deliberately serves as a model and probably more often does so incidentally. The young person, however, is circled by many other models either real or portrayed to him by films, radio, and television. It is enough for us to conclude that much of the behavior of the student is patterned after that of the teacher. It is of especial significance to us that the skills of thinking, more than the social skills, are almost certainly developed according to the example set by the teacher.

The Cyclic Order of Actions

The pedagogical model set forth earlier may be misleading at first glance. It might seem that the behavior of the teacher influences the thinking of the student and in turn produces a pattern of behavior. This is true, but beyond this it must be understood that the dependent variables on the part of the pupils act on intervening variables within the teacher's thinking, which influence his behavior, which starts the cycle once more. Teaching thus becomes a highly complex function of the interaction of teacher and learner which ceases only when the two part company.

In a consideration of the teacher's behavior as related to methods, it becomes obvious that the conventional textbook method is incomplete. The expressive behavior of the teacher is impressed on the learner who cannot, in turn, express himself. The conventional methods are not cyclic in nature, but rather flow from teacher to pupil only. The student is expected to return "correct" answers, but they are more likely to be reiteration of the words of authority than the result of reflective thinking. In the illustration unit presented earlier, and in other illustrations, an interaction is provided in which the growth of knowledge and understanding depends on the contributions from the students. In this frame of reference, the good teacher is one whose behavior elicits from his students contributions of an independent and creative nature.

SUMMARY

The teacher's relationships in the classroom can be so managed that much satisfaction occurs to both the teacher and his charges and their parents. In his role as an employee, the teacher recognizes ethical principles in his dealings with his administrators and the school board. As a co-worker with his fellows, as in all his activities, he follows the Golden Rule and treats them as he would have them treat him.

Several professional organizations serve to help the individual teachers in their efforts to improve the learning conditions for the children and to promote the welfare of the profession.

Each individual has an obligation to maintain his own mental health. While having no more trouble than the population in general, teachers are not free from mental disturbance. It is important, then, that preventive measures be considered.

The teacher is a state employee with particular obligations in the eyes of the law. Although the chance of a teacher's becoming involved in legal action is not great, nonetheless he should be aware of the dangers of his position.

Finally, an attempt has been made in this chapter to present a description of the picture, complex as it is, of the teacher in relation to the people with whom he works.

SUGGESTED ACTIVITIES

1. From observation of a high school class, note the teacher as to the use of sarcasm, degree of severity, and friendliness. Consider your own personality and abilities and determine how you might manage the same situation.

The End: The Graduate is Poised, Sophisticated, and a Mature Thinker

2. Confer with the superintendent of your home high school. Ask him to outline the criteria he bears in mind when employing a teacher. Study an application for employment in the school.
3. In a role playing situation, have an interview with one student playing the superintendent and another a prospective teacher.
4. From a conference with a PTA officer, or from his visit to the class, determine the aims of a local PTA chapter and their program to achieve these aims.
5. Attend, if possible, a meeting of a local or state education association meeting. Look for ethical and legal considerations in the agenda.
6. Determine if there is a local union of the AFT in your vicinity. If there is, seek a conference with one of the officers in order to determine their policies.
7. Study the financial support system of a local school. Learn how the state allotment to each school system is established.
8. Attend a school board meeting, paying particular attention to any action which involves teachers directly.

QUESTIONS FOR SELF EVALUATION

1. In a paragraph or two, organize your own outlook on the place of punishment in the high school classroom. From class discussion based on this assignment, try to draw conclusions consistent with the thinking of the majority of the members of the class.
2. What is the legal worth of notes from parents granting the teacher permission to take boys and girls on field trips?
3. State reasons why parents should be asked to come to the school to discuss the progress of their children rather than the teacher visiting the home.
4. What professional organizations have representation in your home town high school? What percentage of the faculty belong to each?
5. Name two magazines in your field of preparation and indicate the type of article they carry. What is the title of your state education magazine?
6. Outline briefly your course of action, if when you were on hall duty, a student fell through the glass pane of a door and cut his arm severely. Assume other students are present.
7. State briefly your concept of academic integrity and relate it to the context of your teaching field.

BIBLIOGRAPHY

1. BARZUN, JACQUES, Teacher in America, Boston: Little Brown and Company, 1945.
2. FLEMING, C. M., Teaching: A Psychological Analysis, New York: John Wiley and Sons, Inc., 1958.
3. FUESS, CLAUDE M., AND BASFORD, EMORY S., Unseen Harvests, New York: The MacMillan Company, 1947.
4. GARBER, LEE O., Handbook of School Law, New London, Conn.: Arthur C. Crofts Publications, 1954.

5. GAUERKE, WARREN E., *Legal and Ethical Responsibilities of School Personnel*, Englewood Cliffs, N. J.: Prentice-Hall, Inc., 1959.
6. HAMILTON, ROBERT, *Legal Rights and Liabilities of Teachers*, Laramie, Wyo.: School Law Publications, 1956.
7. JOHNSON, EARL A., AND MICHAEL, R. ELDON, *Principles of Teaching*, Boston: Allyn and Bacon, Inc., 1958. Parts 1 and 6.
8. PATTERSON, WILLIAM H., *Letters from a Hard-Boiled Teacher to His Half-Baked Son*, Washington, D. C.: The Daylion Company, 1939.
9. REMMLEIN, MADALINE K., *School Laws*, New York: McGraw-Hill, 1950.
10. SANDERSON, CLARA WILSON, *The Great Adventure of Pedagogy*, Caldwell, Idaho: The Caxton Printers, Ltd., 1942.

Appendices

APPENDIX A

INFORMATION CONCERNING COLLEGES AND SCHOLARSHIP EXAMINATIONS

It is important to our country that the boys and girls with ability continue their education after graduation from high school. Unfortunately, however, some of our best students never enter college or other institutions for further education. In many cases the reason is simply financial inability. Many colleges are crowded, too, and this fact prevents some students from progressing. On the other hand, some colleges have room for more students than attend and scholarships are available which are not used.

This appendix is an attempt to tell the teacher of sources of information about colleges and scholarships so that he can help his students in making decisions about their futures. Only a few sources are listed because a complete compilation of titles of guidance materials would fill several volumes. Some of the books referred to are expensive and it is not suggested that the teacher, or the prospective teacher, add them to his personal library. They can be found in the guidance department of the high school or in the library of the college or university.

College and University Directories

There are several titles in this category and it may be that any one will suffice. In general, these directories are published periodically and it is important that a recent edition be used.

1. BURCKEL, C. E., *The College Blue Book,* Yonkers-on-Hudson, New York: Christian E. Burkel.

This standard reference lists not only colleges and universities but also technical institutions, extension and evening colleges, and other organizations providing opportunities for study beyond the high school.

2. FINE, BENJAMIN, *American College Counsellor and Guide*, Englewood Cliffs, N. J.: Prentice-Hall, Inc.

This work is of especial help to students because there are chapters dealing with self-analysis, college ratings, scholarships and ways to earn money while in college. It also offers information on admission to colleges and opportunities in military service. Descriptions of colleges and estimated costs are also included.

3. KARL, S. D., *The College Handbook*, New York: College Entrance Examination Board (c/o Educational Testing Service, Box 592, Princeton, N. J.)

The *Handbook* is a listing of the colleges associated with the C.E.E.B. Each college submits information concerning location, size, terms of admission, and costs. "This is a book for students who have already decided to go to college and who are now trying to narrow their choices to two or three..." (quote from page ix)

4. LOVEJOY, C. E., *Lovejoy College Guide*, New York: Simon and Schuster.

This volume includes descriptions of more than 2,500 four-year colleges, universities, junior colleges, technical colleges, and other institutions. It tells about the location, accreditation, enrollments, and faculties of these colleges and indicates scholarships available.

5. COLLEGE ENTRANCE REQUIREMENTS AND COSTS OF ALL ACCREDITED COLLEGES AND UNIVERSITIES. Moravia, New York: Chronicle Guidance Publications Inc.

This instrument is in chart form and can be affixed to a bulletin board. It tells of admission requirements, costs, curricula, and control of the many universities and colleges listed.

There are other directories for junior colleges and vocational training institutions. In addition to this, many colleges of all types are glad to send brochures depicting their offerings to high schools.

Guides to Scholarships, Fellowships, and Loans

While it may be impossible to identify all of the scholarship offerings in this country, several volumes are available which list a great many of them. Several are annotated here.

1. ANGEL, JUVENAL, *National Register of Scholarships and Fellowships*, New York: World Trade Academy Press, Inc.

This register lists the scholarships available from private organizations and from the federal and state governments. It also offers advice to the student in reference to leads which can be followed and sources to be tapped in pursuit of scholarship funds.

2. FEINGOLD, N. S., *Scholarships, Fellowships, and Loans,* Boston: Bellman Publishing Company.

This book lists about 300 organizations which offer scholarship aid. It tells of qualifications needed, funds available, and where applications are to be made.

3. LOVEJOY, C. E., AND JONES, T. S., *Lovejoy-Jones College Scholarship Guide,* New York: Simon and Schuster.

This guide gives facts about thousands of scholarships, fellowships, grants, loans, assistantships, and other awards. In addition there is published monthly the *College Guidance Digest* (1475 Broadway, New York 36, N. Y.)

Testing Programs

Once upon a time a boy was assured of admission to a college if his father were an alumnus. Today there are too many boys and girls seeking entrance for this to be true. Each high school student in the country, however, has opportunity to get his name and a measurement of his ability to several colleges which he chooses through nationwide testing programs.

It is generally known that many scholarships are available in this country but just how to obtain one is not general knowledge. Help is available in the search, however, through several testing programs administered to high school students.

1. *The American College Testing Program*

The American College Testing Program is an admission, guidance, and placement test battery designed to provide information to colleges, high schools, and students.

The battery includes tests in English, mathematics, the social studies, and the natural sciences. These tests are designed to measure reasoning and problem solving rather than factual recall.

The results of the tests are reported to the three colleges that the student names as those he may attend. The colleges use them for admission and placement.

The tests are administered in November, February, April and May throughout the country. Most centers are college campuses.

Detailed information can be obtained from The American College Testing Program, Inc., Iowa City, Iowa.

2. *The College Entrance Examination Board's Scholastic Aptitude Test, Achievement Tests, and Writing Sample.*

The purpose of the College Board's examination is to furnish an opportunity for the high school student to present to four colleges of his choice a measurement of his ability and his preparation in one or more areas of the high school curriculum. The Writing Sample is a test of composition rather than of handwriting.

Supplementary Achievement Tests are offered in the less common curriculum areas.

The College Board has test centers in many parts of the country and lists five dates for administration during the academic year.

The College Board address for that part of the country east of the Rocky Mountains is The College Entrance Examination Board, Box 592, Princeton, N. J. The western states are served by The College Examination Board, Box 27896, Los Angeles 27, California.

3. *Preliminary Scholastic Aptitude Test.*

This is a test designed to provide an indication of verbal and mathematical abilities. It measures much the same things as does the Scholastic Aptitude Test and the results of one can be related to those of the other.

The major purpose in this test lies in guidance within the high school but a number of sponsored scholarship programs also make use of the test scores in their consideration of candidates for awards.

This test is produced by The College Entrance Examination Board whose address is noted in Item 3.

4. *The National Merit Scholarship Examination.*

The National Merit Scholarship Examination Program is a nationwide search for students who demonstrate extraordinary ability to benefit from a college education.

Juniors in high school may take the Qualifying Test, which also serves as an application for a scholarship. The test is given in March in each secondary school that registers for it. It consists of examinations in English usage, mathematics usage, social studies reading, natural sciences reading, and word usage.

About 13,000 of the top-scoring students are named semifinalists. The names of these students are listed in a booklet sent to all colleges, universities, and other scholarship agencies.

Approximately 30,000 students receive Letters of Commendation. These students are eligible for special scholarships. Their names are sent to two colleges of their choice.

From the semifinalists are selected finalists who receive National Merit Scholarships. In general, a finalist may use his award at the college of his choice.

The address is: National Merit Scholarship Corporation, 1580 Sherman Ave., Evanston, Illinois.

APPENDIX B

THE CODE OF ETHICS OF THE EDUCATION PROFESSION*

PREAMBLE

We, professional educators of the United States of America, affirm our belief in the worth and dignity of man. We recognize the supreme importance of the pursuit of truth, the encouragement of scholarship, and the promotion of democratic citizenship. We regard as essential to these goals the protection of freedom to learn and to teach and the guarantee of equal educational opportunity for all. We affirm and accept our responsibility to practice our profession according to the highest ethical standards.

We acknowledge the magnitude of the profession we have chosen, and engage ourselves, individually and collectively, to judge our colleagues and to be judged by them in accordance with the applicable provisions of this code.

PRINCIPLE I

Commitment to the Student

We measure success by the progress of each student toward achievement of his maximum potential. We therefore work to stimulate the spirit of inquiry, the acquisition of knowledge and understanding, and the thoughtful formulation of worthy goals. We recognize the importance of cooperative relationships with other community institutions, especially the home.

In fulfilling our obligations to the student, we —

1. Deal justly and considerately with each student.
2. Encourage the student to study varying points of view and respect his right to form his own judgment.
3. Withhold confidential information about a student or his home unless we deem that its release serves professional purposes, benefits the student, or is required by law.
4. Make discreet use of available information about the student.
5. Conduct conferences with or concerning students in an appropriate place and manner.
6. Refrain from commenting unprofessionally about a student or his home.
7. Avoid exploiting our professional relationship with any student.
8. Tutor only in accordance with officially approved policies.

---

* Adopted by the NEA Representative Assembly Detroit, Michigan, July, 1963

9. Inform appropriate individuals and agencies of the student's educational needs and assist in providing an understanding of his educational experiences.
10. Seek constantly to improve learning facilities and opportunities.

PRINCIPLE II

Commitment to the Community

We believe that patriotism in its highest form requires dedication to the principles of our democratic heritage. We share with all other citizens the responsibility for the development of sound public policy. As educators, we are particularly accountable for participating in the development of educational programs and policies and for interpreting them to the public. In fulfilling our obligations to the community, we —

1. Share the responsibility for improving the educational opportunities for all.
2. Recognize that each educational institution may have a person authorized to interpret its official policies.
3. Acknowledge the right and responsibility of the public to participate in the formulation of educational policy.
4. Evaluate through appropriate professional procedures conditions within a district or institution of learning, make known serious deficiencies, and take any action deemed necessary and proper.
5. Use educational facilities for intended purposes consistent with applicable policy, law, and regulation.
6. Assume full political and citizenship responsibilities, but refrain from exploiting the institutional privileges of our professional positions to promote political candidates or partisan activities.
7. Protect the educational program against undesirable infringement.

PRINCIPLE III

Commitment to the Profession

We believe that the quality of the services of the education profession directly influences the future of the nation and its citizens. We therefore exert every effort to raise educational standards, to improve our service, to promote a climate in which the exercise of professional judgment is encouraged, and to achieve conditions which attract persons worthy of the trust to careers in education. Aware of the value of united effort, we contribute actively to the support, planning, and programs of our professional organizations.

In fulfilling our obligations to the profession, we —

1. Recognize that a profession must accept responsibility for the conduct of its members and understand that our own conduct may be regarded as representative.

2. Participate and conduct ourselves in a responsible manner in the development and implementation of policies affecting education.

3. Cooperate in the selective recruitment of prospective teachers and in the orientation of student teachers, interns, and those colleagues new to their positions.

4. Accord just and equitable treatment to all members of the profession in the exercise of their professional rights and responsibilities, and support them when unjustly accused or mistreated.

5. Refrain from assigning professional duties to non-professional personnel when such assignment is not in the best interest of the student.

6. Provide, upon request, a statement of specific reason for administrative recommendations that lead to the denial of increments, significant changes in employment, or termination of employment.

7. Refrain from exerting undue influence based on the authority of our positions in the determination of professional decisions by colleagues.

8. Keep the trust under which confidential information is exchanged.

9. Make appropriate use of time granted for professional purposes.

10. Interpret and use the writings of others and the findings of educational research with intellectual honesty.

11. Maintain our integrity when dissenting by basing our public criticism of education on valid assumptions as established by careful evaluation of facts or hypotheses.

12. Represent honestly our professional qualifications and identify ourselves only with reputable educational institutions.

13. Respond accurately to requests for evaluations of colleagues seeking professional positions.

14. Provide applicants seeking information about a position with an honest description of the assignment, the conditions of work, and related matters.

PRINCIPLE IV

Commitment to Professional Employment Practices

We regard the employment agreement as a solemn pledge to be executed both in spirit and in fact in a manner consistent with the highest ideals of professional service. Sound professional personnel relationships with governing boards are built upon personal integrity, dignity, and mutual respect.

In fulfilling our obligations to professional employment practices, we —

1. Apply for or offer a position on the basis of professional and legal qualifications.

2. Apply for a specific position only when it is known to be vacant and refrain from such practices as underbidding or commenting adversely about other candidates.

3. Fill no vacancy except where the terms, conditions, policies, and practices permit the exercise of our professional judgment and skill, and where a climate conducive to professional service exists.

4. Adhere to the conditions of a contract or to the terms of an appointment until either has been terminated legally or by mutual consent.
5. Give prompt notice of any change in availability of service, in status of applications, or in change in position.
6. Conduct professional business through the recognized educational and professional channels.
7. Accept no gratuities or gifts of significance that might influence our judgment in the exercise of our professional duties.
8. Engage in no outside employment that will impair the effectiveness of our professional service and permit no commercial exploitation of our professional position.

Index